Monograph 62
THE AMERICAN ETHNOLOGICAL SOCIETY
Robert F. Spencer, *Editor*

*

THOSE WHO LIVE FROM THE SEA
A Study in Maritime Anthropology

Edited by
M. Estellie Smith

WEST PUBLISHING CO. 1977
St. Paul • New York • Boston
Los Angeles • San Francisco

Library of Congress Cataloging in Publication Data

Main entry under title:

Those who live from the sea.

    (Monograph—American Ethnological Society; no. 62)

    Bibliography: p.

    Includes index.

    1. Maritime anthropology—Addresses, essays, lectures.

    2. Fishing villages—Addresses, essays, lectures.

    3. Fisheries—Addresses, essays, lecture. I. Smith, M. Estellie, 1935–

II. Series: American Ethnological Society. Monographs; no. 62.

GN386.T47   301.5'5   77–2223

ISBN 0–8299–0139–6

The Contributors

Chris Baks. Chris Baks was born in 1931 and studied at Amsterdam University, The Netherlands. In 1962-1963 and 1970-1971 he conducted field work in Gujarat, India on land reform and bureaucracy. He is currently at Utrecht University. During his former work at Leyden University he and Els Postel-Coster guided students in anthropology in fieldtraining courses in Scotland.

Bradley A. Blake. Bradley A. Blake is professor of anthropology and department head of sociology and anthropology at New Mexico State University, Las Cruces, New Mexico where he received the Robert L. Westhafer Faculty Award for Excellence in Teaching. His research interests have included solar energy application on the Colorado River Indian Reservation, technological innovation among the coastal marine fishermen of Madras State, and technological adaptation of the marine fishermen of the Republic of Ireland.

Professor Blake received his Ph.D. in anthropology from the University of Wisconsin, holds double masters degrees in anthropology and India area studies, and specializes in Southwestern ethnology, applied anthropology, and anthropological theory. Aside from his professional commitment to anthropology, he is also a commercial pilot and flight instructor as well as an adamant sports fishing enthusiast. Professor Blake intends to continue his research in the area of fisheries training and performance in the Republic of Ireland.

Yvan D. Breton. Yvan D. Breton was born in La Durantaye, County Bellechasse, Quebec. Educated at College St.-Jean Eudes, and the Univérsité Laval, he received his Ph.D. degree from Michigan State University. He is currently professor and chairman, Department of Anthropology at the Univérsité Laval. Dr. Breton's research in fishing, economic anthropology, and peasant societies has taken him to fishing communities on the lower north coast of the St. Lawrence in Quebec, to Yucatán, and to Venezuela.

James B. Christensen. James B. Christensen is professor and chairman, Department of Anthropology, at Wayne State University. He obtained his Ph.D. in anthropology from Northwestern University in 1952. Within the area of cultural anthropology he has specialized in Sub-Saharan Africa, with his first field research being carried out in Ghana in 1950-51. He has also carried out research in East Africa (Tanzania), and has returned to Ghana for subsequent field trips for research among the Fanti, with the paper included in this publication dealing with change over the past quarter-century.

He is a fellow and member of numerous professional associations, and his publications include a book, *Double Descent Among the Fanti,* and numerous articles on the Fanti and other ethnic groups and aspects of Sub-Saharan Africa and Afro-Americans. More recently he has been involved in an analysis of expatriate Fanti fishermen and their families who have migrated to Liberia.

George M. Epple.   George M. Epple is chairperson and assistant professor of anthropology at Rhode Island College and holds a doctorate in anthropology from Brandeis University. Dr. Epple has done fieldwork in fishing communities in Trinidad (1966) and Grenada (1969-70) and is the author of articles, papers, and reviews on maritime anthropology, socioeconomic aspects of West Indian fishing communities, and Caribbean literature.

James C. Faris.   James C. Faris, a native of Colorado, received his B.S. from the University of New Mexico (1958) and his Ph.D. from the University of Cambridge (1965). He has taught at McGill University, the University of Khartoum, and the University of Connecticut where he is now associate professor of anthropology. He has carried out field research in north Atlantic maritime communities and in the Democratic Republic of Sudan. His

publications include the books, *Cat Harbour* (1972), *Nuba Personal Art* (1972), and works on cognition and materialist perspectives in anthropological theory.

William L. Leap.   William L. Leap is associate professor of anthropology at the American University (Washington, D.C.) and is director of Indian Education Projects for the Center for Applied Linguistics (Arlington, Va.). He has carried out extensive field work within the Tiwa and Keres speaking pueblo communities of the Southwest, where his interests have focused on the community English vernacular ("Indian English") and on development of programs for native language maintenance within the local school. His interest in maritime anthropology stems, in part, from an 18 month comparative study of linguistic adaptation and linguistic acculturation within Portuguese speech communities in New York State, Massachusetts, and London, England.

DeWight R. Middleton.   DeWight R. Middleton is assistant professor of anthropology at the State University of New York, College at Oswego, where he has taught since receiving his Ph.D. from Washington University (St. Louis) in 1972. In addition to extensive field work in Manta, Ecuador, he has field experience in Colombia and in a slum neighborhood of St. Louis. His principal research interests are in urban, political, social organization and theoretical aspects of ethnology, particularly as they relate to processes of sociocultural change. Dr. Middleton has authored a number of articles, including those in *Urban Anthropology* and *American Ethnologist,* and has read research papers at many professional meetings.

Peter A. Munch.   Peter A. Munch is professor of sociology, Southern Illinois University, Carbondale, Illinois. He was born in Norway, 1908, and received his education at the University of Oslo, Norway (Ph.D. 1946); Oxford University, England; Universität Halle-Wittenberg, Germany; and the University of Chicago. In 1937-38, he was a member of the Norwegian Scientific Expedition to Tristan da Cunha. His positions have included: instructor, University of Oslo (1939-46); research associate, University of Wisconsin (1948-49); associate professor, St. Olaf College (1949-51); professor and head of department, University of North Dakota, (1951-57); professor, Southern Illinois University-Carbondale, (since 1957).

His major publications include: Sociology of Tristan da Cunha, Oslo 1945 (dissertation); Landhandelen i Norge (The Country Trade in Norway), Bergen 1948; A Study of Cultural Change: Rural-Urban Conflicts in Norway, Oslo 1956; The Song Tradition of Tristan da Cunha, Bloomington (Indiana) 1970; Crisis in Utopia: The Ordeal of Tristan da Cunha, New York 1971.

Oriol Pi-Sunyer.   Oriol Pi-Sunyer was born in Barcelona, Spain. In 1939 he moved with his parents to England where he attended secondary schools and later studied at the University of London. In 1951 he went to Mexico to study anthropology at the Escuela Nacional de Antropología and México City College (now University of the Americas). His graduate training was carried out at Harvard University, from which he received a doctorate in 1962.

For the past 14 years Pi-Sunyer has taught at Canadian and American universities and is currently professor of anthropology at the University of Massachusetts, Amherst. In addition to research in Catalonia and other parts of Spain, he has done field work in México, Guatemala, Venezuela, and among New England fishermen. His professional interests lie in economic and social change in modern and modernizing complex societies and he is the author of *Zamora: Change and Continuity in a Mexican Town* and co-author with Thomas R. De Gregori, an economist, of *Economic Development: The Cultural Context.*

Els Postel-Coster.   Els Postel-Coster was born in 1926 and studied at Leyden University. She is now senior lecturer at the same university. Her research has been mainly on women's roles as reflected in belles-lettres, especially of the Minangkabaunin in Indonesia. She is currently studying emancipatory movements of women in the Third World. A current research focus is a project comparing the socio-economic position of women in four countries. This project, begun in 1976, is sponsored by the Dutch Government.

Courtland L. Smith.   Courtland L. Smith is associate professor of anthropology at Oregon State University,

Corvallis. His research, teaching, and publications have concentrated on human adaptations to changing marine and riverine ecologies in complex societies. He is author of _The Salt River Project: A Case Study in Cultural Adaptation to an Urbanizing Community_ as well as a number of journal articles. Smith received his Ph.D. in 1968 from the University of Arizona.

M. Estellie Smith. M. Estellie Smith received her Ph.D. in 1967 from SUNY-Buffalo. She was initiator and original editor of _Abstracts in Anthropology;_ and is currently book review editor for _Urban Anthropology,_ on the editorial board of _Political Anthropology_ and the _Linguistic Forum._ She is author of _Governing at Taos Pueblo,_ "Questions of urban analysis," "Networks and migration resettlement: Cherchez la femme," "Cultural variability in the structuring of violence" and various other papers on maritime communities, Portuguese enclaves, and Pueblo Indians of the southwest—all dealing with her primary concern, the study of cultural change and stability in anthropological theory. She is married to Charles A. Bishop.

Paul D. Starr. Paul D. Starr studied at the Univérsité d'Aix-en-Provence, France, received his B.A. degree from the University of the Pacific and M.A. and Ph.D. from the University of California, Santa Barbara. He taught and conducted research in the Middle East for three years while on the faculty of the American University of Beirut and is currently assistant professor, Department of Sociology and Anthropology, at Auburn University. His previous work has appeared in _New Society, Human Relations, The Journal of Social Psychology_ and other publications, and he has also contributed to volumes on social stratification in the Middle East and human nutrition. His forthcoming publications are concerned with ethnic relations in Lebanon, Eurasians in West Malaysia, and the nature of stressful interaction.

David R. M. White. David R. M. White was born in Pensacola, Florida. He studied anthropology at Florida State University (B.A., 1966), the University of Florida, and Southern Methodist University (M.A., 1972) where he is a Ph.D. candidate. His doctoral dissertation is entitled "Social Organization and the Sea: A Gulf Coast Shrimp Fishery." He has also done fieldwork among Pueblo Indians in New Mexico and migrant Algonkin mink-farm workers in western New York State.

Contents

THOSE WHO LIVE
FROM THE SEA

A Study in Maritime Anthropology

†

1

Introduction

M. ESTELLIE SMITH

SUNY-Oswego

The purpose of this collection of papers is to explore the ethnography of maritime populations. The emphasis is on those peoples who earn their living by exploiting the resources of the sea; live in self-identified fishing communities; are facing especially rapid change in life styles due to technological-environmental evolution. Although the contributions, on the whole, stress ethnographic data, they are all at least implicitly concerned with the broader implications which the study of maritime peoples may hold for those concerned with the need for increasing analytical sophistication in anthropology.

The papers themselves represent a diversity of foci—ethnographical, methodological, and theoretical—sustaining unity because of a common emphasis on the processes of change and stability, particularly as those are affected by technological factors. In order to emphasize the variability that can be shown to be manifested within a single subsistence sphere, I have simply arranged the papers in geographical sequence, beginning with Europe, moving through Africa, Asia, and into the Americas, concluding with a cross-cultural study. This not only groups several papers which deal with data similar because of their common sociocultural setting (e.g., the remote fishing communities in industrialized European countries), but, I think, gives contrasting approaches to the handling of such similar ethnographic settings.

I emphasize the ethnographic base for these studies; such a grounding

1

in the data themselves is necessary for reasons which should be examined.

First, maritime communities have been greatly neglected in the anthropological literature; even societies which depend on marine exploitation for a major portion of their annual subsistence often have this focus noted only in a footnote—after which the author goes on to stress the land-based subsistence pattern. I will return to the problems which this has created in the development of broad-based analytical models; but for the moment let it suffice to point out that the mixed exploitation pattern of hunting, gathering, and horticulture which is often found in such fishing communities can play havoc with a naively conceived evolutionary model of social organization—particularly when such communities are wholly encapsulated in industrial societies.

It must also be stressed that (despite our heavy emphasis in the social sciences today on the need to develop our methodological and theoretical perspectives—with many writers arguing that we have more than enough ethnographic data to move beyond the primitive and simplistic level of data gathering) the majority of anthropologists prefer to derive their more abstract generalizations from observations which they and others have made in the field.

Beyond the significance of the data in and of themselves there are both broader and more pragmatic considerations for studying the maritime econiche. It is being increasingly brought home to anthropologists that it behooves us to become explicitly conscious of those social and cultural forces which structure our research interests and foci (and of which, all too often, we have been unaware). The world today is facing a complex crisis created by combinatorial forces such as the food shortage, the population explosion, the economic vectors of Third World nations in opposition to the industrialized giants, and ideological-nationalistic forces in conflict. We have suddenly become aware that the sea is the new frontier—and like all frontiers it is also the new battleground in the ancient quest for more territory. The sea is a source of food for the protein hungry; it is a source of materials necessary to grow land-based foods, especially as land-derived, finite minerals for fertilizers become increasingly necessary and increasingly scarce; it contains a wealth of untapped resources, such as metals and oils, which are not only needed to maintain the entire life style which man has evolved, but which also may mark the difference between a nation's political and economic continuance or collapse; and it is an international highway for the transmission of trade goods and tactical forces, as well as a territorial extension of specific nations. Thus, the multiple importance of the sea cannot be underestimated and several examples will serve to emphasize this.

India's last census lists one million persons whose occupation is full time fisherman. Critical protein needs, as projected in the current (fifth) Five-Year Program, are to be satisfied by increasing fish production to three million tons per annum within the next five years (Anon. 1974:37–8). In the face of India's internal political unrest, which stems in no small measure from the less-than-successful "Green Revolution," this program, if successful, will play an important part in the well-being of the people—not to mention that of the body politic. One has only to look at the dramatic events which have taken place in other countries when they begin to expand exploitation of their marine resources to understand the economic, political, and humanitarian implications of this developmental trend.

Peru serves as another example: a significant portion of this country's GNP in recent years was derived from her fishing industry. Peru became the world's leading producer of fish meal, a fertilizer vital for the success of the Green Revolution planned in Third World nations. The fishing industry has had a significant impact on, and altered the nature of, the national economy; e.g., in 1970, Peru produced 42 percent of the total world fish meal production (Kolhonen 1974:36–40) and the number of Peruvians tied into that pattern was estimated to be almost 15 percent of the total employed population. As the industry gained momentum, coastal boomtowns appeared overnight and sleepy villages of a few hundred people mushroomed into industrialized port towns of 30,000 or more within a matter of months. In 1972, however, a shift in ocean currents led to a dramatic decline in the catch, which had a catastrophic effect on the Peruvian economy. The ripple effect throughout Peruvian life cannot be fully calculated but it should be noted that (despite the research potential inherent in the boom, its collapse, and its current resurgence under more cautious governmental guidelines) few scholars have dealt with the data or applied it to studies of social control, technological innovation, ecology, cultural change, or the host of other research foci derivable from the situation.

Another example from the maritime sector is drawn from Lake Rudolph. This is a semi-desert area of Africa which traditionally has been inhabited by transhumant peoples. The Kenya government instituted a program of planned change which centered on the occupational shift of these tribesmen from pastoralism to fishing. By 1970, 2,500 men were occupied as fishermen in this newly developed subsistence base (Anon. 1973:54–8). The government's program was based on the argument that fishing, particularly in the lakes which abound in many parts of Africa, will provide a more reliable subsistence base than the rearing of cattle or agriculture, both of which are subject to drought, disease, parasitic insects, and the like.

Kenya is not alone in the move to increase the production of fish; planners in other African countries are arguing that it is far easier to force a sharp disruption on the cultural life of tribal peoples than to try to work within the traditional subsistence-economic parameters. They maintain that imposed changes in historically-embedded patterns of a subsistence style are likely to be resisted to a far greater extent than the introduction of a totally new food-getting technique. Thus, goes the argument, *tabula rasa* learning of scientifically derived programs, centrally planned and administered, is the only realistic approach for new nations striving for economic modernity. So far, the Lake Rudolph experiment seems to be proceeding as planners have predicted.

Whether a new subsistence and economic focus (as in the case of Lake Rudolph, Malawi, and Volta) or one which has existed since prehistoric times (e.g., the Shetland Islanders), it is clear that far-reaching changes are occurring in the maritime sector of world subsistence patterns and economic configuration. One reason for this is the growing need for food. The per capita consumption of fish on a world-wide basis, during the period of 1960–72, showed a 67 percent increase; the world catch, however (despite substantial industrialization of the fishing process), increased by only about half that amount (Miller, 1973:20–5). In part, the differential is due to the resistence of fishermen themselves to change in techniques—changes which, while far more productive in the short run, are economically risky and demanding of changes in life style which the target population finds undesirable.

Part of it is due to economic and environmental variables which national governments must take into account. Newfoundland, for example, has the lowest per capita income of all the provinces in Canada (Brox 1972:5). Implying a still-valid ratio, Brox cites 1949 figures which show that per capita income for a Newfoundlander was $1,065 per annum as compared to that of an individual from Ontario who earned $2,125 per annum (1972:6). Newfoundland's main subsistence focus is fishing but the province is only one econiche within Canada's broad geographic spectrum—a spectrum which allows that country to be classed as a "have" nation with a high standard of living based on industrialism and agriculture. Thus, when one shifts from this national to regional perspective, it is easy to see why Brox can write that:

> In many ways, Newfoundland reminds one of the truly underdeveloped ...
> countries, such as are found in the Middle East, where the Arab herdsman
> tends his goats in the same way as in biblical times, within view of electronically controlled oil wells (1972:6).

After reviewing the literature Brox concludes, "Most commentators seem to agree that [fishing] is a problem-ridden 'sick' industry . . . [and] stress its 'backwardness' (1972:20). To complicate this picture, people of the maritime provinces seem generally convinced that the government is incapable of solving their problems and/or is selling them short for other national and international trade-offs. Attempts by Ottawa to aid the economy while conserving resources have not been notably successful and, in the meantime, programs designed to alleviate Newfoundland's economic plight are a substantial drain on federal funds for that area.

As indicated, fishing per se is not the only input to the international maritime scene. For the last five years the nations of the world have attempted to resolve present and potential disputes arising from the growing need to exploit mineral resources of the sea and deal with management of sea lanes through current or national waters. A series of conferences dealing with the law of the sea have been held. Each conference has led to new rounds of talks in successive years and, particularly in the case of the 1974 Caracas meeting, each seems to acerbate rather than resolve existing difficulties. (Those anthropologists interested in government, politics, and juridical studies would do well to study the proceedings of these conferences!) But, while diplomats and scholars debate and maneuver in an international chess game, the men of one community and one fleet or boat struggle with their foreign counterparts over exploitation and territorial rights. Fishing boats and their crews are captured and held for ransom; gunboats and warships steam to protect their fishing fleets in foreign waters; and hostile confrontations stand in the making, ranging from the little known "fishing war" between Floridians and Cubans in the Caribbean, to the so-called "comic opera Cod War" between Iceland and Great Britain, and the explosive situation in the Near East between various countries (such as Greece and Turkey) and internally (as in Lebanon).

In short, from the perspective of today's world and tomorrow's survival needs, the maritime sector should not be viewed as a bit of exotica. It is not simply linked to an obsolete or anachronistic form of primitive or peasant food getting, but will become increasingly important as the need for minerals and food—protein-rich food—increases concomitantly with the world population.

As with any study which deals with men in their primary quest for food, the ecological factors loom large. In all of the papers in this volume the interface between man and his natural and man-made setting is a basic theme. Quite aside from the economic practicalities, it is fishing which leads many environmentalists to resist attempts to exploit the oil resources of the continental shelves of the world's land masses. Thus, despite the fact that neglect of the fisheries has led the United States to (a) fall from first to sixth place among the fishing nations of the world, and (b) reach a point of declining production which forces Americans to import two-thirds of the fish they consume, the fisheries of the United States coastal waters are still used as a major argument for not exploiting the energy potential of the oil reserves which lie within those regional fishing grounds (cf., Wallace 1973: 11–14). On the other hand, some individuals maintain that fishing is declining in the United States at such a rapid rate that Americans need not concern themselves with the long-term implications of international treaty trade-offs which use access to fishing grounds as a bargaining lever for oil imports, foreign missile bases, and similar negotiating points. Scholars and bureaucrats; diplomats, industrialists, and lobbyists; from all categories there are those who argue there will be no fishing or at least too little to let it weigh heavily in what are seen as significant multinational negotiations. And such thinking—pro, con; right, wrong; long- and short-sighted—is influencing the projections of other countries as well, despite the fact that relatively little is known of fishing communities, fishermen, and subsistence and exploitive patterns developed around the marine biomass. As with the future of American fisheries, we are simply guessing in the dark and much more work needs to be done if the decision-makers are to make rational decisions.

Again, to complicate the picture, the fisheries of some countries are declining but catches of others are up significantly. Some of this is due to incompletely understood biological and ecological factors but much is also due to the industrialization of fishing—nationally financed or maintained fishing fleets which operate with factory ships to process at sea the catch from each day. Since such industrial fishing can catch more, and catch it more cheaply than traditional methods, it is clearly the way which most fishing will go in the next few years. Yet it is exactly this sort of extreme industrialization which may, as ecologists point out, ultimately destroy those very fleets which are being created for this purpose. Overexploitation can destroy the breeding potential of the biomass, including those species not actually utilized by man but needed to sustain the marine food chain.

Of equal concern to the social scientist are the problems emerging from the creation of industrialized fishing fleets. Large concentrations of aquatic proletariat, working within the confines of floating factory units, are not proving as "efficient" as was initially projected. The extensive exploitation not only causes greater environmental waste but also increases operating costs because of shipboard and fleet dissonance which these labor conditions create. As in the agricultural sector we may find that "less efficient," smaller social units are overall more productive and more economical. Studies of these phenomena may not only force us to tighten our definitions of *efficient* and *economical,* they will also lead to a greater understanding of the effects of the growing mammothization tendency in man's subsistence production and exploitation patterns. To observe this process, ongoing, may cause anthropologists to revise some cherished models of objective criteria for the categorization of societies by sociocultural complexity. This is especially so, I think, in the case of simplistic and often erroneous formulas derived from such models as the ratio of energy expenditures to energy productivity.

Thus, the study of the shift from traditional fishing patterns to industrialized fishing has much heuristic utility. In addition to the theoretical input the data demonstrate that human beings, working as cooperative social units, must have the type of structure and organization which makes for positive, affective links within the work unit. Without such links man through illness, group conflict, accidental (or more consciously malicious) abuse of the tools and machines involved—destroys the ambitious productivity projections of "the planners." It is clear, then, that many of the problems inherent in a maritime subsistence pattern are germane to those in occupational analysis. However, the research of those working in the more general field of maritime studies differs from that of occupational sociologists in that it focuses not on the job and/or the ramifications of performing that job in a social milieu, but on the sociocultural setting for an entire community which is created by the dominent subsistence style for the men/women, young/old, seafarers/land-based co-community members who interact within that setting.

COMMONALITIES OF ADAPTIVE STRATEGIES

Occupational demands, as well as the commonalities of the interdigital relationship which members of that occupation *structurally* hold vis-à-vis those in other occupational positions in the macro-system, lead all fishermen to have a great deal in common when viewed in a cross-cultural perspective. These commonalities may be traced to such cross-cutting factors as: uncertainty of the resource because of lack of knowledge and/or control concerning the actual determinants of the availability of the biomass involved (e.g., unknown breeding habits), ambiguity of territory (e.g., unmarked water boundaries) territorial openness (e.g., mobile marine biomass movements are difficult if not impossible to direct or limit) and multiple subsistence potential (e.g., land *and* sea exploitation are usually involved in a fishing community's subsistence base and individuals usually select one or the other pattern on the basis of age and/or sex).

The last point is particularly important because its significance has been minimized in most studies. As suggested earlier, it is not uncommon for societies which exploit the sea to have those maritime activities totally discounted or, at best, mentioned in passing in texts which go on stress, for example, the yam-growing activities of the community. Paradoxically, however, many studies of fishing communities pay little attention to other work which young, aged, and especially women do to round out the subsistence focus while the men are fishing. In one village which I visited in the Azores women gardened intensively, produced cottage crafts for the tourist trade, and—along with children and aged males —cared for small herds of dairy animals. Taken all together these "subsidiary" activities actually constituted as great a proportion of the village economic base as fishing, but (as was also the case with another such village in Ireland) this community was considered by resident and outsider alike as a fishing village. This may be because the traditional emphasis on males as breadwinners allows their primary activity to assume the greatest importance, whether in fact it is.

Returning to those sociocultural characteristics which fishermen share, we find that most possess an explicit awareness that danger is an omnipresent element in the performance of their work. The actual risk varies from econiche to econiche, with some localities suffering relatively little loss of man-hours or life, and others, such as Gloucester, Massachusetts, having a recorded history of several thousand men lost at sea. Whatever the statistical reality, however, there is a cultural perception in the majority of the world's fishing communities that fishing is a dangerous occupation, one in which a man may leave the house in the morning with all well, and have a catastrophe strike before nightfall. There are few land-based subsistence activities which carry this constant threat in a routine performance of one's tasks. As Fricke (1973:1) points out: "A seafarer rarely lives and works alone. . . . He works and lives with others because this reduces the level of risk inherent in working alone." (It is possible that it is this same perception of a high risk factor which leads males to exclude women from shipboard participation, a pattern which leads to a polarization of sex roles in maritime communities which seems sharper than that of agricultural or industrial groups.)

Yet another commonality of maritime peoples stems from the fact that those who fish often represent only a segment of the total community—and a denigrated if not despised segment, at that (c.f., Nishimura 1973:5 and Brandt 1971:65). When community decisions must be made, particularly those patterned by governmental formulas (e.g., council meetings, village forums, town hall discussions) fishermen are commonly unable to participate. As one New England fisherman told me:

Hell! I went to four meetings at the town hall; missed at least two good fishing trips just to be there when they voted on whether to put in a new town dock. Damn fools spent so much time on other folderol that they never did get to talking about the dock—'til the night I *wasn't* there.

Often, then, in communities which emphasize a nonmaritime subsistence pattern, the occupational demands of the fisherman's job inhibit his participation in activities whose occurrences essentially are geared to the temporal cycle of land-based workers—who, it should be pointed out, are not above deliberately scheduling such activities to exclude fishermen. Such exclusion, in fact, may extend to the national level.

The commonalities discussed above are partially the result of what Goldenweiser once called "the range of limited possibilities": given a specific subsistence focus there are only certain techniques available for the efficient performance of the tasks involved in the job performance. There are, in short, certain technological and societal directives, prerequisites, or imperatives which cross cultural boundaries, leaving differences which are relatively superficial when compared to the valid etic elements which may be established.

Another reason for these commonalities is the analysis itself. Built into the observation of occupational groups there is an emphasis on technology and on economics and on the systemic relationship between these two (i.e., on technoeconomics). The study of maritime peoples, like those of other groups whose subsistence patterns put them into a primary occupational relationship with the environment, also emphasizes the complex ecological system within which the human segment functions. A brief look at the history and current status of the Atlantic bluefin tuna will help to illustrate the interactional complexity of ecology, subsistence mode, technology, economics, and societal organization.

Originally these tuna were primarily fished in the Mediterranean and Bay of Biscayne where the same locations had been fished for centuries by traps and a trolling fleet. Following World War II the coastal fisheries of the Atlantic countries greatly increased their catches in these areas through the introduction of the purse seine, live bait methods, and the use of larger, more efficient, longer-range vessels with generally more sophisticated equipment. Soon, longline vessels expanded into the waters of the previously unfished Atlantic. As one writer points out:

Typically, as each new fishery, or modernization, was introduced, the catches increased rapidly for a few years, then decreased almost as rapidly. Since these changes occured at different dates, some fisheries were on the

increase while others were declining. Thus . . . the total catch did not
decline precipitously (Mather 1974:6).

As scientists became more concerned about this economic resource
they began to study the habits of the bluefin tuna; predictions about the
tuna supply were (and still are) complicated by the limited knowledge of
the migratory pattern of this fish whose routes seem to change errati-
cally. We do know however that

> . . . [a] group . . . moves from off easternmost Brazil in March–April to
> off the Bahamas in May–June, perhaps merging there with another group
> which has wintered near the Greater Antilles and in the Gulf of Mexico.
> These fish pass Cape Hatteras in late June. It has generally been assumed
> that they then move into New England and Canadian waters for the sum-
> mer. . . . [In] some years at least, some of these fisheries . . . off southern
> Spain [and Portugal and Morocco] depend, at least partly, on the fish
> crossing the Atlantic to Norwegian waters (Mather 1974:6–7).

Thus, we are aware that a wide variety of fishing communities are vari-
ably affected by what the same fish do, and by what is done to those fish
in widely separated, diverse communities. The diversity can be emphasized by noting that, although the much-declined, traditional trap
fisheries are still in operation in the central Mediterrean and west of
Gibraltar, there are now highly mechanized fleets from Japan, South
Korea, Nationalist China, Cuba, Venezuela, and the Soviet Union competing for the same Atlantic waters (Mather 1974:110).

Such an onslaught cannot help but affect the fisheries involved; overfishing is apparently beginning to diminish even the newest fishing
grounds. From a peak in the mid-1950s when the catch amounted to
about 150,000 fish annually, the catch declined in the early 1970s to a per
annum average of about 1,800 fish. Mather described some of the situations which have arisen as a result of the multinational hunt:

> The Norwegian seine fishery . . . produced over 10,000 tons in the 1950s . . .
> [and] only 100 fish in 1973. . . . The Portuguese traps which have yielded
> over 20,000 fish in some recent years, produced only one or two fish in 1971
> and 1972 and were not set in 1973.
>   The Moroccan traps produced over 30,000 fish in 1958 and only 12 in
> 1973. . . .
>   The Sidi Daoud traps in Tunisia, which averaged about 8,000 fish per

year from 1863–1963 . . . reportedly took only 100 fish in 1972 (Mather 1974:111).

Despite the fierce international competition in the Atlantic, some fleets opted to ignore the tuna. Gloucester, Massachusetts is a major United States fishing port, yet, in the midst of this multinational scramble for tuna, Gloucestermen ignored the fish. What makes this more remarkable is that Gloucester was chosen as the site for the U.S. Atlantic Tuna [Sports] Tournament in 1972. This disinterest by professional fishermen, however, is long standing; as early as 1960, personnel of the U.S. Bureau of Commercial Fisheries had tried to interest Gloucester fishermen in the commercial prospects of bluefin tuna and were frustrated by the "irrational" refusal of the fishermen to pursue this lucrative catch. The position held by Gloucestermen was that fishing was unpredictable enough (shown by the drop in the Gloucester herring catch from 33.7 million pounds in 1972 to 10 million pounds in 1973); why ask for more trouble by shifting over to the notoriously elusive tuna? "Leave those prima donnas to the weekend [sports] fisherman," I heard one fisherman tell another; "They haven't got enough sense to know better!"

On the other hand, sports fishermen were interested and their interest demonstrates the complexities of both the economic aspects of fishing and the difficulty in defining *work*. In 1972, just prior to the official opening of the tournament, the fourth largest tuna ever caught by rod and reel (1,000 pounds) was taken (by a woman). The international publicity which this feat received attracted buyers from all over the world, hoping to make a financial killing from the marketing of the thousands of pounds of tuna which the amateur fisherman would be landing. The Japanese, in particular, bid what seemed outrageous prices in an attempt to corner the market before the tournament began. They succeeded, in only a few days, in escalating the price from $.35 to $1.35 a pound.

What kind of income did the commercial Gloucester fishermen pass up? Enos (1974:9) describes a typical scene, once the tournament began:

> A guy with his own boat, like John Aldrich, could not afford to leave. He brought in a pair of tuna totaling 983 pounds on one trip and sold them for $1,032.
>
> Pete Johnson out of Salem, Oregon hated to leave. Taking a little time out from a business conference in New York to do some fishing, he landed five bluefins in a week. Totaling 3,395 pounds, they sold for $2,673. . . .

This ecological input is, obviously, heavily emphasized in this volume for, as Vayda and Rappaport (1968:476–97) have pointed out, the anthropological study of ecological factors emphasizes human populations and "ecosystems and biotic communities in which human populations are included" (1968:494). They go on to say that:

> Human populations as units are commensurable with the other units with which they interact to form food-webs, biotic communities, and ecosystems. Their capture of energy from and exchanges of material with these other units can be measured and then described in quantitative terms. No such advantage of commensurability obtains if cultures are made the units, for cultures, unlike human populations are not fed upon predators, limitied by food supplies, or debilitated by disease (1968:494).

In other words, we should aim to produce studies of human population units which exist in a particular ecosystem rather than emphasize the more traditional community study approach. This model is particularly apt for the study of modern fishing communities since the systemic relationship linking the interdependent communities, the exploited biomass, and the macroeconomic and political system(s) offers a most attractive analytical elegance. A mobile food source must create a sociocultural pattern different from those whose work is based on a bounded resource, whether the latter are agriculturalists, industrial laborers or territorially prescribed pastoralists. This is true even when viewing land hunters, a situation where we are more likely to be aware of the factors which affect the movements and availability of the exploited resource(s).

The above discussion has emphasized the resource factors which lead to sociocultural commonalities in fishing communities. We may also look at other ecological and sociocultural elements such as those discussed by Andersen and Wadel (1972:2–3). They list features variously true across cultures, which hold for North Atlantic fishing societies (their major concern) but may be more broadly applicable.

> [1.] . . . fishing peoples inhabit relatively small coastal settlements often accessible only by sea. . . .
> [2.] There are often no roadways linking the settlements. . . .
> [3.] The surrounding land is commonly unarable or, at best, suitable only for small gardens and production of feed for a few grazing stock. . . .
> [4.] The fishermen . . . operate from areas with little or only recent development. . . .
> [5.] . . . settlements have poor communication links with the outside. . . .
> [6. populations are small,] culturally diverse, yet relatively simple with regard to specialization and complexity. . . .

[7. there is a stress on] self-sufficiency and adaptability manifested in seasonally pluralistic economic pursuits. . . .
[8. there is]minimal local-level political development.

They suggest that these traits exist because "the ecological and technological problems and circumstances are often similar" despite the variability in attendant social, political, and economic frameworks (1972:6).

THEORETICAL ASPECTS

Thus far I have been discussing the parallels which exist at the ethnographic level—setting, subsistence focus, occupational demands, and the like. There are, however, other commonalities. One is superimposed on the data, and results from the limitations which stem from our current analytical capacity to deal with cultural data. One such restriction occurs because each reader will bring to his understanding of these papers a different concept of culture. Despite the years which have elapsed since Kroeber and Kluckhohn (1952) did their review of concepts and definitions of culture there is still no scholarly consensus on what the term means. This is probably beneficial as it continually forces each of us to limn out our definition to clarify the particular perspective in this or that study. Such working definitions have the potential of ultimately adding rigor and elegance to our work.

Without implying that the other authors in this work agree (which, as will be seen, several emphatically do not!), let me offer one such definition of culture. It may also clarify why I find the study of maritime peoples so productive from a methodological and theoretical perspective.

Culture is a macrosystem of a people's values and beliefs which shores up or leads to changes in the microsystems which make up the total social structure. Each microsystem has an internally consistent system of its own and we may isolate language, economics, religion, kinship, government, and technology as representative of microsystems. Given that each is an internally consistent system it follows that each is capable of being analyzed in isolation. If, however, we are to meet the rather idealistic and grandiose goals of our own disciplinary value system, an approach to the understanding of any socioculture requires us to integrate these various structures, one with another, into a processually perceived macrosystem.[1]

Thus, one may analyze the subsistence-getting patterns, the redistributive and reciprocity patterns, and the related interactions both intra- and intersocietally, and arrive at a structural statement (in the traditional, pre–Lévi-Strauss sense of that term) of the microsystem of economics which, in and of itself, is a complete model of that structure. But to understand the *functioning* of that structure, one must put the "same" economic behavior into the context of, say, kinship or religion. Only in this way can the same element be seen to signify different things, depending on the context. It is this inherent analytical complexity which makes our research so difficult: even when the culture-specific microstructures are reasonably comparable, the intracultural juxtapositional dynamics (and our analytical naiveté) may make what are actually the same etic units appear noncomparable cross-culturally.

It appears that of all socioculture aspects the subsistence focus offers the most analytical utility for the development of this model. Fishing and the patterns of life of fisherfolk offers an opportunity for the formulation of etic units to better analyze subsistence patterns. Fishermen as hunters-gatherers, peasants, entrepreneurs, or proletariat may be compared with their land-based counterparts. We may begin by seeking information on work performance and ask such questions as whether tasks must or may be performed by one, two, or several; whether the tasks are seasonal or constant; and to what extent the product is storable (and what effect this has on norms of productivity). None of these questions, of course, is peculiar to fishing but their answers offer the basis for a culture-specific paradigm of any one society's subsistence mode. We do this sort of analysis in a rather intuitive fashion every time we deal with anthropological data, moving from the ethnographic data to a more abstract generalizing level. We "explain" fishing crews with reference to economics.

The analytical utility of subsistence patterns of which I spoke earlier is probably why all the scholars in this volume have chosen it for their focus. The particular exploitive pattern they have selected, however, is one which, in today's world, has certain technological, organizational, and economic links that clearly cross more traditional sociocultural parameters (cf., community studies). This may be illustrated by concentrating for a moment on problems of cultural change and stability.

As might be expected when using a cultural perspective, the basic premise that cultural patterns are never static leads the authors in this volume to place a primary emphasis on the effects of the dynamics of change, particularly as that change is localized in and generated from the technological dimension of a sociocultural system. All innovations generate vectors of change throughout the sociocultural field but change in the technological segment—the tools (artifacts) and organizational exploitive designs (mentifacts)—seems especially transformative in relation to the rest of the system. The papers here are concerned with the impact of technological change upon what we tend to call *the traditional culture.*

There is, of course, no such thing as the traditional culture, if by that we imply "long-standing, unchanging, and somehow more authentic than what will be tomorrow." Such traditional-innovative contrast is a heuristic fiction of historical analysis. Yet somehow if we know that a trait is not the same as the one which existed in remembered time, or if we know that a trait has been introduced in recorded time (whether that knowledge be obtained through memory ethnography, archives, or the archaeological record), the more recent form becomes less substantive than its ancestor, the "traditional" trait. The latter, in the same process, then acquires a graceful patina of immutability "from times immemorial." We in anthropology have even dignified this bias by legitimizing studies done in the ethnographic present, that is, formulated in terms of a reconstruction of *the* traditional culture.

Just so, a small fishing community in the Netherlands was described as "a closed community [where] tradition remains strong" (Anon. 1975:12), despite the statement in the same article that the prosperity of the town could be measured by the number of Mercedes and other luxury cars owned by community members—as well as by the fact that "the fleet is one of the most modern and best equipped in Europe" (1975:11). Thus, for every Sunday blue law (most of which were introduced during the Reformation), long-stemmed clay pipe (adopted about the seventeenth century), or baggy-trouser-wooden-shoe outfit (probably no older than, say, 300–400 years), there is a fisherman who owned a new auto, television set, or boat equipped with the latest electronic gear—all introduced after 1945 (Koentjaranigrat n.d.). So much for the traditional culture of one fishing village!

François Furet has made interesting remarks on the difficulties of studying cultural tradition and change. In a recent discussion on ethnology and history (1975:5) which emphasizes the complexity of the tradition-modernity concept, he states that "history . . . discovers it is also non-history, . . . change has become a concept measurable in economic terms, in its different aspects; but it uncovers at the same time resistances to change."[2]

Another approach emphasized in many of the papers extends the concept of technology beyond the usual treatment which limits its study to a concern with the material tools which man uses. Earlier in this introduction, I suggested that the technological sector consisted of artifacts *and* mentifacts, the organization and goals of the work force being just as much "tools" of production and technological system as material elements. Technological change, then, may be defined as "any alteration in the productive mode which transforms the energy potential of the subsistence focus." This statement, incorporating both material and ideational forces, offers a more powerful model than one which limits technology to the material expressions of man's manipulation of his environment. When one broadens one's field of vision in this way there is greater potential for the anthropological understanding of the dynamics of technological change—its sources and its ramifying, generative strength vis-à-vis the other sociocultural elements.

Technological change seems to operate much as population growth does—by geometric progression. As man moves towards the future, demands for adaptation appear to come with greater frequency and greater intensity. As yet we are unsure whether this is because more of the subsystems are simultaneously subject to innovation or because, as the human network becomes more far-flung and inclusive, the connective nexuses more easily and rapidly transmit those forces which require us to respond adaptively.

The fishing mode, no exception to this, is also increasingly sensitive—and explicitly so—to the forces which impinge upon it from other econiches and other sociocultural systems. It has already been argued that new exploitive techniques seem especially influential in altering a society's style: It is not simply that the tools themselves have drastically altered a fisherman's ways in one lifetime; nor is it simply that he is moving from an occupational style based on creative and interpretive skills to one based on the ability to operate machines. True, fishing is changing from being labor intensive and dependent on slowly acquired lore of the sea; now radar, sonar, winches, factory ships, storage facilities, safety equipment, radios, and government-provided meteorological reports increasingly surround him. More important, however, acquisition of these "trade goods" from the industrial sector are changing the fisherman from hunter-gatherer or entrepreneur to employee of outside managers; from being self-sufficient he is becoming a part of the broader industrial complex. As the dependency on manufactured equipment increases, individuals lose the knowledge of creativity; the boats, nets, and sails, as well as the lore of sailing, weather conditions, currents, behavior of the biomass—all are being replaced by a reliance on tools and services provided by the government agencies or marine suppliers from whom they are purchased.

Equally important, the fisherman is increasingly dependent on the complex variables of the outside market economy. So, for example, to get a better catch he needs a better boat; to finance the boat he must get a loan, which in turn requires that he take out insurance on the boat. To get the insurance the fisherman must have certain safety equipment on board to protect the moneylender's investment; to pay for the boat and this expensive equipment he must go out further, stay out longer, and bring in bigger catches, and often altering the entire social fabric of his land-based existence. The gap between the fast-vanishing, small-scale fisherman and the highly industrialized commercial fleet is growing as the small fisherman finds it increasingly difficult to capture sufficient food to be able to find a buyer for his small catches or finance even the "minor" repairs and purchases needed to maintain the tools of his trade.

Andersen and Wadel (1972:153–54) have pointed out a number of problems which are relevant in a discussion of technological change. Noting that Bohannan (1963:212) describes five basic subsistence forms (hunting and gathering, herding, horticulture, agriculture, and industry), they emphasize that fishermen essentially belong to the first category. Fishermen are hunters (and to some extent, gatherers), but they hunt a prey which "does not occupy the same environment as the hunter" (1972:154). This limits the means of location and capture as well as locomotion.

Further, fishermen are hunters of *today*, which means they are involved in mass processing and marketing. They are hunters who have autonomy in the hunt, but who are increasingly controlled by outside financial managers. As a result the type of fishing toward which maritime exploiters are moving presents us with a subsistence style which "departs from some anthropological classifications of technology or adaptations. . . . [S]ome features of one technological 'stage' may still be present in others" (Andersen and Wadel 1972:154). Again we see the utility of studying change within the maritime perspective since it may be a sector unique in its broad range of "primitive" and "modern" trait mixture.

The insights which such data present seem more easily overlooked in other subsistence sectors. A case in point is made by Andersen and Wadel:

> Somewhat paradoxically, technological advance in fishing might under certain circumstances increase uncertainty rather than reduce it. Even large capital injections have not reduced significantly the hunting nature of fishing. . . . [F]ishing remains risky and, in our industrial age, not always amenable to rational decision-making (1972:154).

As recent events on the international scene have shown, such remarks need not be limited in their application. Thus, when we study cultural change and, particularly, the question of why one innovation is accepted and another resisted or unsuccessful we are often bewildered by what appears to be irrational behavior. Perhaps we are more victims of our own belief system than we know, being deluded as to the amount of "rationality" and "predictability" which an increasingly complex technology and industrialization have actually introduced.

Relevant to the above discussion is the question of economics, or that system which is concerned with productive norms, distribution organization, and concepts such as *value* and *surplus*—all of which the members of a society coordinate into a system which regulates the flow of goods through, and external to, the community. Such a system is closely related to the primary subsistence foci but, regardless of how often the two are confused, they are quite distinct. The caveat is necessary since, too often, we read of such pecularities as "hunting/gathering" or "industrial" *economies*. However, very different subsistence modes may have similar economic systems, and different societies utilizing the same subsistence mode may employ totally different economic systems.

In contradistinction to an economic structure, a subsistence structure consists of the work which humans perform in order to provide the wherewithal to survive. A critical point in societal organization is marked by the shift from primary production to exchange production, whenever such a shift occurs: in ancient Mesopotamia, Central Asia during the tenth century, nineteenth-century Wales, or modern day Yap. Until recently in world history, most humans were engaged in primary subsistence activities and most societies had one dominant mode: hunting-gathering, herding, horticulture-agriculture, specialized exchange production. This list does not itemize industrialism per se, which distinguishes the dominant mode of Euro-American subsistence today as a pattern in which an overwhelming majority of people are engaged in work for which they receive currency. This may then be exchanged for food, clothing, housing, and the tools of production (education, health care, transportation, or anything else which allows an individual to labor and earn the cash to purchase the goods and services of others). Thus, those who are engaged in exchange production include such diverse types as factory laborers, bureaucrats, artists and artisans, traders, priests, scholars, and primary food producers (such as farmers and fishermen) who market their entire harvest. (By "entire" I mean the producer keeps less than, say, 15% of his food output for home consumption.) The shift to exchange production transforms the entire social fabric of a society and such a shift is currently taking place in many of the world's fisheries. Further, the shift to industrialized fishing, growth of nationally- and corporate-owned fishing fleets, the increasing number of fishermen's cooperatives, and the increasing dependency of fishermen on outside sources of capital are all correlated with the transformation of fishing from a primary subsistence mode to an exchange mode, from labor intensive to capital intensive.

CONCLUSION

This brief resume has surveyed the intricacies of the foodweb, the ecological parameters (simultaneously narrow and far-flung), the complex sociocultural network, and delicately balanced economic factors—all of which are part of the maritime subsistence focus. This introduction has attempted to serve as a broad-based review which will give the nonspecialist a perspective from which to view the papers which follow. All, in one form or another, explore the different aspects and implications which have been discussed above. Though the volume cannot treat all aspects of maritime life (such as the closed system of shipboard life in the merchant marine), it emphasizes the potential which this neglected subject holds for important revisions of existing paradigms and rejections of erroneous or fruitless assumptions.

As a final note, the growing emphasis on fisheries requires anthropologists, through the production of needed source materials, to remind those in decision-making positions that a concern for the environment, for food, for productivity, for the economy, cannot exclude man. As A. B. House, Chancellor of the University of North Carolina, pointed out in 1947:

> The problems of the fisheries are not mere problems of fish and shellfish. They are problems of human beings, their thinking, their needs, their aspirations, and their potentialities (quoted by Dunn 1974:45).

NOTES

[1]Put more directly, and using language for our example, one may take the language which a society speaks and analyze its sounds (phonemes), its groupings of sounds (words or morphemes), its grammar (syntax), and its sense (semology). But a complete analysis of the structure would still not permit us to know the meaning of any given utterance. That is, we would not be absolutely capable of predicting the content—the specific *interactionally generative* potential of any piece of communication. Similarly, one never understands the "meaning" of any single microstructure within a cultural system until one juxtaposes it with *at least* one other subsystem. And even then many examples are required before one who is learning the system—native and outsider alike—can get a genuine feel for the full potential of the various elements or traits in different contexts.

Again, using language to illustrate the point, the dynamic or processual dimension of the communication aspects of language, as a structure sui generis, remains untapped until one feeds into any given utterance information from systems external to language itself. For example, if one says, "Put those dogs on the run," any speaker of English will be able to recognize and completely analyze the *structure* of the statement—all the phonemes, morphemes, its syntax, and its general sense. The one who hears the command will even be able to suggest what he thinks it meant, what was intended to be communicated. But the utterance out of context leaves much room for ambiguity, despite its structural complete-ness. In fact, the more the listener knows about the world, the more ambiguous the utter-ance may be until additional information is juxtaposed. To list only a few possibilities, the statement may be a command for this individual addressed to: (1) exercise the dogs in the kennel; (2) chase the animals away from my house; (3) put the attacking enemy in retreat; (4) move his feet rapidly and get away. In short, until one gives information from other parts of the cultural system, the correct interpretation remains in doubt; the utterance may not elicit the desired response. Had the remark been "I was watching one of those old World War II movies last night and really liked the way John Wayne told his men to 'Put those dogs on the run!'" the message would have been far less meaningless—or ambi-guously meaning-full.

²Although this volume focuses on change in a dramatic fashion, most anthropologists are aware that change is constant and usually minor. Minor changes, however, tend to ac-crete; unnoticed they accumulate and the recognition that a major change has taken place comes only when we compare two or more time periods separated by a major time gap. We tend to see change retrospectively. Rarely, for reasons we still don't fully understand, some few innovations cause a major reordering of a total system in a relatively short pe-riod of time. It may be that an entire complex, a total ambience at a given moment in his-tory, triggers some major readjustment (an example of what Furet calls "histoire événe-mentielle"). It may be that societies are like geological structures: All the daily, idiovaria-tions which cause gradual alterations of a societal structure, warp that structure to an identifiable degree, but the elasticity of the structure allows such shifting to go relatively or even absolutely unnoticed. Eventually, however, the cumulative effect of the changes over time creates a strain so great that there can be no further give. As with a geologic fault, there is a limit to the accomodation; it is the dramatic moment of upheaval we note rather than the more finally significant but gradual process (Furet's "histoire non-événementielle"). It may be, as Karl Popper has argued, that we can never predict the fu-ture but simply explain the past. This, however, would argue that our concern with change and tradition is heuristically fruitless. Whatever the case, the dichotomy is a concept which must be used with great caution.

LITERATURE CITED

Andersen, Raoul, and Cato Wadel
    1972   Introduction. *In* North Atlantic Fishermen: Anthropological Essays on Modern Fishing. R. Andersen and C. Wadel, eds., Newfoundland Social and Economic Papers, No. 5. Institute of Social Economic Re-search. Memorial University of Newfoundland. Toronto: University of Toronto Press.

Anon.
    1973   Fishing Brings Hope to the Hungry: Case Histories. World Fishing 22(10):54–8.

Anon.
    1974.   India Plans Three-Million Ton Fish Harvest Before 1980. Fishing News International 13(4):37–38.

Anon.
    1975   The Man Who Seeks More Work for Urk. Holland Herald,
            March:11–13.

Bohannan, Paul
    1963   Social Anthropology. New York: Holt, Rinehart and Winston.

Brandt, Vincent S.R.
    1971   A Korean Village: Between Farm and Sea. Harvard East Asian
            Series 65. Cambridge, Mass.: Harvard University Press.

Brox, Ottar
    1972   Newfoundland Fisherman in the Age of Industry. A Sociology of
            Economic Dualism. Newfoundland Social and Economic Studies, No.
            9. Institute of Social and Economic Research. Memorial University
            of Newfoundland. Toronto: University of Toronto Press.

Dunn, Lewis F.
    1974   A New Day Coming for North Carolina Commercials. National
            Fisherman 55(13):44–45.

Enos, John
    1974   . . . And in Gloucester, Bluefins Stole the Spotlight. National Fisher-
            man 55(13):9–10.

Fricke, Peter H.
    1973   Introduction. *In* Seafarer and Community. Peter H. Fricke, ed. Lon-
            don: Croom Helm Ltd.

Furet, Francois
    1975   History and "Savages". RAIN [Royal Anthropological Institute
            News] 8:4–6.

Koentjaramingrat
    n.d.   Socio-Cultural Factors of Economic Development in Dutch Fishing
            Villages [Spalsenburg and Urk].

Kolhonen, Jukka
    1974   The Bluefin Tuna Is in Trouble! National Fisherman 55(13):6–7,
            110–111.

Mather, Frank J., III
    1974   Fish Meal: International Market Situation and the Future. Marine
            Fisheries Review 36(3):36–40.

Miller, Morton M.
    1973   Factors in the Fish Picture of Concern to Industry and Consumers.
            Marine Fisheries Review 35(1):20–25.

Nicolson, James
1973   Shetland: Part I. Commercial Fishing 4(9):5–10.

Nishimura, Asahitaro
1973   A Preliminary Report on Current Trends in Marine Anthropology. Occasional Papers of the Center of Marine Ethnology, No. 1. Tokyo: Waseda University Center of Marine Ethnology.

Vayda, Andrew P., and Roy A. Rappaport
1968   Ecology: Cultural and Non-Cultural. *In* Introduction to Cultural Anthropology. J.A. Clifton, ed. Boston: Houghton Mifflin Co.

Wallace, David
1973   The Future of the Fisheries: IV. National Fisheries Policies and Programs for Our National Needs. Marine Fisheries Review 35(9):11–14.

2

Fishing Communities on the Scottish East Coast: Traditions in a Modern Setting

CHRIS BAKS AND ELS POSTEL-COSTER

Rijksuniversiteit te Leiden

INTRODUCTION

Fishing villages on the Scottish east coast enliven the coastal scene for the tourist, but they are important for more than their charm. From St. Monace in the south to places such as Buckie on Morey Firth, and even as far north as Wick, fishing industries flourish these days. Past and present changes influence the fisherman's life with technological and organizational alterations obvious to any outsider. The character of the formerly closed fishing communities is being modified; the fishing units, boats, equipment, and sale mechanism are in a process of rapid change. There is unmistakably a tendency toward a greater number of working units and more complexity within the units themselves. These changes, however, have not always caused the disappearance of the smaller fishing communities. Small- and middle-range fishing industries have proved to be viable in the past, and a number of them continue to prosper. In fact, among the present fishing ports of the Scottish east coast, Aberdeen is the only place where a large-scale fishing industry developed.

The small-scale fishing industry is the subject of this paper. We will discuss aspects of this type of industry and its organization and try to es-

23

tablish whether such an industry will be able to keep providing a living to the fisherman. The area of study is from St. Monace in Fife to Lossiemouth, including the southern part of Morey Firth. The area of Aberdeen is excluded for the reason given above.

The prevailing pattern of thinking about economic development due to a rise in production has not been escaped by the fishermen in this area. As part of a wide network of social and economic relations, they fully participate in the general modernization process with its emphasis on economic growth. They too are aiming at larger boats, electronic apparatus and ever bigger catches. In general they are very keen on new technological inventions, but they seem to be unwilling to pay the price for modernization.

Recently, social scientists and economists have become aware of the dangers of unlimited growth. The ecological problems are obvious, particularly for the fishing industry where overfishing has been a generally acknowledged problem for years. But there are social reasons as well. Since man's social well-being has become a factor in economic thinking, the question may be asked whether large-scale organization is always the best for contributing to the satisfaction of its members.

More attention should be paid to smaller organizational units, or sections that are less capital-consuming and perhaps more suited to stimulating their members' well-being. In accordance with more traditional patterns of living these smaller units offer the opportunity for working on the basis of personal relations rather than formal ones, and for individual participation instead of alienation. In this direction a way out of the dangers of a too rigorous growth pattern may be found.

The reasons for our choice of the small-scale fishing industry should now be clear. This type of fishing is in fairly small units, although these are more and more forming part of wider organizational networks. It is furthermore characterized by a number of aspects that can be viewed as a set of interconnected factors: the boats generally do not exceed 80 feet in length and most of them are much smaller; fishing is mainly in inshore waters, trips never last longer than a week; harbors are small and mostly tidal; boats are owned individually or jointly; private ownership is made possible by government loans, subsidies and grants; much of the enterprise is based on family relations or other personal ties; fishermen feel attached to their place of birth and living, where they learned the job and know the sea.

As indicated above, not all fishing communities of this type have survived the changing conditions; a number have vanished. Communities that were situated remote from roads and markets, did not have a proper harbor, or were too tiny to be demographically viable have disappeared in the course of time. Moreover, the increasing availability of new jobs outside the fishery, as well as better chances for education, have worked against the continuance of a number of these communities.

However, some communities could survive without a harbor, the men fishing from other harbors which they reach by car. These fishermen-commuters generally spend weekends at home. Fishing activities have become concentrated in adjacent harbors that are better equipped, both technologically and organizationally. This process of concentration has left no more than a score of fishing communities in our area of study. Concentration is closely connected with the general growth patterns mentioned above. It is difficult to foresee if this process will continue until Aberdeen and perhaps Peterhead and one or two other places will attract all fishing activities, but a tendency toward enlargement of scale is prevalent. In the economic field this is apparent in more mechanization, a growing complexity in technical means, and more rationalization of work. In the organizational field, the rise of few and larger institutions that encompass local level activities is noticeable, for example, the introduction of the National Producers Organization since Britain's membership in the European Economic Community.

This enlargement of scale can be seen as a process of expanding social and economic activities, and as an extension of the social structure in which the fisherman lives. From an economic viewpoint the process entails growth of the individual business, intensification by product concentration, employment of wage earners, and cooperation or fusion between the individual fishing units. This ultimately leads to a dependency on the capital market. The fisherman, who primarily is a seaman and a technician, will be obliged to enter an intricate and impersonal system he will not be able to grasp easily. Social factors in this context are a change from the family-based type of fishing industry towards the limited company type based in Aberdeen; the relations between skipper and crew will no longer be defined by informal contracts; kinship as a means of occupational recruitment will be replaced by labor exchange offices; the fisherman's social network, which influences his decisions, will be wider and less familiar to him.

In other words, widening of social activities implies an increase of different, and often external, means of control of working conditions. This will also seriously affect the way of living of the people involved. Part of this process of change no doubt is unavoidable. But do these changes necessarily lead towards an ever larger scale of fishing industries, resulting in the disappearance of the small unit? Most fishermen would frown upon such a prospect. At the moment there is no need for more concentration in the form of fusion of fishing activities to fight economic depression. Prices in the fish market are high. The fishing communities are having a prosperous time, in spite of a decrease in weight of the total catch.

Further, a series of conditions is working against unlimited growth; there is no longer a laissez-faire economy and the open market situation has lost its bitter competition, at least in the personal sphere. Government nowadays intervenes through a number of activities, for example, Department of Agriculture and Fisheries for Scotland (DAFS) enacts rules and regulations that cover financial, organizational, and technological matters. Government policy thereby protects the smaller fishing industries by subsidizing harbor-construction works in small fishing ports.

Whether the development will be toward an ever increasing concentration and uniformity or whether room will be left for variety in technical and organizational scope, is, to a great extent, a matter of government intervention and therefore of politics.

TRADITIONAL BACKGROUND

The Boat

Private ownership of boats is the rule in all the fishing communities discussed here. There are no big firms owning several boats at a time and acting as the employers of skipper and crews. Such firms are regarded with mistrust and depreciation and one can often hear remarks like: "You can trust nobody like you can trust your own folk!"

With very few exceptions, the skipper is one of the owners of the boat, while the other shareholders are for the greater part kinsmen or crewmembers, or both. Obviously this principle involves a limitation to economic expansion. In the region south of Aberdeen, the financial basis for the purchase of a boat has to be found in the family or among close friends.

Moreover, around Morey Firth there is the institution of the "salesman" who acts as a moneylender and administrator for the skipper-owners. The latter, by accepting the mortgage, get into a position of dependency on this particular salesman for the arrangement of their affairs. This is why Fishermen's Mutuals hardly exist in this area, while they flourish in the southern area[1] where they perform the same services to the fishermen in the domain of administration and trade as salesmen do in the north.

The big salesmen, who are able and sometimes willing to take some risks, may support young promising skippers who otherwise would have to wait a long time before having a boat of their own. The agreement is sealed by means of a contract, the content of which is exclusively a matter between the two parties. Conditions may differ from case to case but usually an obligation to make use of the salesman's services in buying certain requirements and in selling a fixed amount of fish is included. While the relation is a contractual one, and theoretically may be terminated by one of the two parties at any time, in practice it has a high degree of permanence. It is based on personal bonds between skipper and salesman. Even the sons of the skippers often choose to continue their fathers' relation with a particular salesman if they become skipper-owners themselves. It is extremely hard to investigate the matter in detail, as the content of contracts is generally kept secret by both skippers and salesmen.

Government grants and loans support the individual owner to a great extent; the capital he has to provide himself amounts to a minimum of 15 percent of the total expenses, by judgement of the White Fish Authority. With prices rapidly increasing, the building expenses of a boat may be estimated at some £1200 per foot, one-fifth of which, roughly speaking, has to be directly paid by the owner (with the support of his family, mates, or salesman). This obviously limits the size of boats. By the involvement of salesmen as providers of capital, the average size of boats around Morey Firth surpasses that of the southern places. For Buckie it was nearly 60 feet for light trawlers and a little more than 70 feet for seinenetters in 1973. In Pittenween, Fife, the main harbor of our southern area, we found averages of 45 feet and 55 feet respectively, in 1971.

A second factor limiting the size of boats is the obligation for the skippers to have a certificate when their ships are over 25 tons, which roughly corresponds to 55 feet in length. Further requirements exist for ships over 50 tons. For this reason one-third of the Buckie light trawlers are just under 25 tons, nearly half of them are under 50 tons, while none are just over 25 or 50 tons.

A third factor in this connection is the situation of the harbors. Most of these are very old, and built where the natural conditions were favorable. Still, some of them are rather shallow, and some have bars near the entrance, so that they cannot be entered during several hours around low tide. Thus, a fisherman from, say, Arbroath has the choice between either adjusting the size of his boat to the capacity of his harbor, or sailing from a bigger harbor like Aberdeen or Peterhead, and commuting by car. The DAFS seems to be inclined to keep these smaller harbors intact. Several of them have been dredged and improved on the request of fishermen during the last few years.

A fourth factor pertaining to the size of boats is the preferred material. Although some change is noticeable in recent times, most fishermen prefer wooden boats to steel ones. The reasons for this are partly emotional ("Only a wooden boat feels like a real ship") and partly, until some years

ago, economical. Wooden ships were built at simple local shipyards that
worked with a minimum of capital investment. During the last five or ten
years, due to the higher wages and price of the material, this has
changed, but some 90 percent of the boats are still made of wood. This
material limits the size: wooden boats generally do not exceed 80 feet in
length, and it is forbidden to have them longer than 90 feet.

Size and material of the boats, in turn, influence the fishing methods.
Wooden boats, with their greater vulnerability to damage, are unfit for
heavy trawling. They are generally used for seinenetting and light trawling for the catching of prawns. Conservation methods and accomodations
on board make for relatively short trips, of five days at most, in not too
distant waters.

Skipper and Crew

The skipper-owner of a fishing boat on the Scottish east coast is in quite
a different, and safer, position than the skipper-employee of the big trawling industry (see J. Tunstall, Ch. IX), who may be fired when he has bad
luck for several trips at a stretch. For the former the boat is, at least in
part, his own, and he feels a strong personal bond with her as may be illustrated by the following newspaper item:

> Fishermen brothers W. and J. C., of Lossiemouth, have retired from the
> sea and sold their 27-year-old boat, the Guide On. But they were loath to
> part with the craft that had served them long and well. So much so that the
> brothers stayed aboard for a last sentimental trip when the new owner,
> Skipper ( ) headed the Guide On from Lossie to her new home
> port—Aberdeen (The Press and Journal, 3 May, 1973).

The skipper choses his own crew of four to five men from a small circle
of relatives, townsmen, or fishermen from nearby villages. Recruitment
is on a basis of personal acquaintance by word of mouth. In principle the
men sign for one trip only, but in practice crews do not change much over
the years.

The skipper's personal capacities are constantly at stake. The competition for the biggest catch is observed by the whole community. It is not
only the old men, who are always present at the harbor quay to count and
compare the number of boxes unloaded for each boat, but also the fishermen's organizations who put up prizes for the Skipper of the Year, the

one who had the highest score in white fish, prawn or herring, and so on. Newspapers regularly publish the names of top skippers and their boats when they have broken former records. An instance of this is the newspaper report on Skipper (   ) of Arbroath, who was in command of a boat less than one year old, the Ocean Harvest II, with a crew of five men, including two of the skipper's sons. Under 70 feet long, she made a remarkable performance that was reported under the title "Big-hearted little boat":

> Many who follow the fishing believe Skipper (   ) and his crew may well have set up a Scottish record for vessels under 70 ft. The Ocean Harvest's landing at Peterhead yesterday raised her grossing for her first year so far to £90,621—and she could substantially improve on this by the anniversary of her maiden voyage if the weather holds (The Press and Journal, 2 April, 1973).

Although it is understood that it is the unity of ship, crew, and skipper which achieves results, the honors are bestowed upon the skipper alone. His skill as a fisherman, his commercial insight that makes him choose the right harbor to land the catch, and an amount of good luck that is also regarded more or less as a personal quality, are held responsible for a skipper's success or failure. Once he has a good name he will be able to attract the better fishermen as crew members, and thus continue his successful career. There is a good deal of tension connected with the job, but also the possibility of great satisfaction.

The skipper excepted, there is no formal hierarchy on board. In the small-line fishery of former days, every crew member brought his own gear, and got the same share of the total earnings. To a certain extent, this principle of sharing has been maintained. After the running expenses have been deducted, the net production sum is divided into two equal parts. One of these is called "the share of the boat." It is destined for the owner(s) who set apart a certain amount for maintenance costs, insurance, depreciation, and other expenses. From the other half the crew is paid; it is equally divided among the crew members, the skipper receiving exactly the same share as the others. It is only in his quality of owner that he may get an extra share, the upkeep expense for the boat permitting. Thus all crew members get equal shares, and do the same work; even the skipper may join the men in hauling the nets or gutting the fish, since he is not expected to behave in an exclusive way. This is one of the attractions the job has for young fishermen; they do not need to pass through long periods of apprenticeship, but are taken as full workers practically from the beginning. The crew at sea forms a group of equals under the leadership of the skipper with a definite common goal: to get a maximum of production in the shortest possible time.

Striking is an unknown phenomenon in this sector of the fishing industry. While stubborn strikes were going on in Aberdeen some years ago, the rest of the east coast remained unaffected. It should be noted, however, that the smaller places profited by the higher prices paid for the scarce fish.

The Fishermen's Relations Ashore

Fishermen and their families formed a rather closed community in earlier days. They lived in their small houses close to the harbor or beach and intermingled more with the families of fishermen in nearby harbors than with the landlubbers who were their townsmen. As long as they fished with bait, as is the case in creel and line fishing, it was important for them to have a "fisher lassie" as their wife, because she would know how to prepare the bait and mend the gear. The women also sold the fish in nearby towns and villages. Nowadays the fishing community is no longer an isolated unit. Many fishermen have moved to modern houses on the outskirts of the town, and reach their ships by car. Their families take full part in the general activities of the village life.

Still, most fishing families remain firmly attached to their original environment. They are part of a relatively close-knit network of family, friends, and colleagues. In this network the same ideal of equality is reflected that is found in the relations between fishermen on board. Families of the skippers or the rich ones are not supposed to deviate too much in their way of life from the average.

It is a striking feature of old fishing villages (whose harbors are hardly used anymore) that so many fishermen keep living there. Sometimes this results in several hours driving to their ships that may lie in some west coast harbor. In spite of the increasing concentration of boats in some big harbors, we found no cases of fishermen moving with their families to the town where their ships are enharbored.

To sum up, the traditional background of Scottish east coast fishing is one in which private ownership of boats and personal ties in business relations prevail. The fisherman is no wage worker; his income and his success in life depend directly on his own individual performance, technical as well as social. For skippers, in particular, great emphasis is laid on their personal skill as fishermen, as leaders of the crew, and on their commercial ability. Part of the traditional background sketched above has maintained itself in spite of changing circumstances. We might even venture that this background is partly the reason for the limited degree to which changes in the fishing industry have been accepted by Scottish fishermen. In the next section we will describe some of the changes that have taken place and some of the fishermen's reactions to changing conditions.

CHANGING CONDITIONS

After 1945 government influence on fishing activities increased. Long before, though, its impact was felt on issues such as the provision of grants to improve fishing harbors or regulations to guarantee a good quality of the catch.[2] The involvement of government in fishing activities can be viewed as a consequence of changing techniques in fishing. However, one should add immediately that there was little government planning. In the eighteenth century, fishing was a part-time activity; one set sail when fish shoals appeared not far off the coast. Fishing techniques were simple and one did not land in a harbor but pulled the boats on the beach instead. Gradually more complicated techniques developed and fishing grounds were sought farther and farther away. Trips were made for longer periods and consequently larger boats (that could only land in real harbors) were required. With private and government aid a number of harbors were constructed. After the middle of the nineteenth century technological changes appeared on the fishing boats, notably the introduction of steam-facilitated activities; but again larger boats and increase of crew were required. Again, longer periods at sea were possible. This could all be financed by bigger catches.

For economic reasons the better-equipped or geographically convenient harbors were reconstructed with private or governmental means, or a combination of both. In this way a process of concentration began. An example is Buckie on Moray Firth which maintained its position as a fishing harbor, while Portessie, Portknockie, Findochty, Cullen, and Portgordon, all situated nearby, became dead ports. Only six other harbors in the same area were able to survive. This is a good example of the restricted enlargement of scale we think typical for the fishing industry in this area.

It cannot be denied that a protective policy is followed by the government to prevent further concentration. This policy seems to be based not so much on a well-designed plan, as simply a case of giving in to local interests of fishermen. Playing a part may be the conviction that it is worthwhile to protect a type of industry connected with a way of living that is quite different from the big trawling industry (as exemplified by Aberdeen). Therefore, Aberdeen does not easily get the money for improvement of its fishing harbor, whereas the tiny port of Gourdon was restored a few years ago.

Four types of fishing can be distinguished today. Before 1870 two types only were discernable: small-line and great-line fishing. The former remained at a short distance off the coast, the latter went farther and farther away. For the latter, two distinct phases led to the present situation—what we describe as a middle-range type of fishing. In the nineteenth century a rapid expansion of fishing took place coupled with a remarkable concentration on one type of fishing: herring. This development was expressed in larger boats, more crew, differing techniques. Changes in technology resulted in a number of new activities related to the fishing industry. To mention a few: more and bigger shipyards, chandleries, banking, insurance, and transport facilities. A division of labor arose with jobs for intermediaries, particularly in marketing. Two important events represented a severe blow to this expansion and led, at least temporarily, to a reduction in scale: the temporary disappearance of the North Sea herring and the collapse of the Central and Eastern European markets forced fishermen to adapt to the new situation. A new technique provided the solution.

TABLE 1   Types of Fishing, Scottish East Coast, 1973

Type of Fishing (1)	Size of Boat (2)	Number of Crew (3)	Fishing Grounds (4)	Type of Harbor (5)
Creel*	Less than 20'	1–2	Near coast	All harbors, the smallest included
Light Trawling	40'–60'	3–5	Up to 60 miles	Middle-range harbors
Seinenetting	60'–80'	5–8	Near the coast, also: west coast, Shetlands, Norwegian coast	Middle-range harbors, and Peterhead
Trawling	More than 90'	Up to 40 or 50	Deep sea	Aberdeen

*Creel fishing is not of much importance now. It is generally a part-time activity for elder fishermen or amateurs carried out in small boats, mostly not more than a mile off the coast. The focus of our study are the types of light trawling and seinenetting.

The Danish seinenet mainly introduced via Lossiemouth and Pitten-weem proved to be an answer to the growing difficulties. Now fishing was possible in smaller boats with modern equipment (deisel engine); fewer crew members were needed. The expenses were less because seiners were best adapted to the changing conditions. This was a dual-purpose boat: in summer and autumn herring were caught by drifting; the rest of the year the men went seining after whitefish. Of great importance was the maintenance of a more personal type of relationship aboard; larger boats in the past required more crew, which led to more formal contractual relations. The new technique enabled fishing communities to continue a way of life in which primary relations prevailed while still allowing fishermen to use modern equipment.[3]

A second event was related to the same ecological factor. In 1943 the herring that used to spawn in the Firth of Forth and had been plentiful all along the coast suddenly failed to appear. The fisherman's principal source of income increasingly became whitefish. As happened 30 years earlier this concentration on one type of fish caused serious problems. A further division, now within the middle-range type of fishing, occurred.

This division was inevitable because no fisherman wanted to give up fishing altogether, or to join the distant water fishery which had developed as a large scale industry. Since the early 1950s two branches in the middle range have developed and have proved to be viable: seining and light trawling. The first operates in areas as far east as the Norwegian coast but also on the west coast, the boats mainly sailing from Peterhead, Fraserburgh, and Pittenweem. The light trawlers fish for prawns and sprat within an area of 60 miles off the coast (mainly in Morey Firth and the Firth of Forth) and operate from small local harbors. This flexibility within the inshore fishery, which opened up possibilities to continue work in a traditional setting, is remarkable indeed.

This does not mean, however, that within middle-range fishing there will be no enlargement of scale. Among fisherman there is a trend to have still larger motors on their ships. The great majority of boats follow the pattern of ever-increasing technological outfitting: an electric winch, power block, radio navigator, radio transmitter, echosounder, and fish-loop.

Oil Industry

The oil industry was expected to bring more employment and wealth to Scotland, in particular to the northeast, at the end of the 1960s. An industrial rejuvenation was forecast which would influence smaller industries as well, for oil equipment, repairs, building, and so on.

These high expectations were accompanied by a gloomy picture for the future of the fishing industry. One of the consequences of a rejuvenation of industry would be a decline in numbers of fishermen. So, for Gourdon, a mass participation of fishermen and their boats in the oil companies' service was predicted in 1971. By 1973 not one skipper had joined an oil company's service; instead they continued fishing as before. The predictions seem to have been based on naive assumptions concerning the temptation of high-paying jobs and to have overlooked non-economic factors such as the social consequences of contractual relations and the loss of a feeling of independence. In other villages there was no mass participation either. Profits in the fishing industry reinforced social motives; a fisherman can earn a good amount of money these days.

However, a growing concern with the expansion of the oil industry was observable, especially in the area from Aberdeen to Peterhead and even Fraserburgh. About £6 million have been spent in the development of what is called Peterhead Bay Harbor. It is intended to construct quais, sheds, installations, and the like on the northern and southern sides of the bay. Peterhead is to be made an operational base for the offshore oil exploration and exploitation. About £60,000 will be spent to improve the adjacent fishing harbor. This much money and even more would be needed for the development of Peterhead as the major inshore fishing harbor of Scotland.

Concern has developed about the role local authorities have played in granting facilities and space to the oil industry. There is a suspicion "that the consultative process has been stretched very thinly on the ground" (The Press and Journal 5.2.1973). This is expressed in concern over future access to the fishing harbor, congestion caused by the built-up activities in the harbor, the tankers sailing in and out. Moreover, land speculation is causing serious problems to the locals and there is an imminent danger of a shortage of accomodation in the area. There is a feeling that most of the development costs will be borne by local people as in the case of the planned new sewage system of Peterhead. It is argued that the benefits of the oil would go to outsiders and this slogan is also a political issue for the Nationalist Party. Although there is a rather high amount of unemployment in this part of Scotland, the oil industry has done little to bring it down. Actually the demand is mainly for skilled laborers. There is, in fact, a shortage of this category (filled by Englishmen). Even more high-skill jobs in the oil company's service are mainly for Americans. There is a noticeable concern about the increasing obstacles at sea. After drilling, part of the material is left at the bottom of the sea and forms a danger to the nets. Fear of pollution is also expressed by fishermen: offshore drilling and, to a greater degree exploitation might result in accidents that would harm the fishing grounds.

These subjects are often talked about and, though vague, they are an indication of the fishermen's anxiety concerning oil and its problems. The oil industry is more than a mere economic factor leading to a change of professions; it is a threat to the fisherman's way of life.

The EEC

The prospects of becoming a partner in the EEC met with great hostility in the circles of the fishing industry. Between 1971–73 it was hard to find a fisherman who favored the EEC. Politics were followed with great suspicion, particularly by the inshore fishermen. Despite the postponement of an important EEC proposal (the period for a national inshore fishing zone covering an area from Berwick to Cape Wrath was extended from 5 to 10 years and the zone itself was extended from 6 to 12 miles), fishermen remained reluctant to believe in the benefits of international cooperation. This was demonstrated by prolonged and seemingly endless procedures in Scotland to establish a National Producers Organization for fishermen not participating in deepsea fisheries, accompanied by remarks that no change was needed at all as the present organizational setting worked smoothly and satisfactorily.

Fisheries are heavily subsidized and, quite rightly, the fishermen fear keen competition from the continental trawler industry. The EEC regulations were drafted to make this branch of industry more efficient in order to provide a viable living in a foreseeable future. However, if this efficiency is to be realized by enlargement of units as is the case in agriculture, the EEC would almost certainly deeply affect the inshore fishing system sketched above.

Today more capital investment could hardly be achieved by single persons: a light trawler's cost are about £45,000. Private ownership would soon disappear followed by shipping companies with shareholders, well-known in the deep sea section. Labor relations would become more impersonal. Enlargement of scale would again imply bigger boats and more crew; the organizational system would change; changes in the share system and changes in wages would occur; more time would be spent at sea to guarantee a higher production to defray higher capital investment. The smaller harbors would no longer serve these bigger boats, and concentration would take place in two or three great harbors. New infrastructural measures would be necessary. Governmental institutions would be oriented away from the local level rather than adhering to the administrative setup which tends to follow a policy of decentralization by providing each district with a harbor, a governmental body, and infrastructural items.

Seining Versus Trawling

As a last example of the fisherman's inclination to accept change only to a limited degree, we may mention the constant struggles between the inshore and middle water fleet and the big trawlers. Recently this conflict resulted in a permanent boycott of Aberdeen harbor by nearly all the East Coast seinenetters. For years the seiners complained about the treatment they had to endure in this big deep-sea trawler harbor where the Aberdeen Fish Vessel Owner's Association dictates the rules. Trawlers always have priority in using the harbor facilities and this can result in the smaller seinenetters waiting hours to get access to the market. In addition, they were not free to decide how to unload their boxes, as there was an obligation to make use of—and to pay—the professional dockhands who were able to make their demands by means of their trade union. After some years of grumbling resistance, the outburst came in 1970, after the authorities decided to close the harbor on Saturdays, an important day for seiners to land their catch. They resorted in great numbers to Peterhead, where they were free to make use of dockhands or not, and where the atmosphere was still the familiar one of the small east coast harbors. The boycott became a success; gradually the traders followed the fishermen to Peterhead. Soon a new fish market had to be built in that place, and after a few years it became too small for the quantities of fish landed by seinenetters and prawn trawlers from the whole area.

The government recognized the central function of Peterhead as a harbor for these smaller boats by subsidizing a further extention of the fish market, while refusing subsidy for the special quay for seinenetters in Aberdeen. The policy of the DAFS, as usual, followed rather than anticipated the events. The purpose, however, was clear: to give full play to a middle-range type of fishing industry.

CONCLUDING REMARKS

For an analysis of the position of the fishermen on the Scottish east coast we may take advantage of a scheme Benvenuti (1974 passim) developed to deal with the degree of entrepreneurial autonomy of West European farmers. It seems to us that his scheme can also be applied to the fisherman in the middle-scale section of fishing.

The parallel, of course, is not a perfect one. There are differences between fishing and farming, one of the most outstanding being that fish-

ing production is more limited by the natural environment than is farming production. However, the similarities are such that in our opinion the
analytical scheme by Benvenuti contributes to a better understanding of
the fisherman's position.

According to Benvenuti, a farmer's situation is mainly defined in economic terms, the ultimate solution to a cluster of problems being more
production and rationalization. This has ended, as we all clearly know today, in surplus production, in overstock, or destruction of goods. A
farmer is subject to a number of functionally related institutions, among
which are finance, market, technology, commerce. These institutions
highly influence the farmer's decisions as Benvenuti argues. Moreover,
these institutions (materialized in banks, agencies, auctions, scientific in-
stitutes, factories, shops, government offices, and so on) in their turn are
part of a wider interconnected set of institutions on a higher organizational level. This mechanism is such that it leaves little room for a
farmer's personal decision.

The basic unit in our paper is the skipper, his crew, and his boat. This
unit is also surrounded by a chain of interconnected institutions which
regulate finances and organize the market in the same way as the banks,
shops, auctions, and agencies given in the scheme of the farmer. The
chain, in its turn, is connected with institutions operating on a wider and
higher level, regionally or nationally. Benvenuti's scheme could be
visualized by an upside-down cone, the bottom representing our skipper,
the crew, and boat, the higher parts representing the institutions with
which he is concerned. The wider an institution's range, the higher its
place in the cone. These institutions, as in the case of the farmer, define
the skipper's position in economic terms. The metaphor of a cone sym-
bolizes the depressing character the institutional superstructure exerts
on his position.

In this respect there are essential differences between a skipper of the
middle-scale fishing industry and one in the large-scale type. The first
one still has an insight into the functioning of the set of institutions
which surrounds him. He personally knows his salesman; a relative of his
may be a member of the cooperative board; the shipbuilder may be a
former classmate; financial means can still be raised in an informal way
by borrowing money from kinsmen. Briefly, primary relations not only
prevail, but these relations also provide the skipper with a framework for
making personal decisions.

In the large-scale section, this last condition is no longer fulfilled. Of
some importance in this connection is the recruitment of personnel in the
District Fishing Offices. These are local level offices in which functionaries generally are from fishing families, keeping close contacts both with
the fishing communities and with the officials in Edinburgh on DAFS

level. These local functionaries have much sympathy for the middle-scale and small sections of the fishing industry.

Hence, we are now in a better position to understand the fisherman's reluctance regarding the EEC. His anxiety can be explained as a feeling of being unable to grasp the procedures at administrative levels. The way decisions are made is hidden on a level beyond the fisherman's perception.

In contrast to this is a large-scale section. Here a more impersonal social structure prevails. The chain of interconnected institutions, as organized around the basic unit, is more defined by formal rules and procedures. Division of labor within the basic unit is rather strict; the crew's wages and labor conflicts are regulated via the unions, and conflicts can easily develop into strikes. We could summarize this by saying that the basic unit of skipper and crew is subject to management from above. This has consequences for the fisherman's way of life. In economic terms, deep-sea fishing is more susceptible to the market mechanism; the large-scale section leads easily to product concentration and specialization by a further division of functions and labor; often an irreversible process begins because capital investment and labor costs are high. This enforces more production and the fisherman becomes more dependent on the decision-making levels in this type of industry. His flexibility and the possibility to choose between alternatives diminish. In social terms, this highly affects the fisherman's life.

Actions by fishermen, such as the blockades of fishing ports in the spring of 1975, are a clear demonstration of the rage of people who know that formal procedures of protest do not work. Circumventing formal rules becomes necessary to draw attention to their complaints. The complicated set of interconnected institutions works as an invisible mechanism of coercion and it seems difficult to make decisions that satisfy the local fisherman in this way.

To prevent the argument that we present too rosy a picture of fishing in the middle-scale section, we admit that a fisherman in this section, too, is influenced by external factors he cannot control; fish prices and the impact of technological change are only two items. Still there is more room for alternatives by different fishing techniques, relative nearness of fishing grounds, less division of labor along formal rules, a tradition-based sharing of the catch, absence of labor unions, and a pattern of social relationships rooted in village society. Though government policy is not formalized, it sustains the middle-range section. The gloomy picture which emerges from Benvenuti's paper is not fully applicable to this middle-range situation.

It is an understatement to say that prediction is difficult in the social sciences. Still, we venture to dedicate some words to the future of the subjects of our study. We think that unlimited growth creates a fish-trap out of which escape is virtually impossible. Though in the initial stages the consequences of actions are not always apparent, one soon becomes painfully aware of the irreversibility of the process. It is hardly necessary anymore to point to the consequences of overfishing as the first limitation to an expanding industry. Second, problems to raise sufficient capital to compete with foreign fishing fleets will dominate the future of a completely modernized fishing industry. Finally, the nucleus of the problem discussed here is the complicated network of social and economic institutions in which the large-scale fishing industry particularly is enmeshed. Instead of continuing to stimulate this type of industry, it will be necessary to guide the middle-scale section and to prevent its being absorbed by the one-sided development of ever growing units.

A policy for a pluriform fishing industry is more and more required, so that a place will be left for smaller fishing units which can more easily adapt to changing circumstances. In general, thinking about development and economic growth should become more oriented toward small-scale types of enterprise.

NOTES

[1]An interesting example is the new Fishermen's Mutual association in Buckie. It was started in January 1973 and joined by 13 fishermen, all of them, except one, owners of relatively big seinenetters. Soon the association, whose members were chosen by co-optation, got the name of being a clique of rich people minding their own affairs. Presumably, the small fishermen; were not even able to join the cooperative associations as this would interfere with their obligations to salesmen.

[2]In the eighteenth century there was serious unemployment and government tried by Acts of Parliament to stimulate fisheries. Gradually government influence increased, e.g., by the establishment of a Board of Fisheries in 1882, by the establishment of the Herring Industries Board (HIB) in 1935, and by the White Fish Authority (WFA) in 1951. The HIB aimed at the reorganization and development of herring fishing. The WFA aimed at a rejuvenation of the fleet by a new system of grants and loans.

[3]For the concept of primordial relations, see Geertz (1963:105–57).

LITERATURE CITED

Benvenuti, B.
    1974   General Systems Theory and Entrepreneurial Autonomy in Farming: Toward a New Feudalism or Toward Democratic Planning? 1974 Conference of the ESRS, Sept. 2–7. Reading, United Kingdom.

Geertz, C.
  1963   The Integrative Revolution: Primordial Sentiments and Civil Poli-
          tics in the New States. Pp. 105–157. *In* Old Societies and New States:
          The Quest for Modernity in Asia and Africa. C. Geertz, ed. New
          York.

Postel-Coster, E. and J. J. M. Heijmerink
  1973   Fishing Communities on the Scottist East Coast. Leiden.

Press and Journal
  1973   Issues for North East of Scotland.

Tunstall, J.
  1962   The Fishermen. London: McGiffon and Kee.

        *Unpublished reports by the following student-participants in a field work
training course have been used for this paper: G. Barendse, S. Bavelaar, W.
Slikkerveer, P. Sutikno, N. Verbraak.

3

Two Stages of Technological Change in a Catalan Fishing Community*

ORIOL PI-SUNYER

University of Massachusetts, Amherst

INTRODUCTION

The observations contained in this report are based on seven months of field work in the Catalan fishing community of Cap Lloc. For a variety of reasons, it seems valid to consider the fishermen-farmers of Cap Lloc, a village between Barcelona and the French border, as a subtype of Catalan peasantry. This is especially true of the fishermen who work the purse seine boats engaged in lantern fishing for sardines, anchovies, and mackerel. The same can be said of the remaining small-scale inshore fishermen employing a variety of archaic techniques. Stern trawlers are relatively new to the region and are for the most part manned by individuals not native to the community.

*This report is based primarily on research carried out between January and August 1972. It also makes use of information gathered in the course of three shorter visits between 1964 and 1975. "Cap Lloc" is a pseudonym for a community in the province of Gerona (Spain). I am grateful to my former Research Assistant, Jessica Kelly, for valuable help in the preparation of this paper.

41

The people of Cap Lloc, certainly those who are descended from the local population, do not regard themselves substantially different from other villagers of this part of Catalonia, whether maritime or inland. This is evident in the way they speak of themselves in counterposition to city people; and when referring to the country (*el camp*), they obviously include themselves in this category.

The influence of the shore is very strong. Many fishermen, with the general exception of the trawlermen, own smallholdings—olive groves, vineyards, or vegetable gardens—and divide their time between working the land and fishing. In the traditional pattern, fishing is not so much a part-time occupation as one segment of a diversified economic base that includes horticulture and some degree of wage labor. There is no doubt that this pattern is extremely old in the Mediterranean littoral. The physical appearance of many Catalan fishing villages attests to the close juxtaposition of maritime and horticultural activities: villages are often nestled in coves and bays with terraced hillsides forming a backdrop. As Braudel (1972:144) has noted, "This is the traditional wisdom of the old Mediterranean way of life where the meagre resources of the land are added to the meagre resources of the sea." In some locations, although not at Cap Lloc, a "double-village" settlement pattern is present with a hill village built some way up the coastal massif and seaside village, by the shore.

Cap Lloc fishermen have some understanding of the ecological constraints imposed by poor soil. The land is stony, rainfall is inadequate, and other sources of water strictly limited. For its part, the sea is biologically exhausted and there are few shallow shelves and no continental platforms where submarine life can thrive. While fishermen are aware of the limitations of the Mediterranean—for example, fish caught in the Atlantic and shipped frozen are cheaper in the community than most locally caught species[1]—it would appear that their attachment to the land is much more than a reaction to these limitations.

There is no rejection of the land, just as there is no rejection of the sea. In many conversations that I have listened to or participated in, talk among fishermen was as likely to turn to agricultural subjects as to fishing, and fishermen informants indicated in various ways that they regarded their agricultural activities as very worthwhile and satisfying. One young fisherman, who had been through secondary school and was a good mechanic, commented that as a fisherman he was able to join the income from fishing to that derived from the land his father had left him: "a very small patrimony, but it has been in the family for generations." Given his skills and education, there is little question that this man could have found a better-paying job in some urban location, but he would either have had to sell the land or lease it, and neither option was satisfactory. On another occasion, an older man summed things up for the dozen fishermen sitting or lying on their bunks before turning in for the night:

> This life has limitations. We do not work regular hours and sometimes we go to sea two or three nights in a row without catching anything. Until we sell it, we do not know how much money the fish will bring. Still, for us it is very important that we can be fishermen without abandoning the soil.

There appeared to be universal agreement among the listeners.

It should be apparent, therefore, that the fishermen I worked with fit neither the standard categories that have been applied to "Mediterranean countrymen" (Pitkin 1963:128)—alienated from the soil they work, hating their labor, discontented with their condition of life—nor those that have been applied to commercial fishermen. With respect to fishing, the voyages are of short duration and the activities always carried out in home waters. These fishermen are skilled sailors, for the Mediterranean in winter is a difficult and unpredictable sea; but the water and its resources—much like the land—are respected rather than taken for granted. While my informants were not above some minor extralegal activities likely to increase catches, it is worth noting that the greatest opprobrium is reserved for those who grossly exploit the aquatic environment, in particular the former Algerian *colons* who (according to local lore) typically resort to dynamite. Shortly before my field work, one such French boat sunk after a charge went off prematurely—an episode that was greeted with unqualified satisfaction. "If only all those pirates blew themselves up, we would be much happier," one fisherman noted.

Given these attitudes to farming and fishing, the close linkage between the two occupations, and an economic strategy based on a balanced exploitation of land and sea, it seems reasonable to approach the fishermen of Cap Lloc as basically a variant of Catalan peasantry. Technologically and economically, they seem to respond to innovations in a manner not unlike other autonomous peasant groups. There is sufficient concern to maintain a system that has stood the test of time to look upon change with some degree of suspicion, perhaps even to see it as inherently disequilibrating.

Yet it would be wrong to see this community and its inhabitants as outside the mainstream of national life. Catalonia is an economically developed region and metropolitan influences are strong—increasingly so with the advent of tourism, which is now the major industry in Cap Lloc and its environs (Pi-Sunyer 1973). Consequently, before we examine the response to technological change, it is appropriate to examine the apparent paradox of the survival of peasant communities close to zones of advanced industrialization and metropolitan influences in general.

PEASANT SOCIETIES AND ECONOMIC RELATIONS

The ability of peasant economies to coexist with complex economic structures has drawn the attention of various students of modernization and development. Ethnographers, who typically view the situation from the perspective of the local community, have generally approached the relationship between developed and traditional economic sectors as at least in part a peasant adaptive response aimed at maintaining the viability of peasant sociocultural systems. According to this interpretation, among the reasons that peasants participate in the developed economy is the maintenance of their "peasantness." Hence, worker-peasants enter the factory labor force in order to keep their farms, and many European migrant workers leave their villages so that they might return to them, richer. A whole variety of other alternatives, including seasonal labor and traditional crafts, is also open to the peasant who desires to supplement income from farming.[2]

Whether we approach the phenomenon of economic dualism from the perspective of the total system or that of the peasant component is not as important as recognizing that peasantries are not automatically incompatible with high levels of industrialization and urbanization. Certainly, in the course of the last century, the trend in developed countries has been in the direction of a drop in the relative and absolute number of countrymen in the population, and this trend continues in societies such as Spain that are undergoing substantial industrial development. However, what is striking is that these population movements, which typically involve a major restructuring in the life of individuals from rural to urban occupations and a conscious choice to become townsmen, often affect rural inhabitants from the most impoverished peripheral areas rather than countryfolk living in close proximity to centers of long-established industrialization. Thus in Spain, the major shift is from the poor regions of the south and center to the industrialized zones of the north and Madrid. Areas of intensive industrialization, including Catalonia and the Basque country, have experienced a much more reduced rural migration. In short, Spanish industrial expansion draws most of its labor force from noncontiguous rural and small town areas, while local peasant communities have been touched much less by out-migration.

The result is relatively viable peasantries in close proximity to expanding industrial zones. In part, this is because urban economic dynamism underwrites the viability of peasant modes of production: the urban markets are close and the prices for agricultural goods relatively high and relatively stable. Also, the wealth of nearby cities helps to underwrite local economies by the intrusion of the urban middle classes as owners of second homes, tourists, and summer people. International tourism may also play a role in offering occupational alternatives (typically for some designated season) to rural residents.

The transformation of rural communities is thus a complex process and the result of a multiplicity of factors. Throughout Europe, the modernization of the countryside has historically lagged behind the industrialization of the cities, a point that is made by George Dalton (1972) when he dates the onset of "late modernization" in the countryside to about 1900. It is of course from the cities, as centers of political and economic power, that the influences emanate, leading to macrochanges in rural life. However, if our analysis is correct, proximity to the city (as distinct from incorporation within it) may actually help to prolong some variant of traditional rural life. This is not to say that the prolongation is indefinite, and obviously it will call for adjustments on the part of rural inhabitants, but for a time at least, peasant communities may survive, even flourish.

Much depends on how the situation is perceived by individual peasants, in particular peasant societies. Although it is always dangerous to generalize for peasants, I would tend to agree with Wolf (1966) that established peasantries, as distinct from marginal agriculturalists and rural day laborers, do find substantial rewards in their condition of life and that most such peasants engage in economic transactions primarily to continue a life where satisfactions outweigh discontents.

If this is the case, one might expect that Catalan countryfolk would respond to modernization and technical change according to the judgment they make as to whether new technological and organizational influences are potentially disturbing to traditional structures. We should note that the fundamental structures of Catalan rural life have shown great durability and substantial stability, and hence are unlikely to be tinkered with capriciously.

TECHNOLOGICAL CHANGE: 1925–1935

Sometime in the 1920s—perhaps 1926—the first motor was installed in a local fishing boat. Tradition has it that this was the work of the village mechanic and that the motor in question was salvaged from a French

automobile. Whether the specific story is apocryphal or not is less important than the manner in which this technological change was received.

Initially, the impact of small motors powering traditional fishing craft
(vessels otherwise propelled by oars and lateen sails, and of a displacement sufficiently small to allow them to be run on the beach) was not
dramatic. Such motors did not alter the basic fishing technology which
remained dependent on human labor, nor did they have any appreciable
influence on the size and weight of gear.

Some of the physical effort involved in getting boats to nearby fishing
grounds was reduced, but even so, motors did not automatically displace
oars and sails. They were used in an auxiliary capacity linked to traditional technological forms. It would seem that, in the local perception,
the mere addition of a motor (low-powered, probably not very reliable)
posed no threat to the established economic system or to the sociocultural order in general. Motors, while expensive according to the incomes
current at that time, were not beyond the means of many fishing boat
owners, and the craft themselves required only minor alteration to install
them.

Today, there are no sailing fishing craft in the fleet and all small boats
are gasoline or diesel powered. However, except that the sail has been
displaced by the internal combustion engine, the small fishing craft are
remarkably similar in build and gear to the typical vessels of half a century ago. However, while such vessels are numerous, their catches represent only a small fraction of the total landings at Cap Lloc.

If the installation of motors did little to alter traditional fishing technology, the same cannot be said for the introduction of a complex of fishing associated with larger vessels that can be dated to the early 1930s.
Again, my information may not be strictly "historical," but it is history
as passed down in the local tradition. According to this lore, the first
large boats (and crews) to come into the area were introduced from Alicante, an important fishing port in the Valencian region southwest of
Catalonia.

These boats were received with great antagonism by the fisherpeople.
The story is told that the women of the village formed a line—a human
wall—to stop the Alicante boats from landing their catches. It was not
only that the boats and crews were "foreign," but that they posed a very
real challenge to traditional fishing techniques. The species caught were
the same for both classes of craft, so they feared the stocks would be depleted; but more than this, the Alicante boats were much more efficient,
much more mechanized, and of course, much more expensive to purchase.

In due course, boats of essentially the same type were purchased by
some of the more affluent local skippers and, more significant, by mer-

chants and other entrepreneurs. However, ownership of such vessels was beyond the financial means of the majority of owner-skippers. As a consequence of this situation, a socioeconomic division began to emerge between "rich" fishermen (and owners who were not themselves fishermen) and "poor" ones, a distinction that in the technological domain was in part reflected by the types of vessels in use—the new, larger seiners with crews of up to a dozen individuals, and the smaller boats with crews of two or three men. Most of the crew members of the larger boats were not rich, but (in common with the crews of most other boats) worked for a share of the catch.

The introduction of larger boats, while originally greeted by antagonism, occurred at a time of a relatively slow technological displacement. The Alicante boats, I have been told, spent only part of the year at Cap Lloc. Then again (and I would judge this to be an important variable) the depression of the 1930s, followed by the Civil War, precluded a quick changeover and thus, to some degree, helped to cushion the impact of a potentially disruptive new technology.

Also, at a time when wages were miserably low, and the price of fish equally low, the small, essentially subsistence fishermen were not placed at such a great relative disadvantage when competing with larger boats. The situation is akin to that described for subsistence farmers in similar depression situations. Operations that used little capital and could depend in part on kin group labor might remain viable while more complex enterprises found it difficult to keep going. In a manner of speaking, the small inshore fishing boats reverted to a kind of economy in which cash was not a critical element.

The Civil War of 1936 to 1939, with all the disruption and distress that it brought in its wake, was hardly conducive to further technological change in the fishing industry. In fact, some of the larger fishing boats were commandeered for naval service and were lost as a result of military operations. By 1950, the Cap Lloc fishing fleet consisted of a substantial number of small craft and a few aging larger ones. The fears expressed in the 1930s that large craft would displace small ones and that the livelihood of fishermen was in danger were not realized. The technological changes which were introduced during the decade 1925 to 1935 proved to be not so much a radical change as a relatively slow familiarization with more sophisticated equipment. Certainly, any anxieties that might have been expressed concerning the demise of traditional fishing became very secondary as the Civil War progressed.

It was not until well after World War II that a rapid technological transformation and accompanying social change radically altered the fishing economy of Cap Lloc. By this period, though, fishing had become an industry of secondary importance when compared to the boom in tourism.

TECHNOLOGICAL CHANGE: 1960–1972

The changes in fishing technology that have occurred from 1960 to the present are in essence quantitative—a further development of what might be termed large-boat purse seining. However, the technology entails capital expenditures of such an order that very few skippers can ever have the expectation of owning their craft. Only small boats, pleasure craft, and inshore fishing boats are now built in the town, and all large fishing vessels are built in commercial shipyards in Barcelona and other major ports. The seiners vary in size from 14 to 40 tons and are powered with motors from 128 to 360 horsepower. Of the ten boats in this category, a couple of the smaller ones are veterans of an earlier era, but most are less than ten years old.

Catch being rowed ashore on auxiliary. Note lamps for night fishing. New tourist-related construction dominates the village.

Changes have taken place not only in the size of boats and motors, but in the general area of improved and increased mechanization. Except for such tasks as the sorting and packing of fish on board, most of the heavy work is now assisted by machinery. This has permitted the use of equipment that would otherwise be impossible to handle, whether by hand or smaller motors. As a case in point, the seine nets on the larger boats are as much as 200 meters in length, which allow for a surface coverage of some 3,000 square meters. Additional equipment which is now found on all the larger boats includes fish-finders, known as "radar" in the local terminology, and sophisticated navigational aids.

These technological developments involve very heavy capitalization. Although government loans help to defray the initial cost of boat construction, the capital required is such that few fishermen can hope to find the means to become owners of large modern boats. As a result, virtually all of the larger craft are now owned by nonfishermen, although some of these owners come from fishing backgrounds and make a point of stressing their links to the fishing community.

The growing complexity of fishing has also resulted in an upgrading of the requirements for professional certification—the permits issued to masters, mates, and engineers. Apart from high seas fishing tickets, of which I believe there are no holders at Cap Lloc, the Ministry of Marine issues three different categories of skippers' certificates for coastal fishing *(patron de pesca litoral)*. These certificates are acquired through formal examination and are progressively more rigorous for larger and more complex vessels operating further out to sea. For skippers of small boats, who are supposedly never to lose sight of the shoreline, examinations are mostly a formality, but for those who desire to command the larger craft, the examinations pose a difficult challenge. The older skippers, who learned their trade through many years of experience, seldom have the formal education to study for the higher level examinations and thus find themselves at a disadvantage when competing with younger men with many more years of schooling.

Since experience, rather than formal credentials, is considered to be the most important attribute which a fishing captain can bring to his job, strategies exist by which older experienced men who lack the necessary certificates may nevertheless command vessels. The most typical gambit is for a boat to have an "official" captain aboard—generally a younger man who has passed the requisite examination—as well as de facto captain, the man who is given responsibility for the working of the vessel. This system works well enough in most cases, but the older captains recognize that they are the last of a long line of traditional skippers who learned their trade on the job and that after them, as one expressed it, will come "the scholars."

While a situation of this type contains a potential for generational conflict, I have never observed evidence of such friction between de facto
skippers and those crew members who carry the official papers, although
it is true that younger, better-educated men frequently voice the hope
that in due course they will be able to exercise the full responsibilities allowed by their tickets.

To the degree that there is discontent, and in my opinion it is not only
present but growing, it is focused not on the structure of authority
aboard boats, but on a changing relationship between boat owners and
fishermen. It is true that skippers function as intermediaries between
owners and crews, but they identify with other fishermen and are not perceived by them as agents of a shore-bound boss. Most skippers, in fact,
try very hard to meet what are regarded as the legitimate requests of
other crew members and considerable emphasis is placed on maintaining
a happy ship.

Problems arise not so much as a direct result of technological change,
but as a consequence of the structural or organizational demands made
by the owners of large and expensive boats. One should keep in mind that
the traditional fishing-agriculture symbiosis (and other adaptive modes
structured along similar lines) is predicated on a substantial degree of individual choice. The system works well in the case of owner-skippers of
small boats and, in theory at least, should also be applicable to larger vessels so long as fishermen and owners agree to common guidelines, for example, crewman substitutions: "Pere will not be fishing tonight, he put
in a hard day at the vinyard; his cousin Juan will probably take his
place."

However, organizational difficulties are bound to increase as the size
of crews grows and tasks become more specialized. Also, as vessels become more costly (counting not only initial investment, but also over-
head), the less likely it is that an owner will readily tolerate such inefficient practices as late departures or the occasional lost day.

This is viewing the situation from the perspective of the investor; matters are bound to look quite different if the point of reference is a working
fisherman whose income is derived from a variety of sources. What occupational strategy is followed by a given fisherman depends largely on his
evaluation of the advantages to be gained in selecting from the available
options present at any given time. The aim of economic maximization
without foreclosure of actual or potential sources of income is an ideal
that is seldom fully realized in practice since economic activities are not
divorced from social obligations (one is expected to reciprocate favors,
help friends, etc.). The play of cultural factors is another variable; thus, a
fisherman-farmer may well decide to allocate time and effort to a mar-

ginal agricultural holding if he feels that inadequate care of his land would reflect badly upon him. Finally, the generalizing strategy of keeping options open will not always be compatible with the goal of maximization (if a fisherman skips too many trips, not only the owner, but also his crewmates, may decide that it is better to do without his services). The point I wish to make though, is that even when such limitations and influences are taken into account—and to some degree they are present in all socioeconomic systems—determinations respecting work and effort are in large measure individually arrived at.

For the ordinary fisherman, the advantages of such a system are apparent. The fishing-farming combination is, in fact, only the most typical mixture, and any other occupational strategy that can be fitted into the pattern is acceptable. Thus one informant, who can hardly be thought of as representative, divided his time between working on a fishing boat and producing abstract art. As he correctly observed:

> I'm probably the only fisherman who also paints for a living, but all my friends work at some other trade as well as fishing. They think that it is perfectly natural that I work at mine and sell my paintings to those who wish to buy them. As you know, all Catalans admire the ability to turn a peseta; we are a country with mercantile instincts, regardless of whether you are dealing with peasants or capitalists.

No doubt my informant was voicing a conventional wisdom, but one, I believe, not irrelevant to the situation at hand. Granting that the people of Cap Lloc are imbued with a common "mercantile instinct," it does not follow that what is good for the fisherman is also good for the businessman, or vice versa. In fact, a very strong case can be argued that, given essentially similar personal goals among fishermen and owners, the instruments for achieving these goals will be hard to reconcile. The "situational logic" (Prattis 1973) of these two elements is bound to be different, perhaps even incompatible.

THE DECLINE OF FISHING: SUMMER 1975

It was already clear in 1972 that purse seine fishing from large boats was facing some critical difficulties. Prior to that time, technological innovations had been incorporated with relative ease into the existing social and economic structure. The fears that modern technology would disrupt the traditional order proved for the most part to be unfounded.

Some strife was generated, but as long as technology did not pose a threat to a multifaceted pattern of making a living, anxieties were short lived and accomodation was possible.

Such accomodation, though, was becoming ever more problematic. Also, just at a time when the strain was growing, other occupational options were presenting themselves as viable alternatives. Most of these avenues of employment were linked, directly or indirectly, to the tourist boom and the transformation of Cap Lloc into a resort community.[3]

I returned to Cap Lloc for a few weeks in the summer of 1975. While the briefness of this stay precluded an in-depth examination of the fishing industry, some significant shifts and changes were noticeable. Most obvious was the decline in the purse seine fleet, which by 1975 numbered only six large vessels. Some of the veteran boats, retired from service, had not been replaced. Some modern vessels were also gone, including the 1972 queen of the purse seiners, a large and well-equipped craft which I knew well from my previous visit. The owner had decided it was no longer profitable to operate the boat out of Cap Lloc and had sold her to a fish-

Sorting and packing catch on purse seiner.

ing company in Barcelona where urban-dwelling fishermen do not divide their time between fishing and farming.[4]

This decline in purse seiners was in some measure compensated for by an increase in the number of trawlers. Trawlermen are not engaged in the traditional dual exploitation of land and sea resources; instead, they fish on a full-time basis and earn higher incomes from fishing than the crews of purse seiners. Two factors contribute to this income differential. First trawlers are able to operate in much rougher seas than purse seiners, allowing more working days per year; second, trawler crews split 60 percent of the market price of a catch, while seiner crews receive only 50 percent. A number of men who had previously worked on purse seine boats were, in 1975, earning their living on trawlers. The impression I received was that if a quasi-wage labor situation was a trend of the times in all large vessels, one might as well go all the way and ship on a trawler. Such a trade-off, however, precludes significant shore-based employment.

Other former seine fishermen reacted in an entirely different manner. Instead of shifting to trawlers, they reverted to inshore fishing from small boats—the most traditional marine livelihood and the one offering the greatest flexibility of time and effort. While only a few men were involved in this shift, such fishing seemed to be successful. At least ten small fiberglass fishing boats, plus several score wooden ones, were operating in 1975. Although glass boats are virtually identical to wooden boats in form and function, their presence indicates a willingness of some fishermen to invest their own money in a relatively untried technology.

The healthy condition of small boat fishing can be explained, in part, by higher wages and improved standards of living. The ownership of one's own boat, however small, is something most local fishermen aspire to; and it is quite possible that a number of boats are operated, not so much because of the income they bring in, but out of satisfaction of ownership. Economically, such enterprises may not always pay their own way, but a fisherman with money coming from other work may still be willing to subsidize his own fishing operation. In contrast, an owner of a large and expensive boat must perforce run it at a profit.

Finally, the development of tourism, and its consolidation as the major local industry, opened up a series of occupational niches offering reasonable alternatives to working on a seine fishing boat. No fishermen that I had contact with, either in 1972 or 1975, were employed by restaurants or hotels. This is understandable since most of the jobs in these businesses (waiters, bellboys, porters, etc.) are poorly paid and involve long hours. Immigrants from other parts of Spain fill most of these slots. The better paying jobs in the tourist industry call for levels of education that few fishermen can meet, although the children of fishing families are urged to study hard and become proficient in languages. However, fishermen do have certain skills that are very much in demand in a community that expands greatly during the summer and lacks an adequate number of repair and maintenance personnel. The situation is aggravated by the absence of a handicraft tradition among the southern European middle and upper classes; they have not grown up with tools and few are capable of making even the most rudimentary repairs. In marked contrast, fishermen tend to be skilled with their hands and able to tackle a variety of jobs.

As a result, over the past few years, several fishermen have capitalized on their skills as jacks-of-all-trades. This option has the advantage of allowing the individual to budget his own time and be his own boss; the investment necessary for establishing oneself in this line of business is minimal, and such work closes none of the traditional avenues of employment. Tourism and resort development offer many other income opportunities, including marine-related jobs on boats and at marinas. Furthermore, a steadily growing number of urbanites are establishing year-round homes in the area, bringing some changes to the seasonal nature of shore jobs.

In conclusion, the decline in purse seine fishing at Cap Lloc relates to a series of organizational constraints that make it difficult for fishermen to manage their lives in a desireable and satisfactory manner. Although the problem can be approached as one of technological change, it is not technical innovations, as such, that are primarily responsible for the discontent of fishermen and the actions of boat owners; it is the limitations that these innovations impose on an ethic that views labor in a positive light, while insisting that each individual has the right to define what combination of tasks best suits his needs. Clearly, this freedom of choice is hardly compatible with forms of organization that demand increasingly strict standards of labor discipline, or as one of my informants would phrase it, "you are expected to fish even when it doesn't suit you." In short, fishermen working on seiners find it difficult to "make allocations in terms of the pay-offs that they hope to obtain" (Barth 1967:668).

Fortunately, for most of the men I worked with, the local economy continues to offer a variety of culturally legitimate, and personally satisfying, choices—not excluding some fishing. Other men have opted for full-time commercial fishing, but they have shifted to a different kind of vessel which, on the whole, renders a higher and steadier income. In all likelihood, though, the social and economic changes currently under way do not spell the end of large-boat seine fishing; probably a new balance is being struck that reflects the interplay of available options and individual allocative strategies.

NOTES

[1]Much of the "typical Mediterranean seafood" consumed in local restaurants is, in fact, of Atlantic origin; the cuisine may be Catalan, but the species often come from the Bay of Biscay. The higher grade establishments, however, use locally caught fresh fish and charge accordingly. Only some 15 percent of the fish landed in Spanish ports comes from Mediterranean waters.

[2]Among Catalan peasants income diversification is an old pattern. Both the small size of holdings and a tradition of impartible estate inheritance are factors that help to account for this pattern of work and employment in the countryside.

[3]Tourism has been a mixed blessing at Cap Lloc and other Costa Brava towns. Whatever discontents it may have generated in the region as a whole, it has also undoubtedly expanded the range of occupational options open to some fishermen.

[4]It is also likely that boats based in Barcelona render somewhat higher profits because of the proximity to the urban market.

LITERATURE CITED

Barth, Fredrik
    1967   On the Study of Social Change. American Anthropologist 69:661–669.

Braudel, Fernand
    1972   The Mediterranean and the Mediterranean World in the Age of Phillip II, Vol. 1. S. Reynolds, trans. New York: Harper and Row.

Dalton, George
    1972   Peasantries in Anthropology and History. Current Anthropology 12:385–415.

Pi-Sunyer, Oriol
    1973   Tourism and its Discontents: The Impact of a New Industry on a Catalan Community. Studies in European Society 1:1–20.

Pitkin, Donald S.
    1963   Mediterranean Europe. Anthropological Quarterly 36:120–129.

Prattis, J. I.
    1973   Strategising Man. Man 8:46–58.

Wolf, Eric R.
    1966   Peasants. Englewood Cliffs, New Jersey: Prentice Hall.

*

4

Lebanese Fishermen and the Dilemma of Modernization*

PAUL D. STARR

Auburn University

Throughout most of 1975, Lebanon experienced the most serious and bloodiest conflict in its independent history, including the Civil War of 1958. Over 10,000 persons (out of an estimated total population of 3 million) were killed and many more wounded in fighting between heavily-armed groups of predominantly Christian right-wing Lebanese nationalists and leftist forces primarily composed of Lebanese and Palestinian Moslems. Multi-story buildings were flattened, shops and apartment houses blown up, businesses destroyed and the economy and political structure severely crippled.

Although the conflict is the consequence of tensions which have accumulated over the past several years, one incident which occurred in late February of 1975, during a protest demonstration by fishermen and their supporters in the ancient port city of Sidon, was both an immediate

*This research was supported by a grant from the Center for Behavioral Research, American University of Beirut, Dr. E. Terry Prothro, Director. The author is also grateful to Raoul R. Andersen, Nura Almuddin, Samir Khalaf, P. Nelson Reid, and Susan Starr for their helpful criticisms on an earlier version of this paper, but retains final responsibility for its contents.

cause of localized political unrest and an expression of the larger conflict
in microcosm. There are other factors which must be considered in any attempt to explain the bloody fighting of 1975, including the economic disparities between Christians and generally less-prosperous Moslems, differences regarding support for the Palestinian liberation movement and
Pan-Arabist ideologies, and the concerted effort by Moslem leaders to
change the existing political formula and acquire greater power within
the government. The dispute concerning the fishing franchise, however,
reflects both the broader dilemma of traditional seafarers in the eastern
Mediterranean, challenged by technological obsolesence, and political
processes and conditions which are somewhat unique to Lebanon.

Despite conflicting accounts of what happened, there is agreement
that security forces and others exchanged fire during the demonstration
and a well-known former member of parliament and political leader from
Sidon, Ma'arouf Sa'ad, was wounded. His death a few days later pro-
voked further clashes. During a subsequent week of fighting in Sidon and
other areas, scores of people—including civilians, soldiers, and police-
men—were killed or injured. Protest demonstrations were held in many
parts of the country; the Beirut fish *souk* (market) was closed; the northern port of Tripoli was blockaded for several days; and the Beirut offices
of a fishing company were destroyed by dynamite, injuring several
passers-by. The mutual recriminations which followed nearly toppled the
government of Prime Minister Rashid Solh, who resigned a few weeks
later because of further complications.

The main purpose of the demonstration was to show the fishermen's
opposition to the award of a government franchise for fishing and fish
processing activities to a firm, Proteine S. A. L., headed by the prominent politician and former president of the republic, Camille Chamoun.
The decree granting the franchise, made in December 1971 and publicized
two years later, permitted the firm to exploit the Lebanese coast using
modern fishing trawlers which could reach depths of up to 1200 fathoms.[1]
These operations were to take place at least two kilometers offshore, so
that they would not compete with local fishermen using more traditional
methods. The company was authorized to purchase the fish caught by
others in Lebanon and to use modern methods to store, package, and
market the catch for local consumption and export. Its activities were
also to include the production of canned fish, fishmeal, and fertilizers.
The decree further specified that the enterprise would be permitted to improve existing harbor facilities and promote the use of modern fishing
methods among Lebanese fishermen. Negotiations were undertaken with
a Yugoslavian enterprise to provide vessels and other modern equipment
to be paid for either directly or by shares in the company, but little had

been accomplished beyond the initial planning stages before the demonstrations took place.

As a result of the uproar regarding the franchise, the Lebanese Council of Ministers presented a decision a month after the initial Sidon shooting which amended the initial decree and specified that, in order to further protect the interests of traditional fishermen, Proteine was to fish no closer than 16 kilometers from shore. The government also promised funds to improve facilities at some of the smaller harbors and to assist in the formation of local fisherman's cooperatives, plans for which had been made several years ago.

Although some critics described the franchise as granting the firm exclusive rights over all coastal fishing, the management stressed that their activities would not prevent the traditional fishermen from carrying on as usual. In spite of news reports to the contrary, spokesmen for the firm indicated that fishermen using more traditional methods would not be required to sell their catch to the company, but could do so if they wished.

In the eyes of many opponents, the fishing franchise was incorrectly seen to be the same as the franchise conducted by the Lebanese government for the purchase and sale of tobacco. The Regie Libanaise des Tabacs purchases a certain amount of locally-grown tobacco every year. Even though the price of local tobacco is much higher than comparable grades on the world market, thousands of families—some of them Christians from the Akkar and Koura districts, but most located in Shi'ia Moslem areas of South Lebanon—depend on the crop for their livelihood, and it is supported by large government subsidies. The distribution of the annual quota of licenses for tobacco purchase is thought by the farmers to involve favoritism toward large landowners and the exploitation of small growers who sometimes must sell their crop at a very low price to those with a license. Demonstrations and conflicts between farmers and the internal security forces, resulting in some casualties, have taken place in Nabatiyeh, a predominently Shi'ite Moslem community and site of a large Regie installation. Even though the provisions of the fish franchise are quite different and do not provide the firm with a legal monopoly, some opponents have misrepresented it as such, while other critics have more appropriately described it as a "monopoly in fact."

Criticism has also come from other quarters; some merchant shipowners complained that Proteine was given a lease over a highly desirable docking area in Beirut's crowded harbor for its operations while they had no space to carry out even minor maintenance on their vessels.

There is little doubt that Lebanese fishermen are less productive than those from other countries in the eastern Mediterranean. Although Lebanon is probably among the least sea-oriented of coastal nations, a tiny but highly visible portion of the population nevertheless makes its living by fishing from small boats, usually not farther than a few hundred meters from shore. Two types of boats are commonly used: the *filuka*, which has no engine, and the *lensh*, which is motorized and usually larger. Both types are doubled-ended, have a wide beam, and range from three to nine meters in length. There are about a thousand fishing boats in the country, each of which is in some way different from the others. Most have been made to order in either Tyre, Sidon, or Tripoli. Crewed by one to three men, a larger *lensh* will often tow and work in conjunction with two or three *filukata*.

The most common fishing methods in current practice include the use of gill and sardine nets, long lines, hand lines, and to a lesser extent explosives. While the techniques employed in the two types of net fishing are similar, gill nets are larger and have a mesh five centimeters square and are about 300 to 400 meters long by 2 to 5 meters wide. Sardine nets have a finer mesh about one centimeter square and are shorter, usually about 50 meters long by 30 meters wide. All nets observed are weighted at the bottom by rocks and have floats attached to the top. Long lines of about 200 meters have hooks on the ends of 1 meter lengths of line which are spaced every 2 meters totaling 70 to 100 hooks per rig. These are usually baited with sardines and are stretched beneath the surface between floats or boats. Hand lines, which are used over the side of a boat or from floats, have three to five hooks. Lamp fishing, employing lights fueled by gas bottles to attract fish to baited lines, is practiced, particularly during the warmer months. Many fishermen use both nets and lines during the same outing, and a few set lobster traps. Small portions of dynamite, or occasionally, a hand grenade may be used to kill or stun fish so they rise to the surface, where only about a fourth of them are later collected for bait or sale. Even though the market price for such fish is a fraction of that for those caught by conventional methods, and the fishermen recognize it as a wasteful practice, explosives continue to be used all along the coast in increasing amounts.

Over the last twenty years fishermen have increasingly adopted such innovations as motors, nylon nets, styrofoam and plastic floats, and improved methods of lighting for night fishing; but there are no craft of any size which are able to safely fish some distance from shore, and modern techniques of trawling and storing fish are not found.

Most of the fishermen work during the night and set their nets or lines 200 to 400 meters offshore between eight P.M. and midnight. The catch is retrieved between four and five A.M. and the fishermen are usually back on land an hour or so later. If they sell their fish to a broker and have only minor net repairs and other routine maintenance, their work day is typically over between eight and nine A.M.

Because of earlier nightfall and later daybreak, more hours are spent on the water during the winter months of November through most of March, and some days are lost because of poor weather. A few fishermen switch their work regime from night lamp fishing to day fishing during these months, and some of the less serious fishermen suspend their activities altogether.

Boats are usually operated by their owners who are often assisted by their sons, brothers, or other kin. Sharing arrangements are made between an owner whose boat or boats are used by another, with most of the income going to the actual operator, but this practice is not widespread. Incomes are quite low for the vast majority of fishermen, with most earning approximately 100 U.S. dollars a month. Those who can, earn money from other sources, such as part-time cab driving, construction work, semi-skilled or unskilled labor, or other activities which are compatible with their life as fishermen. Some earn additional income by giving tourists and local swimmers rides to small islands or coastal sites during the warmer months or by smuggling untaxed foreign cigarettes throughout the year.[2] In spite of their low incomes, the fishermen generally regard themselves as superior to other persons who are reliant upon and must be subservient to others in their work and do not have to cope with such a rugged environment.[3]

Marketing is either through a broker or direct to the consumer. A large proportion of fishermen regularly sell their catch to a broker who then transports it to the *souks* of Beirut, Tripoli, or the larger towns for resale. Sometimes the broker himself sells from a stall or makes an arrangement with others, usually members of his extended family, to do so. A few of these middlemen carry on a continuing business with restaurants located in the cities or on the coastal highway; but most of the larger restaurants specializing in seafood retain fishermen directly, and buy from others only when the demand is great or cannot be met by their own people. There are accounts of brokers exploiting the fishermen by making the loans at unreasonable terms, by giving them less then fair prices for their catch, and by using false weights and dishonest procedures during the morning weigh-ins. Such complaints do not appear to be widespread or to evoke great hostility, perhaps because the fishermen have always had the option of selling to other brokers or of directly marketing their catch to the consumer, which many of them do.

Fishermen who work offshore from urban enclaves (some of which are literally in the shadow of Beirut's high-rise luxury hotels), or from locations very close to the busy coastal highway usually sell their catch directly to consumers. They generally display their fish by the side of the thoroughfare to catch the eye of passing motorists in the rural areas or, as in Beirut, put up a flag or other symbol on the end of a bamboo pole to indicate to passers-by that they are available for business. As is generally the case with the marketing of local produce in that small country, there is no advertising, yet consumers almost always have an extensive personal knowledge about where, when, and from whom one may obtain different foods; and transactions are usually conducted on a continuing basis between the same producers and consumers.

Most varieties of fresh fish are regarded as delicacies, and the marketing process frequently takes place during the holiday or leisure time of the consumers, so the buying of fish is often regarded as an enjoyable activity in itself. Extended discussions frequently occur between buyer and seller about the important criteria for selecting a fish or about the advantages of one type over another, not unlike the conversations in Beirut butchershops between customers and butchers regarding spring lamb, another Middle Eastern delicacy. During these exchanges there is generally little or no bargaining over price. Both fishermen and clients are aware of current prices and have similar expectations. Reflecting bargaining practices in the Middle East in general (Khuri 1968), it is considered demeaning for persons of high status to be hard bargainers, and as the most frequent consumers of fresh fish occupy the higher echelons of society, elaborate negotiations over price are not common. Bargaining may take place only once between a fisherman and a regular client, during their first transaction. The price negotiated tends to remain fairly stable during subsequent exchanges, with some seasonal variation, providing for a continuing fisherman-client relationship which entails certain advantages for both. It provides the fisherman with a regular outlet for his fish and the buyer with a reliable source at an acceptable price in an otherwise uncertain market, and saves some time for both.

A few fishermen market their catch using a combination of methods, usually by selling the fish they caught during the night to a broker and, if they go out another time during the day, by selling their second catch directly to consumers in the late afternoon.

Aside from being occasional customers, women play no discernable role in the marketing of fish, or in any other activity concerning fishing, including the repair of nets.

Many forces, however, threaten the traditional fisherman's way of life. The holders of the franchise and their supporters, backed by considerable technical expertise, have contended that modernizing Lebanon's fishing industry is vital to economic progress and that it would greatly benefit both the general population and the traditional fishermen. They say that the use of modern equipment would multiply the catch and exploit it much more effectively. Freezing, canning, and the production of fish by-products would drastically cut waste. Volume production and marketing would benefit consumers, lower prices, cut imports, and strengthen the country's economy. The dangerous, wasteful, and technically illegal use of explosives in fishing would no longer be necessary. They have also indicated that fishermen, who now operate independently or in small groups could staff the new vessels and processing facilities, where they would be covered by the benefits of the government social security system and receive a higher and steadier income. Little action had been taken prior to the award of the franchise even though most of these improvements have been put forth by experts over the last few years and have been incorporated into government development plans (Boulos 1967, 1970).

An estimated 50,000 to 60,000 tons of fish could be sold each year on the Lebanese market, but only about five percent of that amount is now caught locally. The remainder needed for the present annual consumption of about 25,000 tons is imported in tinned or frozen form from Japan, Atlantic, Arabian Gulf, or other Mediterranean countries, including nearby Turkey and Greece. Some of the imported fish are caught off the Lebanese coast by modern vessels from these other Mediterranean countries. Lebanon has been spending the equivalent of about 90 million U.S. dollars a year to import fish and over twice that amount to import meats, causing a serious drain on the economy. Since most of the meat and dairy products used in the country are imported, these high protein foods tend to be expensive. Fresh fish, a primary source of protein in many other Mediterranean countries, may cost over $12 U.S. dollars a kilo in Lebanon, making it a delicacy for the more affluent. Only about three percent of the population eat it regularly. Although fresh fish is particularly desirable, tinned and frozen fish have a larger share of the market.

As the Proteine firm has not been able to complete the preparations required for its operations, it is not clear how they intend to market their catch or how their activities would specifically influence established fishing and marketing patterns. It is quite apparent, however, that the traditional fishermen, fish brokers, and their supporters perceive the Proteine franchise as granting the firm illegitimate rights to activities which the fishermen and brokers feel are theirs and that they stand to lose a good part of their livelihood to the Proteine firm as a result.

Leaders of the Sidon, Tyre, and Tripoli Fishermen's Unions have emphasized in their complaints that the franchise would give the firm a virtual monopoly over coastal fishing and create grossly unfair competition for them. They fear, with much justification, that they might be forced by market conditions to sell their catch at lower or unfair prices to those who are competing with them, and further complain that while the company initially said it could hire 6,000 fishermen it later indicated that there might be opportunities for only 360 "qualified" staff, a tenth of the estimated number of fishermen in the country.

Although not mentioned in their public statements, some fishermen feel the Proteine firm would deplete the number of fish off the coast and would catch such a quantity of fish that prices would fall; they fear Proteine would hamper independent marketing and make traditional fishing economically impossible. Having the reputation of being their own men, many reject the idea of losing their independence and, even if positions were open to them, of becoming employees of a large firm. This attitude prevails even though the average fisherman's annual income is much less than the minimum wage specified by the Lebanese government (Republique Libanaise 1972). It has also been suggested that most *Zu'ama* (local political leaders or patrons) in the coastal areas, whose power is based on a combination of traditional sectarian and kinship allegiances, are concerned that such employment would erode some of their present power and influence. They have individually expressed support for locally-controlled efforts to improve current methods, facilities, and equipment, but no specific alternative plans appear to have been formulated.

A different and perhaps more probable outcome of the firm's modernization of fishing is that it would have a relatively insignificant effect on both the price and the volume of fish available on the market. As many locally processed foods and other locally made items are intentionally priced just under that of heavily taxed and expensively transported imported goods (and are often of lower quality), the price benefits of improved local technology to the consumer are often negligible. Aside from the favorable impact such a change would have on the country's balance of trade, consumers would receive little or no benefit. Under these circumstances the bulk of the present income from fishing could then also go to the Proteine company, depriving the traditional fishermen of most of their livelihood.

The issues involving the franchise further reflect some of the human problems induced by technical change and the experience of the occupational groups involved. It is evident that the decline of traditional seafaring life along the Syro-Lebanese coast has accelerated over the last decade, particularly in Lebanon, largely because of increased competition from modern vessels, a reduced fish population due to pollution and ecological changes, and to a lesser extent problems associated with the Arab-Israeli and Cyprus conflicts. A decline in occupational opportunity, similar to that which befell Lebanese sponge divers, is presently occurring among the coastal schooner sailors in the Eastern Mediterranean and may soon be experienced by the fishermen of Lebanon.

Old seafarers in the country are familiar with the rapid decline of Lebanon's sponging fleet, which had over 400 six-man vessels in the pre-World War I era but now numbers under a score. Unable to compete with much more efficient Greek vessels using divers equipped with underwater breathing apparatus in the 1920s and 1930s (Bernard 1972) or later to cope with the drastic drop in the natural sponge market brought about by the development of improved synthetic sponges, the vast majority of sponge fishermen were forced to pursue another livelihood (Solayman and Charles 1972:226–30). Since sponge diving took place only during the summer months, most had other occupations to fall back on.

The graceful Syrian *skayen* (schooners), wooden sailing ships of up to 100 feet in length and 50 to 300 tons gross, which originally had double masts and square-rigging and sailed over much of the Mediterranean in the late nineteenth and early twentieth centuries, are declining rapidly. Converted to simpler rigging, given auxilary engines and smaller crews in the years after World War II, these ships formerly carried on an active coastal trade between Beirut, Gaza, Port Said, Alexandria, Famagusta, Iskunderun, and Mersin (Prins 1965). A few are still able to compete with more modern vessels on some runs.

Having lost some of their trade since World War II to the greatly expanded road transport system, the schooners are forfeiting their existing share to the larger, faster, and more modern steel-hulled vessels. Although *skayen* accounted for about one fourth of all ship movements in Beirut harbor in the early 1960s, their number of movements since has declined by about 70 percent (Tarhini 1975).

Seafarers have also suffered reverses because of the Arab-Israeli and Cyprus conflicts. The 1967 Arab-Israeli War disrupted schooner traffic to Port Said, Gaza, and through the Suez Canal while the 1974 Turkish invasion reduced trade with Cyprus. Fishing boats in the harbors of Tyre and Sarafand were also destroyed in 1974 by Israeli commandos in reprisal for a Palestinian raid said to have used such craft. Over the last several years, Lebanese fishermen have frequently been detained and harrassed by Israeli patrol boats off the southern coast.

The eastern Mediterranean basin has naturally low fertility because of its land-locked nature, prevailing winds, and precipitation-evaporation regime; fishing has been affected by other problems, as well: occasional quarantines, the pollution which has occurred throughout the Mediterranean, and ecological changes. Different studies have shown that only a very small percent of the fish, shellfish, and crustacea caught in the Mediterranean do not contain traces of chemicals used in insecticides or from industrial wastes. The construction of the Aswan Dam in Egypt has also reduced the number of fish in the eastern basin. The amount of nutritive elements carried by the Nile and then pushed by winds and currents along the coast has been greatly reduced since the dam was built, cutting the populations of some species of fish (Conseil Municipal de Beyrouth 1973).

Both fishermen and the Syrian schooner operators have been able to compete with more technologically advanced competitors by substituting low-priced labor for more sophisticated machines and by modifying their equipment by installing motors, using nylon nets, and other innovations, but these options appear to be nearly exhausted. Because of rising labor costs and increasing levels of efficiency on the part of competitors, modified traditional methods will probably become even less practical. Barring unforseen events in a region known for its instability, modern marine technology could complete its takeover of these activities within a few years. Given the political influence of occupational groups which would become obsolete through the introduction of such innovations and their value to political leaders who could exploit them for other purposes, it might take longer.

Even though several different religious sects are represented among the fishermen, the problem also demonstrates the extent to which many political issues in Lebanon's multi-ethnic society become polarized along sectarian lines.

Much of the activities of the zu'ama' (singular za'im) involves mediating between individual followers and larger political institutions, reflecting a state-*za'im*-client community relationship rather than a state-citizen or state-party-citizen relationship which is common to many other societies (Khalaf 1968, Farsoun 1970). In exchange for their support of a *za'im* (usually in the form of votes, political campaign work, financial contributions, and service in the party militia) followers expect to receive protection against governmental and other threatening outside forces, assistance and favors in employment or in securing government benefits, and *wastah,* or mediation, on their behalf to accomplish these and other ends. These relationships have not been seriously hindered by migration or urbanization and have the same character in both rural and urban areas. When *wastah* fails to provide a desired affect, as in the case of those attempting to do away with the fishing franchise, *zu'ama'* may escalate their efforts and order their followers to "take to the streets" in the cities or to cut roads and otherwise disrupt transportation in the rural areas.

Most relationships between a *za'im* and his clients are based on real or fictive kinship ties. Political identity in Lebanon is synonomous with membership in an extended family within a larger sect. Religious communities tend to be federations of large extended families whose economic and political interests largely coincide and are expressed through *zu'ama'* who are frequently elected to Parliament and are appointed government ministers.

It is no exaggeration to say that much of Lebanese politics since the Ottoman Period can be interpreted as the dynamics between Ottoman and French Mandate authorities and different coalitions of *zu'ama'* representing various communities, as well as between different coalitions, as they come into conflict, negotiate, mediate, exchange, and shift support on various issues.

The ex-deputy who died from wounds received at the initial Sidon demonstration was of humble origins, considered a champion of Moslem and Palestinian causes and had the reputation of being almost selfless in protecting and promoting the rights of the urban poor in his district. The head of the fishing enterprise, ex-president Chamoun, founder and leader of the National Liberal Party, primarily composed of Christian Lebanese nationalists, is somewhat representative of the group of privileged political and economic tycoons who comprise the Lebanese elite. As has been repeatedly shown during past crises, the stability of the Lebanese polity is fundamentally dependent upon consensus among the leadership of various Christian, Moslem, and Druze factions which compose the bulk of the population (Binder 1966, Hudson 1968). Frequently a political issue may not initially involve sectarian differences, but the confessional basis of political parties and of the organization of the government, in which the President has always been a Maronite Christian, the prime Minister a Sunni Moslem and the Speaker of Parliament a Shi'ite Moslem, tends to promote confrontations among political leaders with different sectarian constituencies. Political issues are perceived by many as involving confessional rivalries and subsequently tend to follow such forms, suggesting how the definitions and expectations found within each faction help to bring about sectarian confrontations as self-fulfilling prophecies. It is quite likely that, having become a focal point of political concern, the problems regarding the modernization of fishing in Lebanon will serve as an idiom, among other issues, to articulate the larger and very complicated competitive dynamics found in Lebanese politics. Although overshadowed by the later, more serious fighting between Christian and Moslem militants, the issue has been and will probably continue to be exploited in the continuing contest for power by groups both within and outside the government.

The groups who would be most directly affected and who feel the most threatened by changes of this type are, typically, self-employed people with few resources and a limited flexibility to adapt. As has been the case with much of the economic development which has occurred in Lebanon, those already in positions of advantage in the socio-economic hierarchy have not only been able to more effectively protect themselves from the potential disadvantages which innovations might bring, but they can also more easily examine, experiment with and take advantage of newly developed methods and resources. They usually have much greater access to the capital which is required for new ventures, have superior information sources, greater managerial expertise, and influential contacts in both government and business. Under such circumstances, technological change in Lebanon has tended to maintain or further accentuate social inequality. Although many members of the traditional Lebanese elite have been quite effective in promoting economic development through improved technnology and administrative organization, which has increased the size of the middle class and benefited a large proportion of the population, they themselves have been among the greatest beneficiaries. As has been shown in different contexts, modern enterprises in Lebanon continue to be organized as family firms, and economic development has not been accompanied by a significant decline in traditional loyalties to family, village, or sect (Khalaf and Shwayri 1966) which as noted also provides the primary basis for political organization in that society.

The specific outcome of the dispute concerning the Proteine franchise has been overshadowed by more serious conflicts, but it is apparent that, in the long run, seafarers following traditional ways of life in Lebanon are threatened by technological obsolescence and related forces over which they have no control. There is little likelihood that their present means of gaining a livelihood will be maintained over the next few years. As the larger international economic system in which Lebanon operates restricts the options of small nations, even prosperous ones, there seems little practical alternative to the eventual modernization of the indigenous fishing industry. Regardless of the particular method pursued, it seemed only a matter of time before traditional fishing, like the flourishing Lebanese silk industry of the late nineteenth century, will become a part of Levantine history.

NOTES

[1]As is the case with most Lebanese government decisions, there is frequently a substantial time lag between the making of a decision, its formalization, and its implementation. Most government cabinets tend to be short-lived and many decisions made by previous administrations are not carried out by subsequent cabinets. For that reason there is frequently little active opposition to policies or specific decisions until it appears that they may actually be implemented.

[2]Before World War II there was a particularly lucrative trade in the smuggling of hashish from Lebanon to Egypt by boat. At the present time such commerce is carried on using

aircraft which fly from clandestine airfields, usually in the northern Bekaa Valley, to other parts of the Mediterranean, where the goods are subsequently transported to Western Europe and North America.

[3]Sims (1971) has provided a more detailed description of the methods used by fishermen of the Maronite Christian village of Byblos (Jbeil) and discusses selected elements of their social organization.

LITERATURE CITED

Bernard, H. Russell
    1972   Kalymnos: Island of the Sponge Fishermen. Technology and Social Change. *In* P. J. Pelto and H. R. Bernard, eds. Pp.227–316. New York: MacMillan.

Binder, Leonard, ed.
    1968   Politics in Lebanon. New York: Wiley and Sons.

Boulos, Ismat
    1967   La Peche Moderne: Methods Practiquees au Japon, Possibilities d' Adaption au Liban Beirut: Editions du Centre d' Etudes Techniques.
    1970   Le Plan Bleu: Programme de Reorganization et de Development des Peches au Liban. Direction du Service Chasse et Peche, Ministre de l' Agriculture, Beirut. Mimeo.

Counseil Municipal de Beyrouth
    1973   La Charte de Beyrouth. Beirut: Imprimerie Catholique.

Farsoun, Samih K.
    1970   Family Structure and Society in Modern Lebanon. In Peoples and Cultures of the Middle East, Vol. 2 Louise C. Sweet, ed. Pp. 257–307. Garden City, New York: The Natural History Press.

Hudson, Michael C.
    1968   The Precarious Republic. New York: Random House.

Khalaf, Samir and Shwayri, Emily
    1966   Family Firms and Industrial Development: The Lebanese Case. Economic Development and Culture Change 15:59–69.

Khalaf, Samir
    1968   Primordial Ties and Politics in Lebanon. Middle Eastern Studies 4:243–69.

Khuri, Fuad I.
    1968   The Etiquette of Bargaining in the Middle East. American Anthropologist 70:698–706.

Prins, A. H. J.
    1965   The Modified Syrian Schooner: Problem Formation in Maritime Change. Human Organization 24:34–42.

Republique Libanaiese, Ministre du Plan
    1972   L'Enquete Par Sondage sur la Population Active au Liban, Vol. 1. Beirut.

Sims, Jack R.
    1971   The Fishermen of Byblos: The Study of a Marine-Adapted Lebanese Occupational Group. M. A. Thesis, American University of Beirut.

Solayman, A., and H. Charles
    1972   Le Parler Arabe de la Voile at la Vie Maritime. Beirut: Dar El-Mashreq Publishers.

Starr, Paul D.
  In Press Social Change and Social Differentiation in Lebanon. In Commoners, Climbers and Notables: A Sampler of Studies on Social Ranking in the Middle East. C. A. O. van Nieuwenhuijze, ed. Leiden: Brill and Co.

Tarhini, F.
    1975   Les Voilers de Commerce Meurent Pour Entrer dans la Legende. L' Orient-Le Jour, Samedi, (Beirut Weekly) nouvelle serie no. 297, April 5, 1975.

5

Motor Power and Woman Power: Technological and Economic Change Among the Fanti Fishermen of Ghana*

JAMES B. CHRISTENSEN

Wayne State University

This paper discusses some of the changes that have occurred in the Fanti fishing economy since the writer first worked in Ghana a quarter of a century ago.[1] Primarily, it deals with the impact of the adoption of the outboard motor on dugout canoes and some of the resultant technological, economic, and social changes. Not the least of these has been the movement of the market women into positions as entrepreneurs with a prominent role in financing fishing and fishing equipment. Females have always controlled the sale and processing of fish after the catch was

*An abridged version of this paper was read at the annual meeting of the American Anthropological Association in Mexico City in November 1974. The research in 1950–51 was carried out by the writer as a Fulbright scholar and fellow of the Social Science Research Council, and in 1972–73 while lecturing part-time as a visiting professor in Ghana. The research in the summer of 1974 was funded in part by a travel grant-in-aid from Wayne State University. While the correct spelling of the ethnic group under discussion is "Mfantse," the Anglicized version "Fanti" is utilized here as this is the spelling in common usage and the one most commonly used in Ghana when writing in English.

landed on the beach by the fishermen, but now a significant percentage of the crews must consult with, if not answer to, some market women who have either financed some of the crews' equipment and/or advanced them money for food and petrol when the catch is poor.

The Fanti are one of the Akan groups of the southwestern quadrant of Ghana. They are located along the coast in the approximate center of the country, for a distance of about 60 miles on the Guinea Coast and extending inland for 15 to 20 miles. The economy is based on shifting agriculture with yam, plantain, and cassava as staples. In the coastal villages fishing tends to dominate the economy, although farming is also practiced. The major cash crop is cocoa, as the northern portion of the Fanti area extends into the tropical rain forest belt. Like the other Akan, the Fanti are a matrilineal society with a relatively complex social organization. At the time of contact with the Europeans in the fifteenth century they had small autonomous native states, a hierarchy of chiefs, courts, taxation, money in the form of gold dust and nuggets, and an organized military.

Historical Background

Fanti tradition maintains that they migrated from what is now Techiman in the Brong area of Ashanti, arriving at the coast approximately 550 years ago.[1] Segments of what is now the Fanti area were then occupied by groups known as the Etsii, the Effutu, and the Asebu, the latter claiming they came in by sea from the east. Whether the immigrant Fanti learned fishing and use of canoes from the autochthonous peoples is not known, but Bosman, writing at the beginning of the eighteenth century recorded that the Fanti had thousands of fishermen and traded by sea with Accra to the east and Axim to the west (Bosman 1721:47 ff.). Historical accounts do not document the type of equipment (apart from canoes) that were used prior to the nineteenth century. However the Fanti have been known both as fishermen and seamen along the Guinea coast for generations. Brown (1947:23 ff.) reports that the oral history of the Ga, who live east of the Fanti, recounts that fishing was introduced by some Fanti at Labadi in the Accra area in the second half of the eighteenth century, and that prior to that time the Ga neither fished in the ocean nor had canoes. In the nineteenth century the Fanti were the dominant group crewing the large surf boats for the lighterage firms that brought goods ashore from vessels anchored at sea near Accra prior to the construction of the harbor at Tema.

Apparently the size of canoes has increased with technology. An elderly fisherman, reported to be between 90 and 100 years of age in 1950, stated that prior to the turn of the century all canoes were small by 1950 standards: only 20 to 23 feet in length, with a beam of about 4 feet and a depth of no more than 2 feet. Canoes were reportedly obtained most often along the Pra River where they had been floated downstream from the forest area which had the large trees unavailable in the coastal belt.

Before they acquired twine from Europe, the Fanti nets were made from the fiber of pineapple leaves twisted into cord by rolling on the thigh, a task my elderly informant claimed was slow and laborious. The major net at that time was a casting net used from a canoe or from shore. Lining was practiced using hooks made by a blacksmith. Some wall-nets were made from fiber, and were anchored with stones and calabashes used as floats. My informant claimed he could recall sails being made from matting and bark cloth in the nineteenth century, which is possible, as Brown (1947:25) places the introduction of the canvas sail among the Ga around 1875.

The introduction of manufactured twine to make nets, along with lead and cork, and canvas for sails, brought about the first major technological change in the Fanti fishing economy. A major factor was the introduction of a surface drift net called an *Adii* or *Ali*. This net (mesh about .75 in., 600–900 ft. long and 30 ft. deep) made possible much larger catches of herring during the season. Fanti informants claimed that the *Ali* came to their area about 1924, diffusing along the coast from the Accra area. While the provenance is accurate, the introduction of the *Ali* was probably somewhat earlier. Many of the Fanti fought against the adoption of the *Ali*,[2] which initially cost from £50 to £100 while the traditional casting net could be made at the cost of a few pounds. However, it was adopted as the major net for the crews, and in turn it required larger canoes to handle the larger net and larger catch.

Traditional Practices

The baseline utilized here for the discussion of change will be that which obtained in 1950.[3] The main canoe at that time was a dugout made of a soft wood (usually *Triplochiton scleroxylon*) called *wawa* by the Fanti. Then as now, the hull was carved by artisans in Assin or Ashanti in the forest belt, where the fisherman journeyed to place his order. Where canoes were once brought down the Pra River, and later hauled by rail, since the 1930s they have been transported to the coast by lorry. Once the canoe arrived in the town or village of the purchaser, another artisan prepared it for sea. The hull had to be thinned to approximately 3 inches, not too thick and cumbersome, and not thin enough to weaken the canoe.

The outfitting process included charring the canoe inside and out to dry the wood. A number of staves were lashed athwart the canoe to provide reinforcement and seats for the crew. The mast step was nailed to the bottom, and above that a thick board was nailed across the dugout with a rectangular hole for holding the mast (see sketch). On the topsides, the canoe was decorated and lettered in bas relief. The art work frequently depicted Akan proverbs, ·sometimes rendered on stylized gold weights.[4] Most included a proverb or maxim in Fanti, although English was beginning to be used for names and comments in 1950. Not uncommon was having the cost of the canoe chiseled in the decorative strip to remind the owner to be careful. The carved strip was usually painted with enamel. According to the fishermen the primary purpose of the decoration was to identify the canoe and to make it look nice. The symbolism of the art work and proverbs was not considered particularly significant.

Before a canoe could be launched, the appropriate religious cermony had to be observed. An herbalist (*nurnsinyi*) or a priest (*komfo*) would make an offering of eggs and *oto* (yam and palm oil) to the canoe, and pour a libation of native gin. At this time the canoe was supposed to tell the officiant what its name was to be (although the name was already carved), and what foods were taboo and not to be taken to sea. Each canoe would have a *suman* (amulet or charm) to protect it and the crew against witches *(anyenfo)*. A common *suman* was a mixture of medicine in a small glass vial placed in the bow. In addition the crew members would usually have their individual *suman* to protect them and to ensure a good catch.

The Fanti canoe (*hemba*) came in different sizes and configurations, depending on its primary use. The smaller canoes were utilized for inshore fishing, for tending bottom nets, for casting nets or for lining.[5] The same type and size of canoe would have different names in the various localities, but were often referred to by the kind of net most often used (e.g., *tenga hemba*). The major canoe in 1950, and still in use today, is a dugout made of soft wood varying in length from 25 to 30 feet, with a beam of about 5 feet and a depth of 2½ to 3 feet. Under sail the mast is stepped to slope windward with the halyard carried windward as a stay. One corner of the sail is made fast to the masthead and the other corner supported by a diagonal spar or sprit rising from the same hole in the thwart holding the mast. There is a line from the head of the sail and a sheet from the foot leading to the stern, and the tack is made fast to the bow. The canoe carries approximately 250 square feet of sail. The helmsman uses a long steering sweep when under sail, and a leeboard is sometimes used. They cannot sail more than 90 degrees to the wind, but this is no particular problem, since the prevailing winds are offshore when the

Sketch showing rigging for traditional Fanti canoe.

fishermen go to sea between 2 A.M. and 9 A.M. and are onshore from approximately 10 A.M. to midnight when they return. Other equipment on the canoes are the three-pronged paddles originated by the Fanti, and an anchor made of stone or heavy scrap metal. The canoe is very seaworthy and admirably suited for use on a rocky coast lacking natural harbors or shelter.

When using the *Ali,* a crew of five or seven manned the canoe with one or two of them usually boys in the apprentice stage. There was a preference for a crew of agnates, even though the society is matrilineal. For example, a crew might consist of a man, his sons, and a grandson or two, or sons of the same father and their sons and grandsons. Ownership was rarely vested in the entire crew; rather, one or two men would normally own the equipment. Few fishermen had the required capital to pay outright for a canoe or net, and the major source of funds was their clan or some wealthy individual who would lend money for the traditional 50 percent interest plus the share of the catch allocated to the equipment until the loan was settled. Unlike the present, women were not involved in financing equipment or subsidizing crews to any significant degree; female ownership of a canoe was admitted in only one case.

The major investment in 1950 was for the canoe and net, with the canoe costing approximately £50 ($140) and the net costing twice that amount. Since a canoe could be expected to last from eight to ten years, and a net could be repaired or have a section replaced, a major outlay of capital was not frequently required.

The cost of maintenance was not great, but constant care was required. The major purchases were line for repairing nets, and dye for tanning them. The bark of two species of local trees was previously used for tanning, but by 1950 commercial dye was common. The hull of an old canoe served as a tank for dyeing. Then as now old canoes were cannibalized to repair others, and segments up to several square feet would be replaced by a carpenter. Nets had to be spread for drying daily. Tuesdays and Sundays were the days for mending nets, as Tuesday was sacred to *Bosompo,* the sea god. Abstaining from fishing on Sunday originated in Anomabu in the nineteenth century as the result of a serious conflict between a half-dozen of the fishermen who had become Christian and the others. Some men would go to sea to tend their bottom nets on these two days, a practice viewed as permissible. During August and September, the prime season for herring, it was not uncommon for crews to ignore the taboos and go to sea daily.

Space allows only a brief summary of fishing techniques. The crews would put to sea early in the morning, paddling through the surf and then hoisting the mast and sail, taking advantage of the offshore wind. They would watch for herring on the surface and attempt to cast the net in a circle around the school. If none were visible on the surface they would shoot the net in a line and hope for a catch. After the net was hauled in, which would take approximately one hour, they might cast it again if the catch was small. They would return to shore some time after the wind changed direction to onshore.

A crowd of mostly women and children would come to the beach to await the return of the crews. When a canoe hit the beach the rather lengthy process of getting the fish from the net and dividing the catch would begin, and a large catch could require two hours or more to distribute. The catch was divided according to a set formula. The canoe received one share, the net received two shares and each adult fisherman received one share. Boys in the apprentice stage were given a quarter-share or half-share. The net was given two shares because it represented a larger investment than the canoe. The money allocated to an unmarried boy went to his father; his father in turn was expected to use this to pay the bridewealth when the boy got married, and also to provide him with one of the muskets or "Dane guns" when he became an adult and joined the military unit, or the Asafo company, of his father.

A large wicker basket would be utilized for each share of the catch. The fishermen would place 110 herring in each basket in turn, removing any large fish for division later. Equal distribution was assured by the watchful women who followed the count, or by having one of the crew count out the fish for another member of the crew. One fish would be put aside for each 110 counted. The unit of 110 was used for a number of reasons. Fish were sold in bulk per hundred fish, with the price dependent on the size of fish and size of the catch. A person could not complain unless there were less than 100, so the excess minimized disputes. The women who carried the fish back to the wife or sister of the crew member were paid in fish, coming from the extra allocation. Moreover, fish were sometimes mutilated during extraction from the net or during smoking, and thus not fit for selling. When smoked fish were sold wholesale the buyer was given 105 for the price of 100, in accordance with the Ghanaian tradition that the seller should include an additional portion when it involves quantities of a dozen or more.

Women competing for the opportunity to carry fish frequently created havoc by yelling and shoving around the canoe, and the men added to the din with their own shouted comments and orders. Not infrequently they would paddle back out to sea a short distance and anchor while they divided the catch. When the division was completed, the net, coiled on five or six wooden trays, would be carried back to the drying racks on the heads of women, who in turn received fish for this task.

The price per hundred fish was determined daily by bargaining between the women and the fishermen. Every fishing town or village town
had a woman known as a *konkohen* (from *konko* meaning "selling" or
"retailing"and *hen* meaning "chief" or "head")[7] who was elected by the
women involved in buying, smoking, and selling fish. One of her functions was to meet the first canoe landing with a catch and bargain with
the crew over the price of fish for that day. Other early arrivals would
also join in the discussion. The price arrived at was determined by the
size of the catch and the species. The price set for the first arrivals tended
to prevail for the day, although the price might decrease for the last
canoes to land. A fisherman could turn his catch over to his wife or to a
sister or some other female in his *abusua* (clan). Some preferred to deal
with women who were small entrepeneurs and who kept a number of
ovens for smoking fish. Such a woman might handle a catch of several
fishermen, and some fishermen were partial to them because of their hon-
esty and reliability. The alternatives open to the wife or sister of a fisherman were (1) process the fish herself and then retail or wholesale them to
a buyer, (2) sell them to a woman who bought and sold fish on a large
scale, or (3) retail the fresh fish herself. The latter course was not always
practicable in a fishing village because of the competition. The course of
action would be determined by a number of factors such as the price of
fish, size of the catch, availability of wood for smoking, number of ovens
available, and her established trade networks for disposing of smoked
fish. She was expected to return to the fisherman the price of fish for that
day minus ten percent as her share for handling. The profit she could
realize by smoking and then retailing or wholesaling the fish was also
hers to retain.

The fishermen and the women who handled their fish would settle accounts once a week, or sometimes only once each "season," with 9 to 11
seasons per year, depending on locality.[8] The matrilineal Fanti fishermen
indicated that a sister or some female within the clan was more trusted to
give an honest account than was a wife.

Every coastal town or village had an *apofohen* ("fishing chief") whose
main function was to settle disputes between fishermen or crews. Such
disputes might arise over damage from bumping canoes together at the
beach or from running over or entangling nets at sea. The *apofohen* also
collected *amandze*,[9] the fee charged outsiders for temporary rights to fish
or sell their catch in his village. He was supposed to be an experienced
fisherman; and the position was traditionally patrilineal, comparable to
that of officers in the military companies.

Periodic migration, known as *apoye* or *apotwa* (literally "crossing the
sea"), has long been a pattern for Fanti fishing crews. The motive for mi-

grating might be the desire for a better fishing area, such as the mouth of the Pra River (cf., Quinn 1971:93); or it might be an attraction to the more populous areas of Accra or Sekondi-Takoradi where there was a greater demand for fish. A reason for migrating always given by fishermen was saving money by avoiding the constant requests for assistance and contributions that are inevitable when living among one's kinsmen. Major contributions, such as funeral expenses, would have to be settled on return.

The crew, with their equipment and luggage, would go by sea, and often one woman (preferably an unmarried girl to minimize the conflict that would arise if they took the wife of a crew member) would travel by lorry. Her primary function was preparing food for the men, and if time allowed, she would participate in selling fish. The crew would normally make contact with a local woman who would buy their catch. Financial arrangements were comparable to those that obtained in their home town. The period of time spent away from home would vary from a few weeks to a few months, although those who migrated as far as the Ivory Coast, Liberia, or Sierra Leone would often take their wives and children and remain for a year or more, if not permanently.[10]

Social Change

The fishing segment of Fanti towns and villages has always been among the most conservative and tradition-oriented of the Fanti population. While the Fanti have been one of the Ghanaian groups most receptive to change, the fishing community was regarded as "backward" by educated Fanti both in 1950 and in 1974. In 1950 scarcely any fishermen had had any schooling, and no active fishermen who spoke English were encountered. Very few sent their children to local schools, and fishing was not viewed as an acceptable career for any literate Fanti. Few professed Christianity; fishermen generally were the ones most likely to patronize the traditional priests and herbalists. They were involved in the activities of the traditional *Asafo* or military companies, and in local politics regarding the hereditary positions as chiefs. In short, the fishermen were the least acculturated and the most "Fanti" of all the Fanti.

THE CONTEMPORARY SCENE

Beginning about 1960 the Fanti started to adapt outboard motors to their dugout canoes. As one would expect, this has brought about considerable change in the traditional fishing economy. Canoes have increased in size, and the size of the crew has doubled. Nets have increased in size, and some nets and techniques formerly used have disappeared. The cost of equipping one of the larger canoes with a motor and two large nets has increased approximately 1000 percent over the 1950 version. With the increase in cost the pattern for financing, maintaining, and operating the equipment has also altered, as has the procedure for disposing of the catch. One result has been the increasing role of market women as a source of capital with a resultant increase in their control of the industry, although this facet remains rather covert.

Canoes

The canoes utilizing an outboard motor now measure 35 to 40 feet in length with a depth of over 4 feet and a beam of 5 to 6 feet. While the basic hull is still carved from a single log, a greater depth is achieved by building up the sides with strips of three by three inch timbers, and a

Large Fanti dugout canoe showing technique for mounting motor.

hardwood rubbing strake is now added. Thwarts are now of plank nailed to the hull. The motor is mounted on a triangular bracket bolted to the starboard side a few feet forward of the stern, and brackets are normally reinforced with steel. While the names vary with locality, the generic term for these canoes is *hemba kese* or "big canoe;" when they are putting out to sea some have so much freeboard it is difficult for the crew to reach the water with their paddles.

The type of canoe seen in 1950 is still very much in evidence and still being purchased. In a two-week period in 1973 the canoes in five Fanti towns were counted on Tuesday, a nonfishing day; 37 percent of the canoes present and seaworthy were the small or nonmotorized type. However, this does not reflect the ratio of men involved with each, since a large canoe would have a crew of 10 to 14, an a small canoe, from two to four. Moreover, the larger canoes are more likely to be absent due to migratory fishing than the smaller canoes, and thus not be counted.

Some fishermen, particularly the older men, may use the smaller canoes on a regular basis for line-fishing with a crew of two or three or for fishing with the relatively small-drift *tenga* nets, with an individual net for each of the two to four crew members. However, crew members alternate on occasion between the motorized canoes and the small canoes; when a motor is out for repair some men may go out in a small canoe, while others use them on a regular or seasonal basis. Canoes are still decorated in the traditional manner, but there is greater use of English for maxims and names (50 of 120 in the sample).[11] The weight of the larger ones requires steel pipe as rollers and a dozen or more men to move them across the beach above the high tide line.

Nets

The large nets are now made of nylon and no longer need tanning or daily drying. Many crews still use the *Ali*, but the larger canoes accommodate bigger nets of 300 to 400 yards or more. The middle 1960s saw the introduction of a purse-seine net which has a small (3/4 in.) mesh, with lines running through rings. It has several advantages over the *Ali*: it catches all sizes and kinds of fishes; it can be closed up like a pocket, not requiring the fishermen to jump into the water to scare the fish into the net as with the *Ali;* and the fish are not mutilated by the net. It is preferable to have both nets, and many crews do, since the *Ali* is deeper and can be used for some of the larger species of fishes (cf., Quinn 1971:102–04). Many of the nets in use in 1950 have disappeared and are unknown to the younger fishermen.

Motors and Sails

All motors observed on canoes between 1972–74 were American-made 25 horsepower units.[12] Motor maintenance is a major and expensive problem for the crews. Considerable time is lost when a motor goes out, as there is a scarcity of both spare parts and technicians to repair them. When asked if they had experienced motor breakdown in the past six months, 97 percent of the crews sampled reported they had, with an average of 3.45 incidents per crew. Each time involved taking the motor for repair and loss of fishing days.[13] The large canoes are equipped with sails, but they rarely use them to save petrol and avoid wear on the motor. Many crews now rely entirely on their motor and do not take their sail and rigging with them.

Crew Composition

As indicated, the crews have doubled in size with the introduction of the larger canoes and motor. In eight fishing towns and villages the average size of the crew ranged from 9.5 in Elmina to 13.1 in Kromantsi. The average for 196 crews in the sample was 11.2 men per canoe, but since the sample contained 109 crews from Elmina and Biriwa, which have the lowest average crew size, an adjusted average of 11.8 per canoe is probably more accurate for the eight towns. Included in this figure was an average of 1.6 members per crew who were boys or apprentices receiving a part-share of the catch.

The data from 1950 do not include a systematic analysis of the kinship composition of crews. My field notes contain responses indicating the crews either were agnates, or should be patrilineal kin. Even if this ideal norm was the actual pattern at that time, the increase in size would make a crew comprised of the patrikin of a minimal lineage impossible. Beginning in 1972, data were obtained on 184 crews, attempting to ascertain the relationship of each crew member to the recognized leader of the crew. The informant for each crew was a man reported to be the owner of the equipment as well as a crew member, or in the case of absentee ownership, the so-called "bosun." The results were as follows: patrilineal kin (So, Br, Fa, GrSo), 37 percent; matrilineal kin (SiSo, MoBr, MoSiSo), 34 percent; nonkin or friends, 28 percent. Within the two categories of kingroups, the largest in the patrikin was sons (17%) and brothers (14%). In the matrikin the largest was the sister's son (22%). Some crews consisted entirely of nonkin of the canoe leader. However, it should be recognized that these figures do not show the relationship of crew members to each other.[14]

Cost of Equipment

In data collected for a meeting of government officials and advisers concerned with the fishing industry, the cost of equipping a canoe in 1972 was estimated to be in the following range (estimates in cedis, with 1.15 cedis per U.S. dollar): canoe, 500–800; transportation from forest, 200–300; paddles, sail, and other gear (for a crew of 13), 300–400; preparation, 100; seine net (13 bundles) 600–1000; outboard motor, 400–600. The cost totaled 2100 to 3200 cedis. This estimate is low, because at the time of the report the cost of a new motor actually ranged from 617 to 750 cedis, and most crews have an *Ali* in addition to the purse-seine net. By February 1973, the cost of a Johnson motor had increased from 750 to 895 cedis, and nets had taken a drastic increase of 66 percent. Based on this, the cost of equipping a canoe with a motor and two nets (*Ali* and purse-seine) would be 4000 to 5000 cedis.

However, it is not common for an owner or owners to make an expenditure of this magnitude at one time. The life of a canoe is usually rated at ten years. While a net requires constant repair, replacement is usually by sections rather than a complete net. If carefully handled and serviced a motor may last as long as five years, but they rarely do.

Division and Disposal of the Catch

Because of the larger investment required for equipment, the method of dividing the catch has changed considerably from the practice followed prior to the adoption of motors. Each fisherman still gets a share, with a quarter-share or half-share going to the apprentice. The accepted practice is to allocate two shares to the canoe, but the shares accorded the net and motor vary. The net is normally given three or four shares, with the motor usually getting four shares. In some cases the motor is allocated as much as six shares to pay for a repair bill or save for a future bill. The pattern that occurs with the greatest frequency gives the canoe two shares, the net three shares, and the motor four shares. In 79 percent of the cases it was reported that a boy's share still goes to his father, while in the other cases the apprentice retains it himself. Another change is that a share is frequently accorded to the owner of the equipment just for being owner, or because "they run things" (84% of sample). To illustrate the division of the catch, let us take a typical crew of 12, with 2 of them boys receiving a half share. The division would be 11 shares to the crew, 1 to the owner, 2 to the canoe, 3 to the net, and 4 to the motor, for a total of 21 shares.

Another change has been that fish are no longer counted out 110 at a time, but sold by the pan; the standard measure is a large shallow pan with a capacity of 1.17 cubic feet. The practice of selling by the pan at the beach speeds division of the catch and provides money to be divided, rather than fish. Cash makes it easy to deduct the amount spent for petrol, pay off absentee owners who do not want to concern themselves with sale of the fish, and divide up the remaining shares for the crew and equipment (e.g., 21 in the example cited above).

Out of a sample of 120 motorized crews, 85 percent reported they sold their catch to one particular female. This was either the wife or kinsman of the owner or some woman who lent them money when needed. Fourteen percent replied they sold to "customers," usually two or three women on a regular basis. Only one responded that they sold to the wives of the crew. Thus a working agreement with one or two females was the pattern for the seven towns in the sample.

Thus, the pattern of disposal of the catch has altered greatly; the fisherman and his wife no longer constitute an economic unit as they did before. If the wife or sister of a fisherman now wishes to sell or process fish, she is likely to purchase it from some woman who receives the entire catch of one canoe. The exception to this is during the herring season when the number of pans in the catch may be more than double the number of shares and a fisherman may take some of his share in fish. Women no longer carry nets from the beach as the nets are too large and heavy, and this is now a task for the crew. Women still come to the beach to provide porterage for the women who buy fish; they bring their own pans and are paid .20 to .50 cedis per pan, depending on the distance carried. Some buyers will rent a taxi to carry their fish. A regular practice is for fishmongers from Cape Coast to take a lorry or bus to Elmina to purchase fish. The catch is usually larger there for, in addition to traditional canoes, a large number of inboard trawlers operate there because of the harbor provided by the mouth of the Benya River.

Financing and the Economic
Role of Market Women

The financing of equipment has developed into a major problem for the fishermen because of the increasing cost of the basic equipment.

Government financing and planning has been directed more at development of large trawlers which utilize the harbor and cold-storage facilities at Tema near Accra. For the small operator, more attention has been given to those wishing to invest in inboard trawlers than in traditional canoes. This is not only because it represents modernization, but because as a rule this financing has gone to people who represent better credit risks.

Lack of government assistance is in part due to fishermen themselves. The government once made low-interest loans available to fishermen to buy motors, but the program ended in an economic disaster. The fishermen apparently felt little compulsion or responsibility to repay the loans, and the only provision for enforcement in the program was repossession of the equipment. This was difficult because first they had to locate the defaulter, and fishing people were disinclined to cooperate with the government in tracking down the culprit. If they did repossess the equipment, it often meant that the fisherman had had free use of a motor for an extended period, and all the government had to show for the investment was a burned-out motor. The fisherman's credit problem is further exacerbated by the impossibility of obtaining insurance on a canoe or other equipment, and banks are reluctant to give unsecured loans to a member of a group not reputed to be financially responsible.

Few fishermen have the capital required to obtain one of the three major pieces of equipment required (canoe, net, motor), and the high cost makes it difficult to obtain adequate funding from kinsmen. They frequently have to turn to a money lender, and to a fisherman this is usually synonymous with a market woman. To clarify why the fishmonger has capital to invest while the fisherman may have to borrow the money for petrol to go to sea, it is necessary to look at the economic role of women in the economy. Trading has long been the province of women (cf., Christensen 1961), and as Field has commented on the economic status of Akan women:

> They are—unless quite devoid of "drive"—economically independent. Few wives cannot say to defaulting husbands, 'If you want me to leave you, dismiss me at once: I knew how to buy my own headkerchiefs before I met you.'... By and large, men are improvident and open-handed, women both more reliable and close-fisted, for women have a very early training in the scrupulous handling of small sums. little girls of four may be seen in the market selling such wares as kenkey-dumplings, for each one of which they have to account to their mothers (Field 1960:30).

Women have a need for a degree of economic independence. Fanti husbands are not exactly generous to their wives when the latter are in need of funds to meet their obligations to their own clan during funerals and other ceremonial occasions. However, the women as a group are usually well trained in the law of supply and demand and the judicious use of money.[15] Because of hard work and economic acumen, some women become wealthy by Ghanaian standards.

It is extremely difficult to obtain accurate information on financing and ownership of fishing equipment. While the Fanti will freely discuss the patterns and procedure involved, when it comes to obtaining information on who precisely owns some particular equipment, or the source of funding, the responses must be viewed as something less than reliable. When asked who lent the money to buy a canoe or net the response is frequently, "some rich man." As would be anticipated, the Fanti fisherman and money lender are reluctant to discuss income or financing with anyone outside their immediate lineage, and this reluctance extends to other Fanti as well as to foreign ethnographers. Males are reluctant to admit any economic dependence on women; and at the same time women, who could be viewed as wealthy entrepreneurs by local standards, do not wish to acknowledge it. However, there is general agreement on one issue which obtains whether one is talking to a government official, a banker, a fisherman, or the man in the street: market women are the major source of capital for financing equipment.

Data on a sample of 80 canoes and equipment collected in 1973 indicated the following:

Owned by one or more of the crew . . . . 21 percent
Owned by a male, not a crew member . . . . 44 percent
Owned by a female . . . . 35 percent

Insofar as these data are reliable they indicate a high incidence of absentee ownership of equipment. However, it is suspected that the percentage of female ownership is actually higher than reported. It is surmised that in some of the cases reporting equipment as being owned by a male (crew and noncrew), the actual owner may be a female and the male owner referred to is a relative representing her.

One practice that makes ownership open to question is who receives the shares for the equipment. The situation is not analogous to who owns a delivery van, the borrower or the bank that holds the title. Not only does the lender receive a high rate of interest, but he or she also receives the equipment's share of the catch until the loan plus interest is repaid. The traditional rate of interest among the Fanti is 50 percent but it is not per annum; and it can be less, depending on the relationship between borrower and lender. However, the advantage to the market woman who deals in fish to make such a loan is obvious. If she lends a fisherman 800 cedis to buy a motor, he has to repay her 1200 cedis. Until the loan is repaid she receives the share allocated to the motor. Moreover, this would normally give her proprietary rights to purchase the entire catch of the crew if she wished. It is not unusual for the repayment period to equal the life of the motor, and the process repeats itself. In this case, where a fisherman may maintain that he owns a motor, the economic reality is that he is paying a high rate for the use of it plus shares of the catch.

If a fisherman is viewed as a high risk for a government loan, then why not also by the market woman? The role of the lender is important; in Ghana as elsewhere the government is viewed as fair game. More important, traditional attitudes and practices regarding debts come into play. A promissory note is usually negotiated (as in a bank loan), but the transaction is witnessed by other parties and there is an obligation on the part of the clan of the borrower to settle the debt should he die or default. Moreover, the lender or her emissary keeps in constant touch with the crew to make certain she obtains her share of the catch.

To illustrate the relative income of the owner of the equipment and a member of the crew, let us take an example where the market woman owns all of the equipment used by a crew. Let us assume on a given day there was a catch of eight pans of large herring valued that day at 6 cedis per pan. Using the illustration given above for dividing the catch, and deducting 6 cedis for petrol, 42 cedis would have to be divided into 21 shares. When they settled accounts, each adult member of the crew would receive 2 cedis ($1.74) as his share for that day. However, the owner would receive 10 shares (9 for the equipment and 1 for the owner).

This is only part of the transaction, as she would still have eight pans of fish to sell which will bring her additional profit. An entrepreneur on this level would be likely to have ovens for smoking fish as well as dependent female relatives to retail for her. Space will not permit a description of processing and marketing of fish, but by conservative estimate she would realize a minimum profit of 25 percent over the value of the beach price of the fish.[16] She could eventually realize a gross income of 60 cedis from the fish. From this must be deducted the 6 cedis for petrol, and 22 cedis for the crew shares. If we ignore the cost of maintaining the equipment, her income for the day is 32 cedis, compared to 2 cedis for the individual fisherman on that crew.

The number of market women who would operate on this level is a relatively small percentage. However, involvement of women with a crew may vary from ownership of the equipment, to part ownership (e.g. canoe or motor), to financing equipment. Some merely establish a working relationship by regularly purchasing the catch. In these cases it is the market woman to whom the crew will turn in financial need. This might be an ad-

vance to buy petrol, repair a motor, or purchase twine to repair the nets.
A common practice is also for her to lend the crew an amount varying
from one-half to one cedi per day during periods when there is no catch.
Such loans do not carry any interest and are usually paid off in fish at a
later date.

Price Determination

Each town or village still has the *konkohen* (head of the fishmongers)
who, along with her assistants, is supposed to meet the first few canoes
and determine the price of fish for that day. However, there can be considerable variation in price from the first few canoes; the price fluctuates
with the size of the catch, and extreme drops in price can occur (e.g., a
drop from 8 cedis per pan to .20 cedis in a day has been recorded). The
price also varies with the size as well as the species of fishes; the price per
pan for small herring and other small fish is only a fraction of that for
medium or large herring. When large fish such as mackerel are involved,
the buyer and seller determine the value of one fish, then sell them in lots
of 50. The price tends to decline as the day goes on and the sale and processing of fish become more of a problem for the buyer.

While they admit there is bargaining, both the fishermen and their customers accord to the crew leaders the dominant role in price determination. However, one need not spend much time on the beach as an observer
to ascertain that this is not necessarily the case. The women drive hard
bargains, knowing there are few alternatives open to the fishermen. They
can go back to sea and sail to a neighboring town, hoping for a better
price; but they are just as likely to lose by this procedure as profit by it.
More time and petrol are used, and they have to pay a fee to the fishing
chief at the location of the sale. More important, the women there recognize them as outsiders, which gives the buyer an advantage. Since most
crews sell regularly to one particular woman, there is often a relationship
of mutual trust; but if the buyer has loaned the crew money for equipment or for operating expenses, she has an edge in the bargaining.

Income

The elements, the equipment, and the size of the catch seem to con-
spire against the fishermen to prevent them from making a decent income from their endeavors. When the main herring season is on (August

and September) large catches are common, and price decreases accordingly. Data about annual incomes could not be obtained, but it is possible to give some examples of the range and averages of income when a crew does make a catch. In a survey made at Elmina and Cape Coast in January 1973, the gross income for 14 canoes during 12 days of fishing ranged from a low of 8 cedis for 1 canoe for 1 day, to a high of 272 cedis. After deductions for petrol, this would give the nonowner crew member a share of the catch ranging from approximately .23 cedis to 12.5 cedis. The average for all landings in the sample in the 12-day period was 51.45 cedis, which, after an average deduction for petrol, would be approximately 2.30 cedis per share. Other short-term samples showed comparable averages. Extensive data in government archives provided a record for the town of Biriwa for a 2-month period (July 28 to September 22, 1972) which corresponds to the main herring season during which there were 42 days of fishing. The gross income for 1 canoe per day ranged from a low of 8.25 cedis to a high of 208 cedis, giving the nonowner fisherman an income of approximately .40 cedis to 9.90 cedis. The average gross income reported for all landings recorded (848) during the period was 67.85 cedis which would be approximately 3 cedis per share after deductions for petrol.

However, one cannot conclude that the nonowner fisherman would have an average income of 15 cedis per week during this time. Most fishermen try to work during this season as they are assured of a catch even though the price per pan may be low. However, in the Biriwa data cited above, the number of canoes with a catch varied from 4 to 58 per day. It must be remembered that equipment failure, bad weather, poor fishing, illness, and sometimes lethargy may create periods of weeks or months when a fisherman will not be part of a crew. During some seasons some fishermen may alternate fishing with farming, day labor, or periods of inactivity. Sometimes they join the crew of a smaller canoe, particularly when catches for motorized canoes are small. While they may not obtain much more than "eating fish" they do not run the risk of spending more on petrol than they make from the catch.[17]

Social and Religious Change

Space limits the treatment of social and religious change in contemporary Fanti culture, but some points may be noted. The military companies (*asafo*) comprised primarily of fishermen are still the most active, as are their female auxiliary components. Ties to the matrilineal clan remain strong, but inheritance preferences for the Fanti in general are un-

dergoing change (see Christensen 1974). While customary law indicates
the preferred heir in the next generation should be the eldest sister's eldest son, there is a marked preference for patrilineal inheritance of fishing
equipment.

The question of preferred heir was discussed by 118 men who were the
bosuns of crews, or were reported as equipment owners. The majority, 75
percent, indicated they would leave any equipment they might have to
their sons, 19 percent preferred their sister's sons, and 6 percent indicated both. This correlated with which of the two were actually members
of their crew. All but two percent also indicated they would make a verbal
will (*samansiw*) to implement the inheritance.

While no structured sample was taken regarding marriage and divorce,
data available indicates that divorce is common, even to the extent of being the norm rather than the exception. One contributing factor is the
economic independence of women. With the practice of each canoe selling
fish to one particular female, the fisherman and his wife or wives no longer constitute an economic unit to the former extent. If the wife of a nonowner fisherman wishes to deal in fish, she is likely to have to buy from
some other woman. If a woman has the capital to obtain two or more
pans of fish, and can realize the minimal 25 percent profit (and most
make at least that gain) she will make more from selling fish than her
husband will from catching them.

Regarding religion, 25 percent of the heads of crews sampled claimed
to be Christian, but such a figure does not say anything about beliefs and
practices, and is rather meaningless. Membership in a Christian church
does not imply rejection of traditional beliefs and practices, or even any
conflict. Reference should be made to Field's work on the Ashanti, for her
description and analysis are still applicable to the Fanti (Field 1960).
Eighty-one percent of the informants admitted they still had *suman* (protective amulets) for their canoes. These are primarily for protection
against witches (*anyenfo*), and there is a tendency to journey some distance to obtain them from a traditional priest or herbalist so the efficacy
of the *suman* is more likely to remain a secret. Normally one crew member is in charge of the *suman*, taking it from his room to the canoe for
each day of fishing. A number of taboos and restrictions are associated
with the use of this magic, each *suman* having its own particular foods
that should not be carried to sea, with abstinence from sexual intercourse
prior to going to sea also a common requirement.

Cooperatives and Needs

Let us briefly review the role of the cooperative in contemporary Fanti
society. The government has plans for establishing viable cooperatives in

each of the towns and villages, but a shortage of finances and lack of co-operation on the part of crews has hindered development. The government sees future cooperatives as being involved in catching, processing, storing and selling fish, as well as financing equipment. The average fisherman does not comprehend all of this, and although a majority view cooperatives as desirable (even though they do not join), they see them primarily as a source of low-interest loans for equipment. Cooperatives existed on paper for most of the towns in the Fanti area, consisting of a committee headed by the fishing chief and with a literate secretary. However, only Elmina and Cape Coast had progressed much toward providing funds for members to purchase motors. The advantage of financing through a cooperative as opposed to a bank or government agency is that the debt is then owed to the townsmen and neighbors of the borrower and the obligation to repay a loan is much greater.

It is hoped that cold storage facilities in conjunction with a cooperative would mean less fluctuation in the price received by the crew. Freezing fresh herring in not viewed as practicable because of the high fat and moisture content, and cold storage of smoked fish would appear to be most feasible. This would still involve the women, who would process the fish, and it is anticipated they would also become members of the cooperatives. However, much of this is still in the planning stage but even if financing were available, the extent to which a majority of the fishermen would become functioning members of cooperatives remains debatable.

Summary

When they had to rely on local resources, the equipment of the Fanti fishermen was a small dugout canoe with a variety of small nets made by hand from local fibers. The introduction of the canvas sail and twine from Europe induced some technological change, as a large drift net was adopted and canoes became larger. However, the crews were relatively small (five to seven men), and equipment was owned by some of the crew. The adoption of the outboard motor in the 1960s has precipitated technological and economic changes of even greater magnitude. Canoes became larger, as did the nets, and the size of the crew doubled.

The cost of the equipment increased to a point where the fisherman could no longer manage financing from his own resources or from kinsmen. Defaulting on loans by some of their number made financing from banks or the government difficult to obtain, and the fishermen turned to "money lenders," most of whom are market women. In return for loans to buy equipment these women receive, not only a high rate of interest (50% being traditional), but also the share of the catch allocated to the equipment financed. Some women own the major equipment (canoe, net, and motor), while others own part of it. Some women lend a crew money for operating or living expenses when the catch is poor and in return have the right to purchase their entire catch at a favorable price.

The change to selling the catch to one or two regular buyers, and selling by the pan instead of counting out the catch according to shares has changed the traditional pattern of a fisherman and his wife or sister as an economic unit. The economic role of women, and their influence, has increased greatly with the adoption of motorized equipment and the resulting increase in cost and operating expenses.

NOTES

[1]See Christensen (1954:7–18) for a summary of Fanti migrations.

[2]The *Ali* came to the Accra area around 1900 (Brown 1947:26) and it seems unlikely that it would have taken a quarter-century to reach the Fanti since they often worked in Accra. However, resistance to change is not uncommon. The Fanti have not used the seine net from the beach since prior to World War II. This was attempted once after the war near Anomabu, but the fishermen stopped it as a threat to their investment in the *Ali*. Today a large village of immigrant Ewe from Eastern Ghana operate seine nets near Cape Coast where the absence of rocks on the shoreline permits this type of fishing.

[3]Research on fishing in 1950–51 was done primarily at Anomabu, with some observations made in neighboring coastal towns.

[4]Rattray's (1923:300 ff.) discussion of the form and function of Ashanti gold weights is applicable to the Fanti. Nunoo (1975) discusses canoe decoration among the Fanti with illustrations.

[5]In 1950 the fisherman at Anomabu knew at least 17 different kinds of nets for use in the sea, although some were no longer used. One of these was called *telegrafo*, a bottom net that got its name because it stretched along the coast like a telegraph line. It diffused from Eastern Ghana where it was known as *tengiraf* among the Ga (Brown 1947:25).

[6]While the Fanti are matrilineal, there is also an emphasis on the paternal line to the extent they have been described elsewhere as manifesting a system of double descent (Christensen 1954). Preston (1975) also emphasizes this, although instead of the Fanti *egyabosom* ("father's deity") he uses the Ashanti *ntoro* which the writer never encountered among the Fanti. The same publications contain a discussion of the *asafo* military companies, an aspect of Fanti culture that stresses the paternal line.

[7]In the large markets along the coast there is a *konkohen* for each of the major categories of market women. Thus those who sell trade cloth, vegetables, and the like would each have a *konkohen*. One of the functions of this elected leader is settling disputes between the women.

[8]Each "season" or *nworaba* (literally, "star") is marked by a particular constellation and/or meteorological phenomenon. Certain species of fishes are best caught in certain seasons. There are differences in the number of seasons (11) the writer obtained in 1950 for Anomabu and verified in 1973, and the number (9) and names listed by Quinn (1971:90) for Biriwa. However, the differences are not major. In addition to using stars for navigation, fishermen wishing to return to land can use their knowledge of wind direction (*mfar* or *ahwento*), steer toward the cloud bank *(eminiminim)* over the land, or take soundings with a long line (*esusunsu*) to ascertain whether they are headed inland or not.

[9]*Amandze* is literally "trouble," and since strangers bring their troubles and misfortune with them they have to pay a fee to the host village to compensate for the problems they bring. The amount of the fee varies with the locality and with the purpose and duration of the visit (e.g., selling fish for one day or residing for an extended period). Part of the fee goes to the fishing chief and part to the *oman* (native state).

[10]There are large settlements of Fanti in the Ivory Coast and Liberia, and until they were repatriated in 1971 as a response to the expelling of non-Ghanaian Africans from Ghana, Sierra Leone also had a colony. The families of some of the returnees from Sierra Leone had been there so long that, while they knew they were Fanti and knew their clan affiliation, they did not know their specific ancestral locality. The Fanti in Monrovia are much more efficient fishermen than the local Kru as they have brought large motorized canoes and large nets with them. Of the Fanti interviewed in Monrovia, some were recent immigrants but others were first and second generation born in Liberia whose children reportedly did not speak Fanti.

[11]Names, maxims, and proverbs on canoes are similar to those on passenger lorries and buses (see Field 1960:134–45). Names in English reflect the times, for example: VC 10; Television; Toyota; C.C. Mysterious Dwarfs (a football team); 5.5. (abridged name of a cigarette); C.K. Mann (name of a popular rock-music group).

[12]Apparently firms in the United States, because of the large market for motors for fishing, boating, and water sports, have developed the most efficient outboard motors at the lowest price.

[13]According to the European supervisor of a project at Biriwa which includes a motor-repair installation, one of the major causes of motor breakdown is lack of attention to the proper oil-petrol ratio. Quinn (1971:95) claims that the 18–20 hp. motors in use at the time of her research (1967–68) were adequate, as larger motors and higher speed would capsize the canoes. This is confusing the potential for speed at maximum rpm with the power needed to propel a large craft with an offset motor for extended periods at a power setting that will not burn out the motor. According to Ghanaian officials and German and Canadian advisers, the 25 hp. motor is not adequate. The Fanti in Liberia were using 40 hp. motors on the same size canoe. The term the Fanti fishermen have adopted for an outboard motor is "ahead" reportedly because that is the direction in which it propels the canoe.

[14]I am indebted to Dr. W.E. Vickery for making available data on size of crew and relationship to the owner for approximately 50 crews in Biriwa. Quinn (1971:136 ff.) presents some very good material on intracrew relationships. Several incidents were encountered where adult males without experience as fishermen were taken on as crew; in one case all but one of an entire crew was made up of adult apprentices. In these cases they usually did not receive a fraction-share of the catch, but rather what the owner called a "dash"—a variation on the normal meaning, which in this case referred to a living allowance until they proved themselves.

[15]While trading across the borders of contiguous countries has long been a practice, the air age has added a new dimension for the female trader. They are a common sight on flights between Ghana, Ivory Coast, Liberia, and Sierra Leone. The writer has filled out landing cards on aircraft for illiterate traders who make frequent trips by air.

[16]See Christensen (1961) and Gladwin and Gladwin (1971) for examples of the preparation and marketing of fish. Smoked herring often sells for twice the amount of fresh herring of the same size, and the cost of wood for smoking and transportation is not that great. Highest profit observed was on the sale of fresh mackerel, where a markup of 75 to 100% over the beach price was common. As an indicator of the conservatism of the fishermen and maket women, they still quote prices in pounds and shillings even though the cedi was adopted as the standard currency in 1967. Two cedis equal one pound.

[17]The intermittent nature of fishermen's income is aptly illustrated by Quinn (1971:113) on a sample of 233 fishermen for a period of 13 seasons or approximately 17 months. In the sample, 101 fished only 2 seasons and the maximum was 3 men who fished only 7 out of 13. Income from fishing varied from £ 0–20 for 78 men to £ 151–200 for only 8 men.

LITERATURE CITED

Bosman, William
    1721   A New and Accurate Description of the Coast of Guinea (English translation). 2nd Ed. London: (n.p.).

Brown, A. P.
    1947   The Fishing Industry of the Labadi District. *In* The Fishes and Fisheries of the Gold Coast. F. R. Irvine, et al. Pp. 23–44. London: Crown Agents for the Colonies.

Christensen, James Boyd
    1954   Double Descent Among the Fanti. New Haven: Human Relations Area Files.
    1961   Marketing and Exchange in a West African Tribe. Southwestern Journal of Anthropology 17(2):124–139.
    1974   The Change in the Avunculate in Two African Societies. Ghana Journal of Sociology 7(2):30–36.

Field, M. J.
    1960   Search for Security. Evanston: Northwestern University Press.

Gladwin, Hugh, and Christina Gladwin
    1971   Estimating Market Conditions and Profit Expectations of Fish Sellers at Cape Coast, Ghana. *In* Studies in Economic Anthropology. George Dalton, ed. Anthropological Studies, No. 7:122–42.

Nunoo, Richard B.
    1974   Canoe decoration in Ghana. African Arts 7(3):32–35.

Preston, George Nelson
　1975　Perseus and Medusa in Africa Military Art in Fanteland, 1834–1972. African Arts 8(3):36–39, 68–71.

Quinn, Naomi
　1971　Mfantse Fishing Crew Composition: A Decision-Making Analysis. Ph.D. dissertation, Stanford University.

Rattray, R. S.
　1923　Ashanti. Oxford: The Clarendon Press.

*

6

Cultural Adaptation and Technological Change Among Madras Fishing Populations

BRADLEY A. BLAKE

New Mexico State University

Madras State has a coastline of 620 miles on which are located 242 marine fishing villages, housing some 236,000 salt water fishermen. The area is divided into the Coromandel Coast, Palk Bay, and the Gulf of Mannar. This paper is concerned with a portion of the Coromandel Coast which I call the Tamil-Telugu fringe area; specifically Madras and northern Chingleput Districts, including Pulicat Lake, which forms a part of the Madras-Andhra border.

The coasts of Madras and Chingleput Districts cover an area of 100 statute miles, containing 58 marine fishing villages with a total population of about 50,000 fishermen. This portion of the coast produces an annual catch of approximately 4,000 tons, as opposed to 68,000 tons for all of the coastal districts of the state; the area is heavily surf beaten, lacks natural harbors and bays, and requires specialized kinds of water craft for both shore and offshore fishing. The Madras State Fisheries Department is attempting to increase fish production by introducing certain modern technological concepts and materials to marine fishermen through cooperative societies.

With certain modifications in fishing techniques and water craft, these marine fishermen represent a sample of a larger pattern seen nearly everywhere on the coastal littoral of southeast India. Tamil- and Telugu-speaking fishermen seldom cross their linguistic borders for mates, marketing, or new fishing grounds, except to a limited extent in the linguistic fringe area where bilingualism is fairly common.

Social structure is characteristically south Indian, with a preference for caste and subcaste endogamy, patrilineality and locality, and the joint family system. Breakdowns in the systems are understandably higher in and near Madras City than in the outlying areas. Kinship terminology is essentially the same as anywhere in nontribal Tamiland. Though they call themselves "Chettiars," the caste name for this area is *Pattanavan,* which includes two traditionally endogamous subcastes known as *Chenna Pattnavar,* and *Peria Pattnavar.* Caste identity and oc-

Tamil coastal marine fishermen with two-man catamaran, Bay of Bengal, Madras.

cupation is maintained irrespective of Christian conversion. Marine fishing is not exclusively confined to Pattanavans, and Harijans and Moslem fishermen are found on the coast as well.

These marine villages have a long tradition of both subsistence and commercial fishing; the name *Chettiar* has merchant overtones. Though in a sense they are geographically isolated, in reality contact with non-fishing peoples has been constant and purposeful. Pottery and brass utensils, cloth, logs, foodstuffs (other than fish) are obtained from inland merchants or bazaars. None of these things are produced in the marine villages. There is a well-defined division of labor; men fish, and women handle and market the catches either with or without the intervention of middlemen.

There are two basic kinds of water craft: catamarans and masula boats. Fishing gear consists of hooks and lines, and at least seven types of nets. Briefly, the masula boat is a sewn, sailless, plank craft which has neither floor nor frame ribbing; carries a crew of 10 to 15; and is used exclusively for shore seining. It is extremely stable, able to withstand heavy surf, and lands well on the hard sand beaches. The catamaran is a nonrigid, keelless craft formed by lashing together trimmed wooden logs (*Melia dubia*) originally imported from Ceylon, but recently taken from Mysore and Kerala. There are four basic types of catamaran presently working this area; differences are in size and numbers of logs rather than design.

The catamaran fishermen leave the shore at dawn, run the surf, then proceed under sail to the fishing grounds anywhere from 3 to 15 miles out, fish for the better portion of the day, then return under sail around four o'clock in the afternoon. Some prefer to fish nights and return to shore at dawn. The fishermen are not known for their precise navigation, and dislike being out of sight of shore. Catches are placed in palmyria frond bags, and tied to the craft as the surf is run. Later the fish are placed in wicker baskets on the beaches, where the process of sorting, bargaining, and selling takes place.

The problem of getting the fish from the shore to the markets is pressing, since decomposition begins as soon as the fish leave the water. The catch may be turned over to the wife for sorting and sale in the closest bazaar, or auctioned on the spot to merchants or other fisherwomen. Or, the catch may have to be turned over to a middle man for loan repayment. Wherever one finds fishermen, one finds the middleman, be he Moslem, Hindu, Christian, or a fisherman within the village itself. He is in constant demand (especially during the slack periods from October through December); and is usually able to provide ready cash for a variety of purposes, with the understanding that when fishing picks up, the catch is his.

Tamil coastal marine fishermen with three-man catamaran at sea, Bay of Bengal, Madras.

Traditional social patterns combined with craft and associated gear structurally fitted to specific uses had brought about a delicate ecological balance. Since about 1956, attempts to improve the fisherman's lot have threatened this balance. Middlemen are a part of life, as are poverty and indebtedness, and there is an understandable reluctance to invest in new materials which may not prove as effective as their present equipment. The average fisherman makes only two or three rupees a day. There is fear of becoming involved in long-term loans which place financial loads on the family. An individual can handle the subsidized cost of nylon netting and the occasional expenses involving small loans, but a Pablo boat trawler with engine costs 30,000 rupees. As a consequence, trawlers are frequently purchased under the names of local fishermen, but are financed by Madras merchants and middlemen. Traditional fishing grounds are being overfished, and the catamaran fishermen complain that their nets are torn and the catches depleted; thus frictions develop. During the northeast monsoons the trawlers illegally head for Cochin and take advantage of lighter seas where they make their money while the catamaran fishermen sit at home.

Some fishermen say that nylon nets cut the fish, which in turn increases spoilage, and drives other fish out of the area. Others complain that those using nylon take larger catches than their cotton nets. However, the majority of fishermen questioned maintained that the nylon was simply too expensive. Attitudes toward change are positive for the most part providing fishermen feel that they can meet the expenses, that the change is obviously for the better, and that in the last analysis it will raise their income. This may appear overly simple at this point, but decisions involving the investment of money in a joint-family system must not be handled lightly.

The Madras Department of Fisheries, the oldest in India, was established in 1907. Reasons given by the Madras presidency to justify creation of the department were: (1) every civilized country possessed a fisheries department, and (2) fishing was the third most important industry in the country. The orientation was of course technological. Over the years the department has attempted, with varying degrees of success, to introduce and maintain fishermen's cooperative societies, unions, and federations among both inland and marine fishermen; through these organizations the department has introduced government subsidized nylon and cotton twine, motorized trawlers, ice-making plants, transport and cold storage facilities, improved marketing systems and some halfhearted attempts at social welfare. In addition, the department wants to construct housing blocks and harbors for fish landings, and eventually to eliminate the middleman.

The department prides itself on its technical orientation, yet is appallingly understaffed with trained and competent personnel and is in many ways vastly overextended and divided between the marine and inland fishing activities. Decentralization of authority and the matrix of lesser officials has produced a bureaucratic situation patterned for the most part after the British system, yet intrinsically Indian in its philosophy and action. Prerogatives of caste and job status are of course operative.

Tamil coastal marine fisherman, Bay of Bengal, Madras.

Once a man achieves officialdom above the level of *inspector,* he is reluctant to leave his office for any activity which might be in any way considered menial. As a consequence, those individuals who should be most valuable in a field situation which calls for critical evaluations of action programs often find themselves deeply involved in the mechanics of paper administration.

There has been a recent attempt to try to introduce outboard motors on the catamarans as was done in Ceylon, but this project has yet to get underway. Problems of foreign exchange make it difficult to get parts, breakdowns are common, and trained technicians are scarce. Several fishermen training schools have been set up, but the level of instruction is low, students are ill-prepared for quasi-technical training, and the training trawler is of questionable value.

The department feels that its most pressing problem is the need for adequate harbors and marketing facilities; before trawlers can operate effectively, they must have good anchorage. Madras harbor is presently overloaded, and trawlers must take their chances when anchored offshore. The heavy surf is a constant threat. Fishermen living any distance from Madras city proper—even if they could afford the trawlers—would have to spend a good deal of time away from their village. The department has been considering a plan whereby whole fishing communities could be moved to the site of newly-constructed harbors, but must cope with fishermen in this matter of moving: village sites are difficult to leave, and families are reluctant to move to apartments. This has been tried in Madras several years ago, but without success.

Cooperative societies in most coastal villages are modest and somewhat uneven in operation. Practically every village has a cooperative society, but not all villagers necessarily belong. Periodic visits are made by the departmental cooperative inspector, either to collect money due on loans, check the society accounts, or settle disputes and matters of society business. Visits are also made to advance loans or distribute twine. Factions often develop between the officers and members of the societies and the village headman or local *panchyat.* The most difficult *kuppams* ("fishing village") to administer are of course in the city itself; these fishermen are "city-wise," aggressive, and used to handling cooperative inspectors. Factional disputes are common, political alliances are often explosive, and cooperation with departmental policies largely lacking.

In brief, administrative and cultural barriers exist on both sides. The department must cope with an unwieldy bureaucratic process, an overabundance of inefficient office help, low pay, poor transportation, and the frustrations involved in trying to increase fish production. In some respects they have spread themselves so thinly that it is nearly impossible to maintain effective contact with the villages.

In spite of the growing pains and shortcomings of the relationship between the department and the village, certain positive changes are in evidence. Aside from roads, ice-making plants, insulated vans, and so on,
the department is at least aware of the inadvisability of introducing
change through the traditional and familiar channels; for example, there
has been no immediate need to improve on current net designs, for a kind
of cultural selection has in the long run produced the best net for the
existing water craft. One merely provides the twine, and suggests new
tying techniques.

The most pressing problem appears to be the lack of communication
and understanding between the department and the fishermen. If the cooperative idea is to be at all effective, then a concerted effort should be
made to train and tighten the societies. Frequent visits to *kuppams* are
necessary not only for administrative purposes, but to reinforce departmental policy, listen to village grievances and suggestions, and stay
within the financial capacities of the local society. Factionalism is a constant threat, and there is no easy way out of it; however, an understanding of the reasons for village splits is the first step in effective cooperative planning.

In summary then, what persists is an Indian state agency introducing
western technology to essentially illiterate lowcaste coastal marine
fishermen, through nontraditional cooperative channels.

IMPROVING THE CHANCES OF
SOCIAL AND ECONOMIC CHANGE

Can the effectiveness of change programs be enhanced by having members of one's own culture introduce innovation and technological change?
The answer to this question is affirmative, provided the innovator is
aware of his and the host culture's learned biases. Programs involving
change can be placed in motion and nurtured along for years; however,
the real test of successful innovation rests on the ability of the host culture to continue the change process on its own, without feeling the pressures of constant supervision and forced conformity.

However, as frequently happens in change programs, the people involved in the mechanics often find themselves becoming more concerned
with what has been termed here "work-conditioning" than with the initial goals of the project. Not all persons who become involved with
change programs need necessarily spend all of their time on a face-to-face
relationship with the host culture. It is only realistic to recognize that ad-

ministrators need to administrate, clerks must keep records and type reports, and field personnel need to spend time in the villages with the people.

Attempts must be made on the part of the directors of joint administrations—the Departments of Cooperation and Fisheries in this instance—to recognize the importance of making the effort to understand each other's operations. The premise underlying interdepartmental understanding rests on the proposition that mutual enlightenment can only improve action programs, not only at the administrative and worker levels, but all the way down the matrix of lesser officials to the tip of the bureaucratic maelstrom leading directly into the *kuppams* and the men who inhabit them.

A practical aspect of interdepartmental education might be regular staff-training seminars designed to create a perspective in which project goals, procedures, and problems could be discussed openly and frankly. It is often the case that administrations involved in change programs find it difficult to understand why people can be so tradition-orientated or change-resistant, when at the same time the administrators balk at the very suggestion of changing a single paragraph in any one of their office forms.

Applied anthropologists, as well as other persons and organizations concerned with cultural and technological change, find comfort in the panacea of education, which in the absence of constructive criticism is offered as the only way out of a difficult situation. From this, one might conclude that the answer to the whole problem of *kuppam* administration lies in the mass education of fishermen; that if each fisherman were carefully taught the economics of cooperation and marketing, all of them would somehow see the way and the light, and would as a consequence become models of frugality and cooperative enlightenment. This is pure myth.

What is implied here is that administrators frequently see education as a one-way street, down which comes knowledge, direction, and understanding. In brief, they say, "if we have the 'truth,' then why bother with anything less than that truth?" As noted earlier in this study, the Cooperative and the Fisheries Departments exist in the organizational frameworks which can provide the data necessary to understand the departments, but are not well-enough informed about the fishermen to offer any accurate insights into *kuppam* culture beside statistical accounts of craft, gear, population, and fish production. Why this lack of "soft data?"

Part of the problem lies in the cultural demands on Indian civil servants. Good jobs are difficult to find unless (1) an individual has an education, (2) there is an available employment slot requiring his qualifications, and (3) he knows someone (either in the organization or elsewhere) who will recommend him for the position. Religous and political affiliations are as important as caste in some civil service positions, despite governmental attempts to eliminate those considerations. Employees tend to guard their jobs carefully, and often exhibit uneasiness or despondency when reprimanded for even minor infractions.

When one considers the pressures of civil service job maintenance (not to mention the rarities of promotion), it becomes somewhat easier to understand why there is, on the part of the employee, little time and concern for the lives of other men. There is much more than *dharma* involved in the day-to-day existence in one's job. There is a real concern over the possibility of losing the job because of what may be interpreted by the employer as inefficiency, such as the failure to make loan collections from the fishermen[1].

In spite of the problems surrounding the cooperative inspectors' official activities in the *kuppams,* it would be possible administratively to expand their activities to include more time for each *kuppam,* in order to develop their ability to see *kuppam* problems fermenting before they exploded into open conflict. In short, the Fisheries Department already has a man in the *kuppams* who could function much more efficiently than he does.

The operational structure of the cooperative scheme from the primary cooperative society at the *kuppam* level all the way up through the unions and federations is so loosely organized and poorly supervised that graft and misappropriation of funds runs nearly unchecked throughout most of the organization. Yet, in spite of these problems, the Fisheries Department points with pride to an increase of fishermen's cooperatives and fish tonnage over the years.

It was considered general knowledge in the Cooperative and Fisheries Departments that the Reserve Bank of India would not consider financing fishermen's cooperatives until the societies showed every indication of stabilization. This suggests that the cooperative movement, at least in the area of fisheries, needs considerable tightening. Perhaps the first steps towards cooperative reorganization must take place in the primary cooperative society, right in the heart of the *kuppam.*

A possible beginning in the reorganization of primary cooperative societies might be the development of model societies. Pilot studies could be conducted, placing greater emphasis on the training and supervision of society members by the cooperative inspector. This should create an atmosphere in which both fishermen and inspectors might communicate effectively. There must be close supervision and frequent contact with the fishing communities if there is to be a stable economy in the *kup-pams*.

There needs to be an honest appraisal of the "middleman problem." It is extremely difficult to attempt to eliminate this institution, common in most of India and among fishing peoples in particular. Students of culture change are usually aware of the importance of introducing innovation through traditional channels so as to minimize culture shock and make the transition from the old to the new as smooth as possible. The research period of this study did not allow time to examine the middleman problem in detail. As one might expect, the middlemen would rather not discuss their business transactions with anyone other than their contract holders. Whether the Fisheries Department likes it or not, the middleman has functioned as one of the major distributors of fish in Madras state. He functions not only as a business contact for the fisherman; but also serves as a dependable source of money for weddings, funerals, and holidays, as well as during the monsoon period when a *kuppam's* fishing drops to almost nothing.

In searching all of the bylaws, rules, and regulations governing the administration of cooperative societies and their extensions, and after speaking to a large number of Fisheries and Cooperative Department officials, it is quite evident that there are no funds available anywhere in the coffers of the Madras government to cover anything less than famine in the *kuppams*. One can now begin to understand why fishermen are reluctant to turn over all of their catches to a cooperative scheme for marketing.

Finally, one may ask two questions which illustrate the difficulties in this situation: (1) if the government of India finds that it is technically and economically unrealistic to adapt native fishing craft and gear to motorization and design changes as has proved to be the case along the coast of Madras State, would it not be more effective to focus their attention on trawlerized fishing, leaving the catamaran and masula boat fishermen to their traditional fishing technology? (2) what kinds of problems could be predicted if the government of Madras attempts *kuppam* relocation programs to concentrate marine fishermen in housing units strategically located near natural and artificial harbors?

CONCLUSIONS

The discussion has focused on the problems of fishing technology and induced change in India. Unfortunately, there are relatively few studies devoted to the peculiar circumstances facing the government of Madras

State and other Indian states bordering on salt water. However, marine fishing people, regardless of their geographical location, face similar problems which require similar solutions. Thus, discussions of the problems facing the Madras Fisheries Department in the matter of the total effectiveness of their present change program are not unlike those confronting other countries which are also involved in similar problems. There are questions which might be asked concerning the price a government is willing to pay for improved fishing technology.

In anticipating problem areas in marine fishing technology, can there be a transferability to the broader problems of change programs? In essence, can any of the research results of this study be in any way applied to change programs both in fishing and nonfishing populations?

One positive approach may be expressed best as transferability through the process of data gathering. The significance of personal contacts with individuals and organizations who might be willing to cooperate with the researcher by enlarging his sphere of contacts cannot be emphasized too strongly. Introductions to others who might be in a position to render aid and advice or who are sympathetic with the goals of the project are invaluable. The rationale behind this stems from the proposition that human awareness can facilitate expediency. This is not to suggest that all of one's contacts will prove fruitful or beneficial, but if handled carefully and discretely, associations with persons in positions of power can shorten the data-collecting process considerably. A proficient field researcher should (again, with help and suggestions) be able to carefully select those whom he feels will be most useful in removing the obstacles of bureaucracy, which have been known to bring even the best-intended project to a standstill.

Greater emphasis must be placed on the food potential of marine resources by concentrated research on present world methods of harvesting fish. If there are to be international attempts to increase food production, fishermen will have to be trained to handle the complexities of modern fishing technology. Based on the present study, this transition can be accomplished if proper planning, cooperation, and supervision exist between the fishermen and the government.

Any accumulation of data such as has been presented in the body of this study warrants a theoretical summary which attempts to place the study in what has been termed a framework of transferability or meaningfulness relative to other similar interests in applied anthropology, or within the broader perspective of culture change as a major area of interest under the larger rubric of cultural anthropology.

An important factor which seems to come from most studies of induced change is that hindsight is more valuable than foresight. One might argue that given enough experience and hindsight, there will eventually be a body of theory developed which will have real significance (and perhaps predictability) for applied anthropologists and other agents of change. On one hand, it is entirely arguable that each field study is unique, with its own idiosyncracies and cultural history somehow setting it aside from other studies of similar magnitude and scope. In short, a marine fishing study in one Madras State district would produce somewhat different data than in another district. On the other hand one might say, aside from minor changes in technology, ecology, and methods used for the production and distribution of marine food sources, that a study such as this might lend support to other research projects dealing with marine fishing in general.

It is relatively easy to find fault with technological change programs, but far more difficult to suggest and implement corrective measures for existing programs. The shift from native fishing techniques to modernization is a giant step, but not nearly as large as it appears. Men are capable of learning new techniques, but the manner in which these techniques are introduced and reinforced is crucial in making the transition. Some anthropologists may only regret the loss of traditional technology and cultures but a far more important problem is the price traditional peoples are being asked to pay for modernization.[2]

NOTES

[1]There is no intent in this study to denigrate the honest efforts of the Fisheries Department personnel. Without the full cooperation of the Fisheries Department and their cooperative inspectors little could have been accomplished. The men of this department face monumental problems which can only be partially appreciated. They deserve much more credit than they appear to receive in the body of this study.

[2]The data in this paper were cross-checked against and substantiated by the following bibliography.

LITERATURE CITED

Anugraham, D. D.
    1940   The Fisherfolk of Madras, an Economic Survey. M.A. thesis, University of Madras.

Barlind, F. H.
    1958   Report in Madras State on a Survey Fish-Marketing Situation. Madras Fisheries Marketing Report, No. 4. Madras: Controller of Stationery and Printing.

Beales, Allan R.
  1961   Cleavage and Internal Conflict: An Example from India. *Reprinted
          from* The Journal of Conflict Resolutions 5:1:27–34.

Bhattacharyya, S. N.
  1965   Fisheries in Indian Economy. Delhi: Metropolitan Book Company.

Blake, Bradley A.
  1969   Technological Change Among the Coastal Marine Fishermen of
          Madras State. Ph.D. dissertation, University of Wisconsin.

Byrnes, Francis C.
  1968   Some Missing Variables in Diffusion Research and Innovation
          Strategy. Reprint (adapted from same title), Philippine Sociological
          Review 14:4: (10:66), 242–56. New York: Agricultural Development
          Council.

Desai, M. B., and Pr. R. Baichwal
  1959   Role of Middlemen and Cooperatives in the Production and Market-
          ing of Fish. background Paper No. 3, Regional Seminar on Fishing
          Cooperatives, Oct.–Nov. 1963, Karachi (West Pakistan). *Reproduced
          from* Indian Journal of Agricultural Economics, 14:4 Oct.–Dec. Pp.
          91–114. New Delhi: International Cooperative Alliance.

Digby, Margaret
  1961   Cooperation for Fishermen, a Study Based on Proceedings and
          Working Papers of the Technical Meeting on Fishery Cooperatives,
          Naples, May 12–21, 1959. Holland: Food and Agriculture Organiza-
          tion of the United Nations.

John, V., et al
  1959   Report of the Fishing Experiments in the Offshore Waters of Madras
          State. Madras: Controller of Stationery and Printing.

Karve, D. G.
  1967   Reformulation of Co-operative Principles. Bombay: Gandhi Smarak
          Nidhi.

Kuriyan, G. K., and D.A.S. Gnanadoss
  1962   Motorisation of Fishing Crafts in Madras State. Madras: Controller
          of Stationery and Printing.

7

Changing Economics in an Ecuadorian Maritime Community[*]

DeWIGHT R. MIDDLETON

SUNY, Oswego

INTRODUCTION

This study presents a broad, descriptive view of the changing economic scene on the central coast of Ecuador, where in recent years the maritime sector has undergone rapid development. The central locus of development is the growing city of Manta; the primary impetus for change emanates from the tuna fishing boom and from the construction of a new maritime port. Concomitantly, the traditional fishing fleet of canoes and small sail launches has diminished considerably in size, and the fishermen have responded differently to the presence of new job opportunities. Their differential responses will be explored later in this study. In order to fully appreciate the regional and national significance

*This study was supported by PHS Fellowship MH40446–01A1S1 from the National Institute of Mental Health, supplemented by a Training Grant for field research conducted from July 1970 to August 1971. A return trip to Manta in the summer of 1973 was made possible by a Faculty Research Fellowship from the State University of New York.

111

of these developments, however, it will be useful first to sketch briefly the ecological and historical circumstances that precede them.

ECOLOGICAL SETTING

The arid province of Manabí occupies the central Ecuadorian littoral. To the north, the littoral is cloaked in the heavy rain forests of Esmeraldas, and the margin of the sea is mediated by extensive mangrove swamps. To the south, the central desert region extends to the fertile Guayas River valley where Ecuador's largest city and major port, Guayaquil, is located. To the east, Manabí is bounded by the forested foothills of the Andes. The northern and eastern reaches of Manabí are much more fertile, and are therefore not properly included in the central coast desert.

Both the aridity of the central coast and the richness of its fishing grounds are influenced heavily by the Humboldt current, a cold current flowing northward along the western coast of South America, accompanied by cool, dry winds. In northern Peru, the current swings westward away from the coast. The Humboldt, sometimes called the Peruvian current, is an extremely important supplier of nutrients and is largely responsible for the abundance of *anchoveta* off Peru and of tuna off Ecuador. Its richness is due primarily to the process known as *upwelling*, that is the rise of cold water from the ocean floor (Acosta-Solis 1966). Plankton thrive on the nutrients in the cold water provided by the upwelling, and fish feed upon the plankton only to become prey to larger fish and so on, up the food chain. Upwelling occurs as a result of the action of prevailing winds that drive away the warm surface water from the coast to be replaced by lower layers of cold water. When the winds abate to a point where this action is no longer sustained, the water warms to a greater depth, thus decreasing food supply. Fish are then driven deeper in search of food and thereby become more inaccessible to capture. Such a period is said to reflect the dominance of El Niño (the Child), or warm current from the north, bringing with it increased rainfall (Hurtado 1969:20).

The Humboldt itself periodically alters its course somewhat and, in so doing, precipitates concomitant fluctuations in weather conditions on the periphery of its influence. Manabí, for example, continues to suffer periodic droughts running in cycles of 20 to 25 years, interspersed with short periods of sporadically heavy rainfall. Particularly serious doughts occurred in the years 1865, 1894, 1903 and 1921. A prolonged era of generally marginal precipitation extended form 1940 to 1960 (Alvarada 1971), but torrential rains caused extensive damage throughout Manabí in 1953 and 1971.

Lacking water, power, and natural resources, Manabí has long languished in the shadow of the romance and booms of other regions of Ecuador. Although Manta itself has been known for many years for its brisk, if small scale, economic activity, it has generally been depicted as a small, dusty, and uninteresting town. Today, Manta's image has undergone a complete transformation as it spearheads a province-wide burst of development. The development of Manabí and the discovery of oil in the Amazonian province of El Oriente are extremely important to Ecuador's national economic advance because they both diversify the exploitative economy and geographically spread the rewards.

HISTORICAL BACKGROUND

Major rivers in the Ecuadorian littoral—unlike those in Peru which flow from the Andes at right angles to the sea—tend to follow a north-south axis. Thus, where in Peru such rivers created a series of similar and hospitable environments transecting the littoral, the early inhabitants of Ecuador were constrained to adapt either to an interior riverine environment, or to the sea. This distinction is exemplified particularly on the central coast where adaptation to the sea was well established at least as early as 500 A.D. (Meggers 1966:130). In the absence of dependable water courses, an extensive network of wells supplemented by reservoirs was established throughout southern Manabí and in the vicinity of Manta (Meggers 1966:162-163). By this date, large balsa rafts were used in fishing and continued into the colonial era. Indeed, a detachment from Pizarro's expedition, probing southward from Panama, encountered such a raft in 1525 laden with trade goods (Meggers 1972:89). Fishing and coastal commerce, then, were fully established in the pre-colonial era (Murra 1963:804). The precise relationship between Ecuador and the Peruvian civilization is unknown. Spanish chroniclers are fairly certain that the Inca were unable, if indeed they attempted, to incorporate the Ecuadorian coastal cultures into their empire (Meggers 1966:162-63); but a commercial relationship between them undoubtedly did spring up, and perhaps some additional tribute or recognition was tendered by the coastal peoples.

Under colonial rule the Indians of the central coast remained free for the most part, the majority living near the sea in villages located slightly inland as a protection against pirate attacks. By the 1700s the Indian component may have succeeded in recovering demographically from the effects of the conquest (Hamerly 1970:86), and in the late 1700s and early 1800s the combined Indian and mestizo population experienced a sub-

stantial spurt of growth. This demographic revolution occurred despite
years of drought in 1771, 1790 to 1795, and three more such periods in the
first decade of the 1800s (Hamerly 1970:80). This tremendous increase in
the face of adverse conditions must have been greatly facilitated by a
well-developed utilization of marine resources. However, while chronic
drought no doubt left the maritime adaptive apparatus largely unim-
paired, it surely caused excessive and intolerable fluctuations in the critical balance between fresh water supply and population demand. (In
Manta, water was still being imported by truck and by burro as late as
1963, although subsequently these carriers were replaced by a supply line
from the interior.) In any event, the excess population moved south to
the struggling port of Guayaquil and to the Guayas River valley, which
was then undergoing extensive agricultural development. This migration
appears to have been critically important to Guayaquil's rise to power,
for the area was labor deficient at the time due to the cacao boom
(Hamerly 1970).

Historically, the population of the central coast was not exposed to the
many onerous demands placed on other colonial groups, for the region is
not minerally or agriculturally rich. In addition, fishing does not lend itself well to the oppressive regimentation characteristic of plantation
economies; at least one scholar has suggested that fishermen may frequently have occupied a favored position with their colonial rulers (Price
1966:1364). By the middle 1800s life in the area could be described in the
following manner:

> Most manabitas and santaelenenses, whether cholos or mestizos, com-
> bined fishing with subsistence farming and/or cattle raising. They earned
> the cash with which to pay tribute and/or tithe, and to purchase whatever
> they could not provide for themselves by marketing shellfish and fresh fish
> in Portoviejo and Santiago de Guayaquil, by exporting salt and salted fish
> to the highlands, and by selling the celebrated but misnamed Panama hats,
> hammocks, baskets, and kitchen utensils which they wove out of *paja to-
> quilla (Corludovica palmata)* (Hamerly 1970:129).

Thus, these marine-rich and land-poor conditions constituted the basic
set of problems to which the central coast population adjusted its life-
ways. Lack of water and Guayaquil's ascendancy as a commercial center
and port city left Manta struggling in its wake; but contemporary pressures for national development, the quickening pace of international
trade, and the world's insatiable hunger for marine resources worked in
concert to catapult Manta into the modern era.

THE TRADITIONAL FISHING SECTOR

In this century the traditional fishing focus in Manta as well as in its neighboring communities depends upon the use of canoes and sailboats of a moderate size. Prior to the expansion of the tuna industry and the port, over 400 canoes and perhaps 100 sailboats were used largely on a subsistence basis, supplemented by cash sales on a small scale. Today, the catch from these vessels is still sold on the beach to middlemen who distribute it to the markets of Manta, Portoviejo, and other towns of inland Manabí, as well as to the highlands. The catch from canoes and sailboats is not normally sold to the processing plants, for they have their own boats and make their own arrangements with independent operators.

About 37 sail-powered launches continue to operate in Manta. They are rigged with mainsail and jib, and they can be manned adequately by two fishermen, although at least three are normally preferred because of the fishing technique employed. Crews in the past were comprised largely of relatives, particularly sons and brothers, but today they include many friends as well. Women do not fish; few if any have ever been to sea. Many sons have gone to work on the tuna boats, or taken jobs in any number of other activities increasingly available to them now in the bustling city. Older fishermen lament these changes and worry about securing dependable help; for launches, unlike canoes, are never sailed by a single fisherman.

Prior to the creation of new port facilities, wider and deeper launches hauled freight between anchored ships and Manta's single dock, which was little more than a short appendage to the land and was positioned in shallow water, thus forcing ships to anchor far offshore. The construction of the new port signaled the demise of these service craft, and they were destroyed for lack of buyers.

Launches and canoes work different fishing grounds; canoes work close to shore, while launches sail regularly to a distance of 40 or 50 miles. The distant island of La Plata is a favorite fishing ground, particularly for black marlin. Launch fishermen trawl, that is, they trail their hand lines overboard as the craft continues to sail. Nets are not used, except a landing net. Sailing long distances provides the launch fishermen greater opportunity to catch larger fish. Since such fish may weigh in the hundreds of pounds, the lure of landing 1000 or 2000 sucres worth can make several luckless days suddenly worthwhile. Canoe fishermen also catch large fish, but the chance of doing so is, in their estimation, considerably less the nearer to shore they work. Fishing in the depths off Manta is a comparatively safe enterprise, for the region rarely experiences severe storms; the most hazardous time is faced when landing a large fish. In this case two fishermen must leave the launch for the small canoe (which is trailed along behind the sailboat) in order to tire the fish by letting it pull the weight of the canoe. The third man follows in the launch. The principal danger in this maneuver lies in being tipped over in shark-infested waters; all fishermen are quick to relate stories of such accidents, but they seldom occur in fact. Canoe fishermen, on the other hand, have been known to intentionally leave their craft to land an oversize fish. They slip into the water and tip the canoe, allowing the entering water to force the canoe to ride lower; and the fish is then eased, rather than lifted, into the boat. The water is bailed out once the fish is secured, and the boat returns to its normal displacement.

Launches depart for the open sea sometime between early evening and midnight and sail through the dark to arrive at the desired location by early morning. They frequently do not return until dusk the following day. Launch fishermen spend more time in fishing and in maintenance than do those who use canoes, but while the investment in time and expense is greater for them, the potential payoff is also greater (launches contain more fish, if nothing else). The earnings of the two groups overlap a great deal, but launch owners have the edge. The fishermen themselves generally believe this, and there is an additional status boost in owning the larger craft, which originally took an investment of up to $400 (U.S.) compared to perhaps $40 for canoes.

Canoes are hewn from logs by Negro and Cayapa Indian workmen in the northern province of Esmeraldas, and in southern Colombia. They are found distributed from this area southward to Guayaquil, on the beaches of the sea and on the banks of lower river courses and estuaries. Manabí is the area of most intensive use of the "Manabí canoe, as well as the center of its distribution" (Edwards 1965:47). About 18 feet long, the Manabí canoe is easily confused with the Cayapa or Chocó canoe (the Chocó is a region of the northern Colombian littoral) which is also observed throughout the same area, but not in the same numbers. The Chocó and Cayapa canoes are also frequently confused with one another, although the Cayapa craft is distinguished primarily by small platforms at bow and stern. Rivermen in the north sometimes stand on these lips to paddle or pole their way along; such platforms, however, are not desirable for use at sea. While resembling the Chocó canoe in its basic configuration, the Manabí craft is heavier and deeper, and possesses a bluffer bow and stern (Edwards 1965:47). Introduced during the postconquest period, and replacing the balsa raft, the Manabí canoe is not native to the central littoral. Edwards (1965:49) gives the impression that the Manabí canoe is fabricated in Manabí, perhaps in Manta, but the fishermen deny this. I observed no canoes in stages of construction in Manta, nor did I hear of any. Indeed, they were in short supply and certainly not to be had at a "reasonable" price. Edwards (1965:48) notes that in 1958 canoes were not using outboard motors yet, but speculates that their general use may not be far off. But this innovative experiment has not been widely accepted and probably will not be for some time, if at all. Fishermen do not see any economic advantage in their use and most do not know much about motors—maintenance is a nuisance and an expensive one at that. Those who experimented with motors eventually sold them. During the period of field work, several motor-driven canoes traveled between the port and the nearby village of Los Esteros, but no fishing canoes were thus fitted. Basically a river craft, the Manabí canoe must be modified for seaworthiness. The gunwales are extended in height to provide more clearance above the water line, and to afford better protection against shipping water in choppy seas. The bow and stern are braced to receive the greater force of waves, and a wood receptacle is installed to anchor the mast at the bottom. A triangular mainsail is employed, one which is larger and sronger than the smaller rectangular ones used in Bahía and San Lorenzo to the north. A few canoes are rigged with a small jib, and balance boards are regularly used in all.

Canoe crews consist of two to six men, some of whom may be related. As in the case of launch crews, fewer sons are involved as the years go by and an increasing number of friends are to be found instead. All parties contribute gear, especially lines and hooks, and shares are divided equally from the total sales, or if there is less solidarity among crew members, according to what each man catches.

Although there are seasonal fluctuations, canoe fishing is a year-round occupation. Fishermen remain at home only when there is no bait, when offshore seas are too rough, or when they have something urgent to attend to elsewhere. Since the region is not marked by sudden and severe storms, the cause is more often the lack of bait. Many fishermen believe that the expansion of the tuna industry has caused a reduction in the fish population, as they are finding it increasingly difficult to obtain sufficient bait, and are now forced to ask for, or to buy, it from the tuna boats. Formerly, bait was collected by means of a large beach net operated in the early morning hours before daybreak. According to informants, perhaps ten or more of these nets were once used cooperatively by clusters of families. Today not only are they seldom used, but few actually exist. Tuna boats require great quantities of bait and they harvest it accordingly. Since they conduct their collecting operations in the bay, they reduce the amount of bait available to the fishermen. If the fishermen know the captain well, or if he is generous and bait is plentiful, they might receive it free. Otherwise they must buy bait at four or five sucres per two pounds.

The cash income of canoe fishermen ranges from 100 to 600 sucres ($4 to $24 U.S.) per week. One hundred sucres is considered a bad week; 250 to 300 is a good, or average week; and 400 and up is an excellent week. Although tuna fishing is not as consistent in its income as canoe or launch fishing, many of the traditional fishermen admit that they could probably earn more working the tuna boats, but they prefer to fish for themselves, not liking to work for someone else, or at irregular times. They like their freedom.

THE TUNA INDUSTRY

The fishing industry in Ecuador is based on three types of marine resources: tuna, shrimp, and lobster. Shrimp is taken off the northern coast, in the vicinity of San Lorenzo and Esmeraldas, and southward to Bahla de Carlaquez. Tuna is especially abundant off the coasts of Manta and Salinas (near Guayaquil), while lobster is harvested near the Galapagos Islands. The Ecuadorian fishing industry has grown considerably in the past decade, based particularly on the larger share of tuna caught. In 1955, the tuna industry barely existed, and only one factory in Manta—there are other plants in Guayaquil—was processing fish caught primarily by traditional methods. In that year the entire industry realized only .3 million dollars. After the introduction of motorized boats and improved techniques, production increased sharply, rising to 5.4 million dollars in 1962 and to 6.3 in 1967. From 1965 to 1967 canned tuna production rose from 1,900 thousand tons to 2,100, but frozen bulk tuna production during the same period leaped dramatically from 4.7 thousand tons to 9.5. While some canned tuna is produced for domestic consumption, the greater bulk of tuna and whitefish production is exported. Four major fish processing plants now operate in Manta, and several smaller ones produce irregularly. All but one have been established since 1965. The development of the tuna industry, including the more than 100 tuna boats in the Manta fleet, was a result of cooperation among the Ecuadorian government, the U.S. International Cooperative Administration, and the Food and Agriculture Organization (FAO) of the United Nations.

By current industrial standards, Ecuadorian tuna boats are generally quite small in capacity—about 40 tons. Even the several which can contain over 100 tons are comparatively small. Tuna fishing continues throughout the year, but the best season is the rainy period lasting from December to May. Even during the productive season, however, fishing is not uniformly good each day, for fluctuations in water temperature of only a few degrees determine whether or not tuna move to greater depths. Occasionally, tuna boats spend long days in the harbor waiting for a change in luck; on the other hand, they may be gone for several days at a time when luck is holding. When conditions are unfavorable, owners are reluctant to send out their vessels unless there is a fair chance of at least recovering operating costs. Normally one-third of the proceeds is divided among the crew members and another third is allocated to fuel and maintenance. When there is no catch the crew receives nothing. A tuna crew consists of a captain, an engineer, and approximately 12 men who fish with cane poles. When a school of tuna is sighted, these men seize their poles and position themselves along a narrow, exterior platform located a few feet below topside at about deck level; the platform runs along the port side and the stern of the vessel. Instead of baiting hooks, which are unbarbed, bait is flung overboard in large quantities by the bait man, and the tuna snap at anything moving including bare hooks. The tuna are rapidly hauled or flung on board, and the unbarbed hooks immediately returned to the water. With a normal crew of 12 to 16, and with nearly 100 tuna boats operating at various times, some idea of the impact of the tuna boom in generating jobs can be formed.

PORT CONSTRUCTION

In 1954, the *Camara Comercio de Manta*, an organization of interested business men which has played a key role in Manta's successful growth, moved to form a single agency with centralized power to procure funds for the construction of a maritime port. This initial action led eventually to the founding of the Port Authority, empowered to levy rents for the financial support of its organization and to control the administration of the functioning port facilities. When trouble arose with the national government over the signing of the building contract, the entire city went on a general strike to force the issue in its favor (Cedeño 1969:24). Finally, on February 20, 1959, the construction contract was signed and work began shortly thereafter. The major elements of the complex include a wharf capable of handling two to three ships simultaneously (another wharf was completed in 1971), warehouses and storage aprons, an auxiliary pier for banana exporters, and two small wharves for tuna boats. Several of the larger processing plants have their own docks. An integral component of the complex is the dual lane avenue extending from the port along the beach past Manta and the neighborhood of Tarqui, and connecting with roads to Quito and to Guayaquil. Along this thoroughfare matériel moves day and night, some of it destined for the oil fields in the Oriente, Ecuador's Amazonian province.

The port has provided many new jobs and now serves up to 40 or more ships in one month. The Manta port has the advantage of being a deep-water port, while Guayaquil is a river port, thus subject to tidal fluctuations making long work periods difficult. Manta is fast gaining the reputation for moving cargo faster with less expense and pilfering than Guayaquil, but it still lags behind the well-established river port.

STRATEGIES OF ADJUSTMENT

The principal concern of this section is to construct a simple, low order model of the varied responses among traditional fishermen to the changing maritime sector. In the initial phases of development, entrepreneurs attempted to increase the yields of canoe fishermen by outfitting canoes with motors. This innovation proved ineffective for reasons noted earlier. With the introduction of mechanized vessels equipped with nets, winches, bait tanks, and so on, the economic payoff was amply demonstrated and the tuna fleet began to grow. Wages were attractive and many traditional fishermen quickly abandoned their canoes for the tuna boats. The transferral of fish from dock to plant and back to dock after processing created other jobs, some of which were taken by fishermen, some by townsmen. A few of the launch owners, particularly those having wide experience, were asked if they wanted to captain a tuna boat. At least one individual who accepted such an offer has become moderately rich as a consequence of his decision. Partially because they possessed some of the skills required in these jobs, and partially because tuna fishing and fish handling were defined as fishermen's work, and thus lowly valuated, the traditional fishermen moved rather quickly into these jobs in the early phases of development. Success, however, attracts attention and the skills involved, although unfamiliar to townsmen, are not really difficult to learn and proved to be no real barrier to those who needed jobs.

Several basic strategies were developed by the fishermen in the face of change.[1] Some chose to work only in the factories, or on the docks, or on tuna boats, while others chose to remain in the launches or canoes. A single-job strategy was followed in both cases, emphasizing either the traditional facet, or the new. Those who elected to work a new job frequently shared considerable optimism in their future, to the point of selling their canoes and severing many old relationships; they were earning good money. Fishermen who stayed in their launches and canoes tended to be older and more cautious; some of them felt that the steady reduction in their numbers, accompanied by urban growth, would increase their share in the expanding market. Another group of fishermen, however, chose a second strategy—a multiple-job strategy based on a mixture of new and old activities. Because of seasonal fluctuations in fishing causing periodic idleness, and because of varying work schedules permitting flexibility, these individuals were able to move from one type of job to another.[2] Basically, they work in the industrial sphere when possible, but fish in the traditional mode during slack times. Where there is a conflict between traditional work and industrial work, however, priority always is given to the industrial job because labor is cheap and plentiful, and an undependable worker is quickly dismissed.

The fishing industry has fallen upon hard times in recent years, perhaps because of overfishing (by Ecuadorians and by various foreign fleets) or because of critical fluctuations in water temperature. Unfortunately, this same period has seen Ecuadorians caught up in the inflationary spiral that has spread among rich and poor nations alike, driving up operating costs in both traditional and industrial components of the maritime sector. Now that development appears to be stalled, fishermen have had to reconsider their original response to change. Some who originally opted for work exclusively within the industrial sphere have become disillusioned and returned to a multiple job strategy; they have reverted to traditional fishing, but still work in the industrial sphere whenever possible. In this period of limbo, their initial decisions have proved not to be irrevocable, if they simply stored their canoes under the house, and/or they did not disengage themselves from too many of their former relationships. On the other hand, those who did sell their canoes and stopped cultivating certain established ties are faced with the difficult task of obtaining a canoe at inflated prices—they certainly cannot construct their own—or must somehow convince canoe or launch owners to take them on. The future appears to fishermen to be unclear and alternatives ill defined; they do not understand why the fishing is bad. The present condition of maritime development in Manta lends support to Anderson and Wadel's (1972:154) thesis that during some stages of technological development in maritime groups, anxiety may increase rather than diminish.

The extent of the predicament can better be appreciated by a brief treatment of data derived from genealogical and household survey work in the former fishermen's barrio of Tarqui, now an urban parish of about 4,000 inhabitants. Based on a random sample survey of a section of Tarqui adjacent to the beach, it is clear that about 40 percent of the households are directly engaged in fishing activities of some kind. Perhaps another five percent are employed in the processing plants, and another two percent work more or less regularly on the docks. Of the fishermen sampled, 20 percent are canoe fishermen and 17 percent are tuna fishermen. One-third of the households involved in tuna fishing, however, had 2 or more tuna fishermen in the household. Where traditional fishing is concerned, this condition would not be surprising for extended family households, and to have compounds focusing on fishing was standard in the old fishermen's barrio. But such data for households of tuna fishermen reveal a heavy commitment to new maritime development. Since the tuna industry has reached a plateau in its development, such families have been particularly hard hit economically. As one might expect, household solidarity has been put to the test in some families, and fission has occurred in several cases known to the investigator.

Actually the picture may be somewhat bleaker, for an examination of genealogies reveals that about 20 percent of the extended families have multi-household commitments to the maritime sector. Thus, to the extent that enduring cooperative relationships exist among these households, and therefore constitute a second line of defense against hard times, they have "chosen" a high risk strategy. Families and households, as well as individuals, pursuing a multi-job strategy in times of flux and stall may well fare better than those adhering to a single job strategy, traditional or industrial. The degree to which fishermen themselves are conscious of strategizing runs a wide gamut from not very much to a lot. Clearly, it is much easier to coordinate at the individual household level than at the extended family level. It is safe to assume, however, that in too many cases economic conditions have not permitted the luxury of choices and strategies. After all, to a large degree, the maritime focus is the only game in town for otherwise unskilled urban fishermen.

CONCLUSION

In this study, I have attempted to adumbrate the principal changes taking place on the central coast of Ecuador, particularly in the city of Manta. The maritime focus is an ancient adaptation to a marine-rich and land-poor environment. Lacking a good natural harbor, located in an arid region, and fully exposed to the constant assaults of freebooters, Manta was ignored in colonial times while Guayaquil achieved ascendancy on the strength of her port activities and the agricultural development of her hinterland. The development of the port at Manta serves the central region of the littoral where, in the Andean foothills, bananas have become the principal export crop. World demand for fish has stimulated the development of the tuna fleet which has created hundreds of jobs; however, it has also presented traditional fishermen with some difficulties, such as the decreased availability of bait. Many traditional fishermen have taken advantage of new jobs resulting from maritime development, but fishing is, like the banana crop, not always a predictable resource, especially on the periphery of the influence of the Humboldt current. Under such conditions, forecasting the future course of development is risky enough even for those with technical expertise, not to mention poor fishermen.

NOTES

[1]While these strategies cannot be statistically validated, they do rest on a year of interviewing and participant-observation. Additional insights were gained in conjunction with the sample survey, particularly the section on occupations. Additional information derived from the survey may be found in Middleton (1974 and 1975).

[2]A case study of a fisherman utilizing an effective multiple-job strategy is presented in Middleton (n.d.).

LITERATURE CITED

Acosta-Solis, Misael
    1966   Los Recursos Naturales del Ecuador y su Conservación, Vol. II. Instituto Panamericana de Geografica e Historia. Durango, Mexico: Editorial Stylo.

Alvarada, Raúl
    1971   Manabí: Preparandose para un Futuro Mejor. Anglo 10 (Mach). Pp. 1–2 Quito: Anglo-Ecuadorian Oilfields, Ltd.

Andersen, Raoul, and Cato Wadel
    1972   Comparative Problems in Fishing Adaptations. *In* North Atlantic Fishermen: Anthropological Essays on Modern Fishing. Newfoundland Social and Economic Papers, No. 5. Institute of Social and Economic Research. Memorial University of Newfoundland, Pp. 141–65. Toronto: University of Toronto Press.

Cedeño, J. Viliulfo
    1969   Historia, Tradiciones i Leyendas: Manta-Jocay. Manta: Portuaria-América.

Edwards, C. R.
    1965   Aboriginal Watercraft on the Pacific Coast of South America. Berkeley: University of California Press.

Hammel, Eugene A., and Ynez D. Haase
    1962   A Survey of Peruvian Fishing Communities. Anthropological
            Records 21: 211–30.

Hamerly, Michael T.
    1970   A Social and Economic History of the City and District of Guayaquil
            During the Late Colonial and Independence Periods. Ph.D. disserta-
            tion. The University of Florida.

Hurtado, Oswaldo
    1969   Dos Mundos Superpuestos: Ensayos de Diagnóstico de la Realidad
            Ecuatoriana. Quito: Instituto Ecuatoriano de Planificación para el
            Desarrollo Social (INEDES).

Meggers, Betty J.
    1966   Ecuador. Ancient Peoples and Places. London: Thames and Hudson.
    1972   Prehistoric America. New York: Aldine-Atherton.

Murra, John
    1963   The Historic Tribes of Ecuador. *In* Handbook of South American In-
            dians, Vol. 2. Julian H. Steward, ed. New York: Cooper Square Pub-
            lishers.

Middleton, DeWight R.
    1974   Neighborhood and City in Coastal Ecuador. Urban Anthropology
            3: 184–99.
    1975   Choice and Strategy in an Urban Compadrazgo. American Ethnolo-
            gist. 2:461–475.
    n.d.   Network and Opportunity: Changing Arenas of Recruitment in an
            Ecuadorian City.

Price, Richard
    1966   Carribbean Fishing and Fishermen: A Historical Sketch. American
            Anthropologist 68: 1363–83.

8

The Influence of Modernization on the Modes of Production in Coastal Fishing: An Example from Venezuela

YVAN D. BRETON

Univérsité Laval

INTRODUCTION

In recent years, social scientists have shown a growing concern for the introduction and effects of capitalism in marine zones. Thus far, the significance of the anthropological contribution has been mainly in the study of marine adaptations and fishing communities in coastal regions. I suggest, however, that the specific interest of anthropologists in fishing has its roots in certain modifications that have taken place within their previously accepted theoretical and methodological frameworks. For instance, the advent of cultural ecology has greatly contributed to the development of studies of ecotypes and has led to the rediscovery of the importance of infrastructure as critical element in social change (e.g. Steward 1972, Cohen 1968, Wolf 1966). Another significant redirection has come out of the substantivist-formalist debate that has promoted conceptual links between anthropologists and economists involved in the study of rural development and has led to a significant infusion of Marxist theory into our discipline (Godelier 1974, Rey 1973, Meillassoux 1964, Cook 1973).

In a study of modernization which is of interest to me in this paper, Marxist theory is in direct contradiction with liberal-capitalist approaches to developmental changes in fishing. A review of the content of several anthropological studies of fishing shows clearly, however, that their epistemological underpinning still lies within a functionalist framework which emphasizes the importance of superstructure at the expense of infrastructure; moreover, they provide little information on the interrelationship of the levels. Secondly, it seems that in their desire to build up a strong maritime anthropology, some have followed a tradition already established in our discipline and rejected the utility of models or paradigms applied to peasant agriculturalists. At the same time, they neglect the considerable contribution of Marxism to the study of economic change and development in which modernization is seen as the transition from small scale agriculture to industry.

The following seeks to demonstrate the utility of such a theoretical and methodological orientation for the understanding of the present situation of a group of Venezuelan coastal fishermen. First, I will briefly describe how modernization can be initially explained by an examination of ecological and technological diversity in fishing. A subsequent analysis of capital and levels of production in each community will show, however, that this approach is not sufficient to explain the introduction and effects of modernization; instead, the concept of the mode of production will be used to analyze modernization within a synchronic and a diachronic framework. Such a procedure will permit us to identify the main effects of modernization at the levels of social relations within and among production units.

ECOLOGY, TECHNOLOGY AND MODERNIZATION

The three communities selected for comparison are located near the Gulf of Cariaco, an ecological zone approximatively 60 kilometers long and 20 kilometers wide, in the state of Sucre in eastern Venezuela. This Gulf has a sill at its entrance with a maximum depth of about 75 meters, and the maximum depth in the Gulf is 90 meters. The water is stagnant much of the time; but in the last months of the year, strong northeasterly trade winds remove surface water from the Gulf, and there are influxes of cool and oxygenated open-ocean water. As a consequence, various marine species can be caught at specific times of the year, with greatest diversity during the fall.

Chiguana, the first community studied, is located at the bottom end of the Gulf. The Chiguaneros' marine zone is therefore limited in size and in

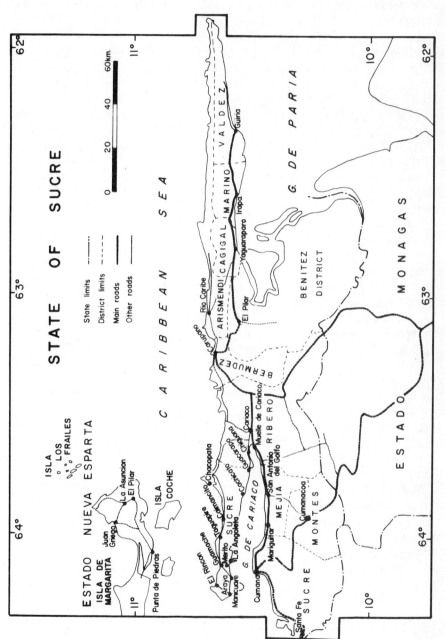

State of Sucre

depth. In addition, the accumulation of mud and detritus due to the periodical flood of the Cariaco River makes demersal fishing (fishing of
bottom-feeding species that yields large species of high commercial
value) and the use of motorized boats on an extensive scale impossible.
With these limitations, Chiguaneros fish mainly for one species (lisa)
with a single technique, the floating gill net (*chinchorro*). This explains
why only 48 out of a total of 154 active males and females in the community engage in fishing, and some of them (22 persons) on a partial basis only. The fishing economy is therefore completed by other activities
such as cattle-raising, agriculture and periodical wood-cutting on a commercial basis.

The second community, Guacarapo, is located eight kilometers west of
Chiguana. Its fishing zone is already wider and deeper. Fishermen can
therefore exploit marine resources on a more significant basis. Their more
varied technological apparatus is adapted to demersal and pelagic fishing
and includes hand lines *(cordel)*, gill nets *(chinchorro)*, shore seines *(man-
dingua)* and a generalized use of motor launches. Of a total of 129 active
adults, 98 are engaged in fishing. Cattle raising is the only significant
secondary activity for some members of the community.

Finally, in Santa Fé, located west of the mouth of the Gulf of Cariaco,
the fishing zone is adjacent to the open-ocean water of the Caribbean sea.
The presence of numerous islands and coves gives the Santa Fesinos an
exploitative zone with an ecological diversity that considerably widens
the variety of the species that are caught and of the techniques that are
used (several specialized nets such as *tren sardinero, tren jurelero,* and
the purse seine, *argolla*). Contrary to Chiguaneros and Guacarapaneros,
Santa Fesinos are specialists who devote most of their time to fishing.
That there are approximately 440 full-time fishermen indicates clearly
the importance of this activity in the community. The selection of these
three villages therefore provides a continuum (not a Redfieldian one) in
which fishing activities are characterized by an increasing ecological and
technological diversity, and take place within a more specialized economy as one moves from the first to the last.

To understand the infrastructure of fishing in these villages, let us
compare their factors of production. Table 1 summarizes and compares
the size of the exploitative zones, the relative amount of capital invested
in fishing, the number of fishermen, and the total annual output.

The table clearly demonstrates an increasing complexity of the factors
of production that is correlated with larger catches. These data could lead
to the assumption that fishing in each community is characterized by a
differential level of development of its productive forces due to the relative influence of modernization. But this type of statement, even if it is

TABLE 1:   Factors of Production in Fishing,
Eastern Venezuela: 1970-71*

Factors of Production	Villages		
	Chiguana	Guacarapo	Santa Fé
Size of Fishing Zone	15 sq km	90 sq km	400 sq km
Capital	67, 340 Bs	185,925 Bs	690,590 Bs
Number of Fishermen	48	98	440
Annual Output	68,970 kg	147,000 kg	1,173,121 kg

*Source: Y. Breton 1973
Bs=Bolivares (=$.225 U.S.)

based on statistical data, does not adequately explain the effects of modernization or its causes. Indeed, it simply constitutes a general framework that indicates the range of the phenomenon under consideration.

In fact, with some slight modifications in the points of comparison, there emerges an interesting relative uniformity that contradicts, to some extent, the significant differences previously assumed. Thus far, I have taken the factors of production individually, comparing them for the three communities. However, an examination of the relations or ratios that exist between these factors within a single community leads to a different interpretation of the influence of modernization. For instance, a simple comparative framework demonstrates that the amount of capital invested in technology in Chiguana (Bs 67,340) is less than twice the amount invested in Guacarapo (Bs 185,925). This is ten times smaller than the total for Santa Fé (Bs 690,590). Identical proportions (1:2:10) apply to the labor force (48 in Chiguana, 98 in Guacarapo and 440 in Santa Fé). The above figures suggest that whatever the community's degree of economic specialization, the combination of productive forces in coastal fishing requires identical adjustments from producers. What at first seems to be a significant diversity based on ecological variations is no more than the application of a single and identical adaptive pattern from which the effects of modernization are barely visible. It is, therefore, obvious that the approach used so far is incomplete to explain the ef-

fects of modernization processes and, furthermore, depending on the
axes chosen for comparison, such an approach can lead to different inter-
pretations. A more dialectic approach is needed to better comprehend
what is transpiring in these communities.

MODES OF PRODUCTION AND MODERNIZATION

One of the striking features of the economic organization of fishing in
eastern Venezuela is that some production units clearly possess all the
characteristics of a capitalist enterprise while others are precapitalist in
their structure and operation. In the capitalist units, work groups possess large capital assets that are concentrated in the hands of a few individuals. They use a diversified and specialized technology and are paid
fixed wages according to their responsibilities in the productive processes work. Their production is sold entirely in a market. In the precapitalist units, which include the majority of fishermen, work groups are
relatively small and rely on a simpler technology. The purchase and
maintenance cost of this technology is shared by several members of the
group. Fishermen are paid on a basis proportional to the amount of production and a good part of the output is used to satisfy domestic and local demand; the surplus is sold on the outside market.

The present influence of modernization in coastal fishing is therefore illustrated by the presence of two modes of production one of which is
clearly capitalist and the other is closer to the characteristics of petty
commodity production. A useful hypothesis of some economic anthropologists who have studied the problem of the articulation of production
modes can be employed to better comprehend the present situation of
fishing in eastern Venezuela. The crux of their argument is that, in spite
of an apparent contradiction, petty commodity production can become an
important sustaining basis for capitalism in its initial phase of expansion; it even maintains itself over a relatively long period, despite the
presence of capitalism, if entrepreneurs find it profitable to invest in com-
mercialization rather than in production (Servolin 1972, Rey 1973).

This is precisely the situation that presently prevails in fishing in eastern Venezuela. The investment in fishing gear, boats, and motors not
only represents a great amount of capital (which increases with the generalized use of nylon nets and bigger engines) but bears serious risks,
given the material conditions of production in fishing. Therefore, the entrepreneurs seem to prefer, in their incipient phase of capital accumulation, to invest their money in the transformation or transportation sectors of fishing, leaving the small producers to invest at the level of production.

This procedure presents a double advantage: While giving the small producer the illusion of independence, it permits the capitalist entrepreneur to control all the fish maketing and thus to obtain a considerable profit through a form of absolute rent. In eastern Venezuela, there exists a mercantile bourgeoisie that purchases the production of almost all coastal fishermen at a relatively low price to resell it at high price in the main urban centers, sometimes as far as Caracas. But, given the profit derived from this type of enterprise, the number of middlemen has tended to increase in recent years. Moreover, their previously privileged position vis-à-vis the producers, which in some cases was a real monopsony, is now undergoing modification from the effects of competition. While the number of producers remains stable or even diminishes in some communities, the merchants must engage in an increased competition to obtain fish from small producers. This explains partially the emergence of some of the previously-mentioned capitalist production units in fishing. They belong to merchants who decided to invest in production to maintain their volume of exchange. These people clearly become "primary climants" (Leclair 1959) who accentuate the mercantile character of capital and greatly modify the relations of work within the fishing teams.

This synchronic examination of the articulation of the modes of production completes what has been observed at the simple level of factors of production in each community. However, since the increased competition between middlemen is only partially responsible for the presence of some capitalist production units, there remains the problem of explaining the reasons underlying the presence of others. This can be done only through an examination of modes of production over a longer period. While providing additional information on the present processes of modernization, this methodological step will permit a more complete description of the degree of economic specialization in a community.

After the war of Independence (1821), the entire marine zone adjacent to the Gulf of Cariaco was granted to a few individuals under the juridical form of "prebendal domains" (Wolf 1966:51). These people then possessed exclusive rights of exploitation of some species (obviously the most important such as *lisa, mero, jurel*, etc.), and they were the only ones permitted to use the techniques of pelagic fishing (i.e., nets and seines). Their monopoly over the marine zone and over the means of production permitted them to control all the production in the region. The individuals organized large work groups (from 20 to 50 fishermen) characterized by a complex division of labor. Therefore, there existed during the nineteenth century, a capitalist mode of production in fishing (mercantile, rather than industrial capitalism, given its labor-intensive character); and the capitalists controlled all the steps of the activity, from production to marketing. Even if these capitalist enterprises were not numerous (seven or eight by the end of the century), they nonetheless prevented the majority of fishermen from investing in fishing and their privileges severely restricted the development of petty commodity production.

As a result, if we try to characterize the participation of fishermen in fishing activities at that time, we arrive at the following conclusions: (1) Some fishermen were obliged to sell their labor to capitalist entrepreneurs, receiving very low wages in return. These fishermen were not able to control the means of production, but were simply wage laborers within a capitalist enterprise; (2) others participated in fishing with a very simple technology (hand-line and cast-net) and fished for their domestic needs only. Their participation in the exploitation of the marine zone has therefore centered around a mode of production characterized by self-sufficiency. Their reproduction was insured by auxiliary activities such as agriculture, cattle raising, or wood cutting.

In 1928, the dictatorial regime of Gomez came to an end. With his departure, the juridico-political basis that legalized the privileges of capitalist entrepreneurs was abolished. As demonstrated by social scientists who studied the effects of liberalism on European peasantry during the nineteenth century, the abolition of feudalism (or its various forms) encouraged, in certain contexts, the emergence of petty commodity production (Lenine 1972:183–84). This is precisely what happened with fishing in eastern Venezuela after the death of Gomez. The majority of fishermen grouped themselves into small production units, fishing first for their domestic needs, and selling their surplus on the regional market. However, even though this period corresponds to a betterment of the economic situation of the peasant-fishermen, the entrepreneurs (or their descendants) who had previously accumulated capital remained in an advantageous position. The juridical reform has not been uniformly applied in all communities, and in some cases, the entrepreneurs succeeded in keeping partial rights of exploitation over productive sites. These sites still provide them with an above-average output. This is the case, for instance, in mackerel fishing in Guacarapo and Santa Fé. Mackerel is a species of high commercial value which can be captured only in specific spots (e.g., in coves with deep water that are surrounded by hills which facilitate the location of schools).

When the foregoing statements are placed within the context of the present degree of economic specialization of the villages studied, a relationship emerges between the reduced importance of fishing in Chiguana and the fact that its inhabitants have been engaged in this activity only since the end of the Gomez regime. In the villages of Guacarapo and

Santa Fé, to the contrary, fishing has always been the main activity for the majority of people, but among those production units which now possess a capitalist character, some are directly related to families who formerly benefited from privileges in the exploitation of the marine zone.

The diachronic examination of the articulation of production modes therefore provides significant additional information on the processes of capital accumulation and gives a slightly different picture of modernization. At least it demonstrates that in eastern Venezuela fishing has known a period of mercantile capitalism in the last century, and that modernization is not an entirely new phenomenon. Even though, after 1928, this mode of production lost its importance at the expense of a mode of production evolving around a petty commodity production, it is now re-emerging. It is essential to keep in mind that part of the present modernization process is the direct result of the outside influence of a mercantile bourgeoisie, and the other part of the process cannot be understood without a reference to a historical context.

In ending this analysis, we can now come back to the microlevel of the communities and see the real effects of modernization within the social relations of production. Instead of comparing a volume of capital in each communities, let us examine how it is distributed. Tables 2, 3, and 4, which summarize these distributions, give additional insight into the dif-

TABLE 2   Allocation of Investment
in Fishing Equipment: Chiguana, 1971.*

Level of Investment	Number of People
Bs 0– 499	7
Bs 500– 999	11
Bs 1000–1499	5
Bs 1500–1999	2
Bs 2000–2499	2
Bs 2500–2999	–
Bs 3000–3499	–
Bs 3500–3999	2
Bs 4000–4499	1
Bs 4500–4999	1
Bs 5000–5499	2
Bs 5500–5999	
Total of Owners	34
Average Individual Investment	Bs, 1980

TABLE 3   Allocation of Investment
in Fishing Equipment: Guacarapo, 1971.*

Level of Investment	Number of Owners
0– 999	8
1000–1999	2
2000–2999	3
3000–3999	1
4000–4999	2
5000–5999	3
6000–6999	–
7000–7999	2
8000–8999	–
9000–9999	1
10000–10999	–
11000–11999	–
12000–12999	–
13000–13999	2
14000–14999	1
19000–19999	1
22000–22999	1
29000–29999	1
Total	28
Ave. Investment	Bs, 6754

*Source: Breton 1973 (Tables 2 and 3)

ferences observed in factors of production. In Chiguana, 34 fishermen out
of a total of 48, or 70 percent, participate in investment. In Guacarapo,
only 28 people out of 98, 29 percent, possess capital assets in fishing. In
Santa Fé, 64 fishermen out of 440, 14 percent, are investors. From the
above, we can assume that the main effect of modernization lies in the
concentration of capital. In all the villages there is a gradual dissociation
between the producers and the means of production. Modernization is,
therefore, illustrated by this basic mechanism of the introduction of capitalism. However, because of the reward system still prevailing in the majority of the crews (i.e., wages proportional to the amount of production),
we cannot conclude too rapidly that there is a proletariat whose importance increases from Chiguana to Santa Fé. The concept of salary, as de-

TABLE 4   Allocation of Investment in
Fishing Equipment: Santa Fé, 1971.*

Categories in Bs	Number of Owners
0– 999	1
1000– 1999	3
2000– 2999	3
3000– 3999	7
4000– 4999	8
5000– 5999	3
6000– 6999	8
7000– 7999	–
8000– 8999	5
9000– 9999	2
10000–10999	3
11000–11999	3
12000–12999	3
13000–13999	2
14000–14999	4
15000–15999	–
16000–16999	–
17000–17999	–
18000–18999	–
19000–19999	1
20000–20999	2
21000–21999	–
22000–22999	1
23000–23999	1
24000–24999	–
25000–25999	1
26000–26999	–
27000–27999	–
28000–28999	1
35000–35999	1
79000–79999	1
Total	64 Owners
Average Investment	Bs, 10790

Source: Breton 1973*

fined by bourgeois economy, exists in only a few production units whose owners do not participate in the activity. The majority of fishermen who do not possess capital assets are friends or relatives of the owners, and remain paid on the basis of a share system; these relations have brought about a relatively informal authority structure. Nevertheless, independent from the existence of fixed or relative salary, the fishermen who invest in technology receive a part of the total output for their investment, and a concentration of capital is necessarily linked to a concentration of income. The form of remuneration now prevailing in these communities is therefore in a transitional period which corresponds to the present articulation of the modes of production.

Last, it is worthwhile to underline the marked differences that exist at the levels of capitalization and the peaks within the distributions. These levels are Bs,5,000, Bs,30,000 and Bs,80,000 in Chiguana, Guacarapo, Santa Fé, respectively. Similar features are found in the average investment per owner (Bs,1,970; Bs,6,754; Bs,10,790).

Even if petty commodity production still seems to be the prevailing mode of production in the area, it is now undergoing strong modifications that can be seen in the social relations of production. When the productive forces will be renewed on a more extensive scale, there will no doubt be an even greater concentration of capital and the emergence of additional capitalist production units in which fishermen will become truly proletarianized.

CONCLUSION

The previous analysis seeks to demonstrate that a Marxist framework for the study of economic and social changes in fishing presents some analytical advantages. Rather than emphasizing a typological approach which results in a superficial identification of links between infrastructure and superstructure as do too many functionalist studies, this framework permits us to explain apparent contradictions inherent in the modernization process, and gives us better conceptual tools with which to pinpoint macro and microtransformations.

The analysis at least shows that capitalist modernization, even if it leads to an increase in productivity, is not always an optimal adaptive strategy, if there is no counterpart in the distribution processes. This is the challenge with which these coastal fishermen, located at the periphery of capitalism, are now faced.

LITERATURE CITED

Breton, Yvan
    1973   A Comparative Study of Rural Fishing Communities in Eastern
            Venezuela: An Anthropological Explanation of Economic Specializa-
            tion. Ph.D. dissertation, Michigan State University.

Cohen, Y. A.
    1968   Man in Adaptation: The Cultural Present. Chicago: Aldine.

Cook, S.
    1973   Economic Anthropology: Problem in Theory, Method and Analysis.
            In Handbook of Social and Cultural Anthropology. J. Honnigman,
            ed. Chicago: Rand McNally.

Godelier, M.
    1974   L'Anthropologie Économique: Un Domaine Contesté. Paris: Mou-
            ton.

Leclair, E.
    1959   A Minimal Frame of Reference for Economic Anthropology (Re-
            vised). N.Y.: Rensselaer Polytechnic Institute. Mimeo.

Lenine, V.
    1969   Le Développement du Capitalisme en Russie. Oeuvres, Tome 3.
            Paris: Editions Sociales.

Meillassoux, C.
    1964   L'Anthropologie Économique des Gouro de la Côte d'Ivoire. Paris:
            Mouton.

Rey, L. P.
    1973   Sur l'Articulation des Modes de Production In Les Alliances de
            Classe. Paris: Maspero.

Servolin, C.
    1972   Aspects Économiques de l'Absorption de l'Agriculture dans le Mode
            de Production Capitaliste. Paris: Mimeo.

Steward, J.
    1972   The Theory of Culture Change. (1st ed. 1955). Urbana: University of
            Illinois Press.

Wolf, E.
    1966   Peasants. Englewood Cliffs, New Jersey: Prentice-Hall.

*

9

The Marginal Group as a Medium of Change in a Maritime Community: the Case of the Glasses in Tristan da Cunha*

PETER A. MUNCH

Southern Illinois University—Carbondale

INTRODUCTION

When modern Western industrialism establishes an outpost within the territorial habitat of a traditional folk community, it comes as a powerful agent of change. Most important, with its superior technology and its promise of material prosperity, it appeals to one of the basic universal needs of man—that of life sustenance and physical comfort with the least possible expenditure of effort and body energy.

However, before it can penetrate the receiving community and gain acceptance among its members, the value system of industrialism must break through the natural defenses of traditional society. Seldom, if ever,

*Revised and abbreviated from "Agents and Media of Change in a Maritime Community: Tristan da Cunha," a paper presented to the Society for Applied Anthropology, Amsterdam, March 19–23, 1975. Financial aid was gratefully received from Southern Illinois University, Carbondale.

are the material values associated with industrialization rejected out-right. But modern industry needs for its continued operation a committed and reliable labor force and must demand that the contract relationship involved in accepting a wage-earning job in the industry take precedence over most other obligations. This demand for an undivided devotion to the economic enterprise, which Max Weber recognized as the outstanding characteristic of modern capitalism, is likely to collide, in a traditional folk community, with established personal relationships and obligations. A conflict of values ensues, which is not so much concerned with the acceptance or rejection of innovations as with the priorities of obligations (see Munch 1974).

The intensity and outcome of this conflict between the new and the old depends, of course on a complex multitude of factors.[1] We shall here concentrate our attention on the social structure of the receiving community as a factor in social change.

We will assume, as a matter of definition, that a "community" is integrated to the extent that its members share a sense of common identity. As far as this common identity is disturbed or weakened by factional identities within the group, there is "structural tension." Such structural tensions, more or less latent, are normally present in any collectivity, from the largest nation to the smallest family unit, and they may take a variety of forms. At the community level, they often become manifest in the form of a class structure, a minority group structure (racial, ethnic, or otherwise), or in the formation of cliques and "social sets," more or less sharply differentiated. When any such structural tension is polarized and develops into a categorical differentiation of subgroups, it may have a disrupting effect on the community.

"Sociocultural symbolism" refers to a "symbolic group," being a strictly ideational phenomenon of shared collective identity, finding its most important symbolic expression in the commitment of its members to certain selected culture traits (values, norms, patterns of behavior, and appearance) that are considered characteristic of the group. The conformity to such a symbolic norm then becomes crucial to the acceptance of an individual as a member of the group.[2]

Because of the subjective nature of collective identification, however, the boundaries of symbolic groups are seldom sharply drawn, membership being a matter of degree of loyalty and ascription. Laxity in conforming to the symbolic norms, therefore, and even a direct deviation from them (although it is usually regarded as a sign of weakness in the loyalty to the group and even sometimes as a symbolic expression of identity with an outgroup), seldom leads to a total ouster from the group. Regularly, however, it results in some greater or lesser degree of marginality and estrangement, depending on the flagrancy and consistency of the deviations.

Such marginal elements are probably present in most communities, since they usually consist of people who appear to have a weaker identification with the community and a fragile commitment to the traditional values and symbolic norms. They may find the rewards of a new social order greater than the possible negative sanctions associated with the abandonment of the old, and may become an important factor in social change, especially if they form an identifiable group with its own internal cohesion, thus causing a structural tension in the community. Such a group seldom has the power, authority, or prestige to function as an *agent* of change by presenting new alternatives in values and patterns of conduct. But it may very well become an important medium of change by being more receptive to new alternatives presented by strangers to the community, thereby mediating the infiltration of new ideas into the community itself and possibly undermining the traditional values.

THE SOCIAL STRUCTURE
OF THE TRISTAN COMMUNITY

Atomistic Integrity

The community of Tristan da Cunha, on the shoreline of a volcanic island in the middle of the South Atlantic Ocean (population, February 1970: 275), was founded in 1817 as a utopian community built and organized on the principles of anarchy and equality, and with communal ownership and operation.[3] It was, however, never firmly integrated as a community. It appears that the idealistic combination of a communal enterprise with complete freedom from authority and control was impossible to realize; as one of these principles had to yield, anarchy and freedom prevailed, and the community developed into a loosely joined aggregate of independent households, fitting quite well the definition of an "atomistic community" whose members "recognize only individual allegiances" and "lack the social forms necessary for group action."[4]

Individual allegiances are indeed what hold this community together. Economically, each household is in principle independent of the rest, and there is no apparent sense of obligation to the community as a whole or to specific collectivities within the community. But like most agrarian and fishing communities, the Tristan community is tied together by a network of selective, reciprocal relationships between individuals involving joint ownership of boats, cattle, orchards, and huts, as well as various patterns of cooperation and mutual aid. These relationships run through the whole community, overlapping and interlocking in such a way that they leave no one untouched. The result is a community where a person belongs, not by some collective identity at the expense of his individuality, but—on the contrary—by virtue of a personal identity which is expressed and confirmed in those individual allegiances which he chooses to reinforce in a pattern of selective reciprocity.[5]

The all important basis for these individual allegiances is kinship, which in the case of Tristan da Cunha as in most Western societies, is bilateral, with equal importance given to relations through mother and father, and which is recognized in some cases as far as second cousin once removed (usually under the generic kinship term "cousin"). These kinship ties, of course, are ascribed by birth; but not all are recognized to the same degree. They are reinforced or counteracted by a number of uniquely personal factors, such as marriage and in-law relations, relative prestige, and even personal compatibility. And kinship does not always prevail. With the firm structure of the nuclear family, however, and with the importance that is given to kinship relations in general, it is not surprising to find that people tend to be identified with certain family lines of descendancy, which thereby acquire a certain degree of collective identity in the minds of the islanders.

Social Sets

Since kinship relations are recognized bilaterally, they do not result in the formation of clearly defined and mutually exclusive groups like patronymic "clans" following exactly the lines of the seven existing surnames Glass, Swain, Green, Rogers, Hagan, Repetto, and Lavarello. But the islanders do indeed talk about "the Glasses," "the Greens," "the Swains," and "the Repettos," referring to vaguely defined groupings consisting of those who are identified, and identify themselves, with certain lineages, whether they happen to be affiliated through their mothers, fathers, or spouses. And since kinship ties through the mother may be just as strong as or, in some cases, stronger than the paternal ones, a well integrated family may indeed command the loyalty of most of its offspring both cognate and agnate, through several generations. The result is the differentiation of more or less well-defined social sets, each identified with a particular lineage but including persons of different surnames.

None of these social sets, of course, has sharply defined boundaries. Although the core members of certain social sets are easily identified, affiliation is a matter of degree and frequently overlaps. Besides, most of these groupings are probably quite spurious in composition, subject to shifts and realignments as new generations take over. Two or three of them, however, have remained fairly constant over several generations and stand out with relative clarity in the minds of the islanders as more or less sharply differentiated social entities. It appears that in these cases, the social differentations based on kinship have been reinforced by cultural, ethnic, and possibly even racial differentiations in the past (Munch 1972).

THE GLASSES

The Historical Background

The founder of the settlement of Tristan da Cunha was a Scotsman named William Glass. He had been a gentleman's servant in his youth, but enlisted in the Royal Artillery where he became a corporal. In 1816, Britain took possession of the island of Tristan da Cunha, which was uninhabited at the time except for a lone settler, the only survivor from a previous abortive attempt to establish a settlement, and Glass became a member of a small garrison dispatched from the Cape Colony. When the garrison was removed the following year, Glass and two companions decided to stay and form a corporation dedicated to the principles of anarchy and equality, with communal ownership and operation. They drew up a brief document of agreement, which was solemnly signed in the presence of witnesses, stipulating among other things

> that in order to ensure the harmony of the Firm, No member shall assume any superiority whatever, but all to be considered as equal in every respect, each performing his porportion of labour, if not prevented by sickness.

While stationed at the Cape, Glass had married a young "Cape Creole" of Dutch ancestry, and he brought her and their infant son with him to Tristan. Before the garrison left, they also had a daughter. The other two members of the "firm" were bachelors. They did not stay long. But Glass and his rapidly growing family were soon joined by others, mostly sailors and navy-men, and in 1827 five women from St. Helena, most of them of mixed but undetermined racial origin, were persuaded to join the company on Tristan in search of husbands. When William Glass died in 1853 at the age of 66, he was the father of 16, the grandfather of 25 or more, and the more or less recognized patriarch of a community of 83 people in 10 households, 6 of which were of his own family.

In the meantime, important changes had taken place in William Glass's utopian dream. Some of the sailors and navy-men who had joined the party in the early years had been more attracted by the prospects of equality and anarchical independence than by communal ownership and management. Glass had difficulties making the newcomers "perform their proportion of labour" in the communal enterprise, and only four years after the establishment of the egalitarian commune, a new agreement was drawn up containing the following paragraph:

> No person subscribing to these articles are [sic] to cont[inue reminding?] particular p[ersons?] of their Duty in point of Work, or otherwise, as in such Case nothing but *Disunion* will be the consequence; Wm Glass being at the head of the firm, will allot to each individual every evening, his work for the following Day, not by way of task but merely for the purpose of causing all to do their best for the general good, which will be the means of insureing peace, and good will among the people, as well as benefitting the Establishment, in which all are concerned.[7]

The document also pronounced that "it is . . . to be understood that the whole of the Land, Stock, &c &c is the sole and joint property of Wm Glass and John Nankevile"—Nankevile was the one remaining original companion of Glass. Soon he also left the island, and Glass presumably became the master and sole proprietor of all material assets of the "firm," including livestock and all cleared and cultivated land. A few years later he even set up a last will and testament, witnessed by a sea captain and a passenger from a passing ship, in which he assigned one-third of his property to his eldest son, the rest to be distributed among his other children (Gane 1933:713).

It appears later arrivals largely ignored William Glass's claim to authority and exclusive property rights. Clearly, they had not settled down on the island to help build an empire for the Glass family, and together with the few older settlers who remained, they strongly embraced the original principles of freedom, equality, and anarchy. It was during the following few decades that the community developed its present atomistic structure as each newcomer established his own independent household, cleared his own piece of land, and even acquired some cattle and sheep, although Glass still had the most (Taylor 1856:86).

It is not known whether William Glass resisted or even resented the development that took place. A certain social distance, however, and perhaps a slight tension seems to have developed between the well-mannered

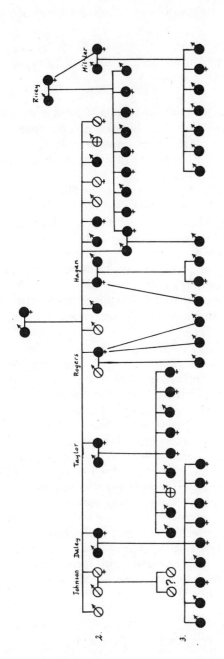

FIGURE 1 The Glass Set, 1853

⊘ -emigrated

⊕ -died on Tristan

landlubber Glass and his company of fiercely independent sea-dogs, an estrangement that was peculiarly accentuated when American whalers arrived on the scene.

American Whalers

The first American whaler appeared off the shores of Tristan da Cunha in 1828. The traffic increased slowly at first but reached its peak in the 1840s, when the island became one of the most important fitting stations for the New England whaling fleet, with ships calling for fresh supplies of water, vegetables, and meat.

A peculiarly close relationship developed between the Glass family and the American whalers. Most of William Glass's children got involved with whalers and whaling. One of his eight sons died in infancy, but of the seven who grew up, at least six went whaling in the American ships and eventually made thier homes in far-away New London. Five of his eight daughters married Americans, four of them whalers. Some of his whaler sons-in-law settled down on Tristan for a while, one of them for the rest of his life. There were even three or four illegitimate grandchildren by whalers (Fig. 1). Two of the remaining daughters also eventually settled in New England.

The other settlers appear to have been totally excluded from all this. None of their numerous children sought or found a spouse among William Glass's children during his lifetime, and not one of their daughters married an American whaler. Two or three of the boys went whaling, but they did not ship out in American whale ships. Instead they went to South Africa, where they engaged in whaling from established land bases. And most of them eventually returned to Tristan.

There is no evidence to show that this structural tension in the Tristan community between the Glasses and the rest caused an open conflict or even a noticeable friction as long as William Glass was around. From all accounts, William Glass was a gentle man, and it seems that the social code of dignity, kindness, and generosity, for which the Tristan islanders have been known over the years, was already then well established. After the founder's death, however, the split appeared to be deep enough to cause the first great fission of the community. In January 1856, practically the whole of William Glass's family including his widow left Tristan da Cunha in two whale ships bound for New London, Connecticut, and perhaps for a couple of decades, the name Glass was absent among the settlers of the island.

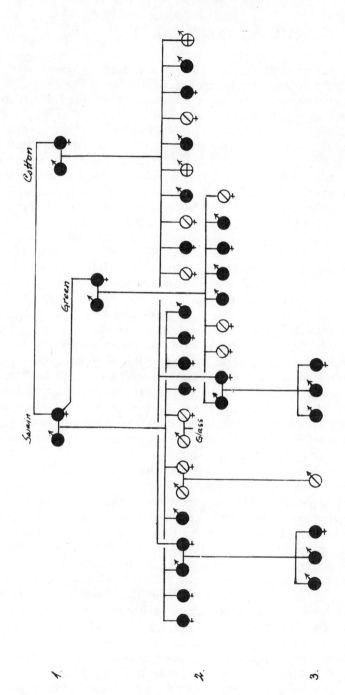

FIGURE 2   The Swain-Cotton-Green Set, 1860

SAILORS AND WHALERS

The departure of most of the Glass family removed almost all structural tension that may have existed in the community in the 1850s. The dominant element now consisted of a single social set of three closely interrelated families. Alexander Cotton and Thomas Swain, two salty seadogs with boisterous careers in the Royal Navy behind then, had arrived in the 1820s and were among the five men who in 1827 persuaded a ship's captain to bring them five women from St. Helena. The two chosen by Cotton and Swain were sisters. A decade later, a Dutchman named Pieter Groen was shipwrecked on the island. He decided to stay, changed his name to Peter Green, and took for his companion a daughter of Thomas Swain's woman, who as a little girl had arrived with her mother (Fig. 2). And the ties of kinship and common spirit that united these three families were reinforced in the second generation. Three of Peter Green's four sons married daughters of Alexander Cotton, and with the marriage of a fourth daughter of Cotton to Thomas Swain's oldest son who was her cousin, an intricate network of socially significant relationships was established and maintained between the three families, to the complete exclusion of the Glasses and their whaler friends (see Fig. 5).

Prominent among them was Peter Green, who soon became the undisputed "grand old man" of Tristan da Cunha. But he apparently had no design on taking over William Glass's position as "the head of the firm." On the contrary, he went out of his way to explain to the British authorities and other outsiders that he was *not* the "governor" of Tristan da Cunha; and in the eyes of most of the islanders for some generations to come, he and his family came to stand as in incarnation of the traditional principles of anarchy and individual integrity.

One family of the Glass set remained on the island (Fig. 3). Captain Andrew Hagan was the master of an American whale ship. He arrived at Tristan in 1849, and leaving the ship in the hands of the mate, he settled down and married one of Williams Glass's daughters. Upon the departure of the rest of the Glasses, Captain Hagan became the sole heir to William Glass's property, including herds of cattle and sheep which, by Tristan standards, were considerable. Whether he had designs on a position of authority in the community we do not know, although he appears to have presented himself to visiting ships as the "headman" of the island. But he clearly had ideas about promoting his own prosperity in direct competition with the other settlers. By prudent management, his herds continued to increase, and he soon established himself as a "cattle king" and the owner of nearly half the cattle on the island.

This in itself was apparently felt as a threat to the egalitarian ideals of the community. It soon, however, became a real threat to the economic

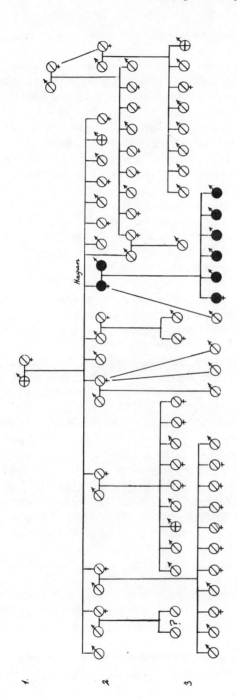

FIGURE 3 The Glass Set, 1860

⊘ – emigrated

⊕ – died on Tristan

welfare of the community, as well as to the voluntary consensus on which its anarchical order rested.

Trading with passing ships was the one remaining activity in which this now atomistic community still performed as a collective unit. However, since the community as such no longer owned cattle or raised a crop as a communal enterprise, a system had developed by which each family took its turn in providing the necessary supplies for the trade, while the proceeds of the trade in clothing, stores, or money were each time equally divided among the families. Individual islanders could trade with individual crew members and passengers, but the trade with the ship's stores was considered a prerogative of the community as a whole. In accordance with the anarchical ideals of the community, of course, there was no formal agreement to uphold the arrangement, nor was there any established authority to enforce it if necessary. It was just a custom that had developed, had proven itself workable, and was upheld by common consent.

It appears that Andrew Hagan was attempting to ignore the arrangement. He seems to have gone into private business with visiting ships, offering his own beef for sale to the ship's stores, to the prejudice of the communal barter. This, of course, was a direct challenge to the anarchical order of the community as it put in jeopardy its very foundation in a voluntary consensus. What made it even more serious was that Hagan did not stand alone. He apparently had received support from two other members of the Glass set who had returned from whaling to settle down on the island. One dissenter is a threat to any anarchical order; a group of them might easily turn it into chaos.

Hagan's two supporters were Tom Glass and Joshua Rogers, a son and a grandson of William Glass, who had left with the rest of the Glass family in 1856 but returned several years later and each married a daughter of Thomas Swain. It appears that the three of them, Hagan, Glass, and Rogers again formed with their families a separate coterie based on close kinship ties, which were further reinforced when Hagan, now a widower, married a third daughter of Thomas Swain (Fig. 4). It was a restored Glass set, marginal and in opposition to the dominant Cotton-Green set, with the Swains now split between the two factions (Fig. 5).

By now, it is quite clear that the marginality of the Glasses in relation to the rest of the community had an important foundation in a strongly felt difference in the settlers' social backgrounds and former occupations. It is well known that, in the days of the windjammers, the sailor had generally an overbearing contempt for the landlubber, but for the whaler he had nothing but bottomless scorn. What sharpened the cleavage of the Tristan community and created a structural tension that might have threatened to split the community again was evidently the fact that the

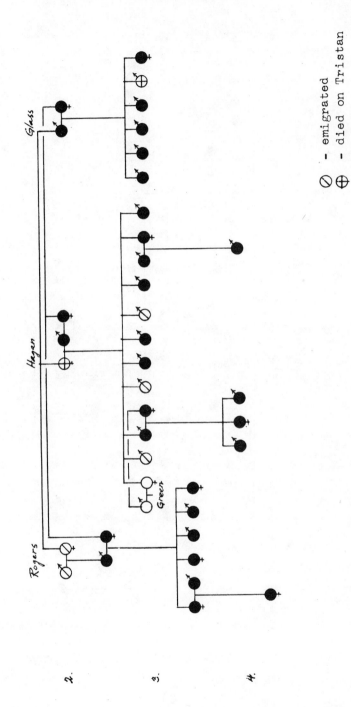

⊘ - emigrated
⊕ - died on Tristan

FIGURE 4 The Glass Set, 1885
"The Whaling Boys"

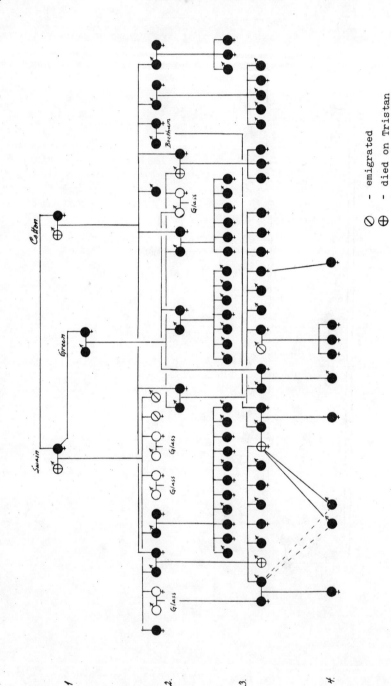

⊘ - emigrated
⊕ - died on Tristan

FIGURE 5   **The Swain-Cotton-Green Set, 1885 "The Sailor Boys"**

dissenters were identified as "whalers." This time it went as far as having Peter Green write to the British Admiralty asking for the removal of "the three whaling boys" (Correspondence 1887:35, Brander 1940:263). Obviously, he was referring to Hagan, Glass, and Rogers.

It is not known whether the structural tension existing in the Tristan community broke into any kind of open conflict. The tension was once more removed by the departure of most of the principal actors, this time in a more tragic way. In November 1885, in one of the unresolved mysteries of the sea, a lifeboat was lost with 15 men on board, comprising two-thirds of the adult male population at the time. As it happened, there were mostly Greens in the boat. Within a year, Peter Green had lost all of his sons. A son-in-law, three grandsons, and three brothers-in-law were also in the boat. But among the lost men were also Tom Glass and three of Andrew Hagan's sons. Joshua Rogers had "gone mad" with fits of violent convulsions. He died a few years later after a fall from a cliff during one of his fits.

After the lifeboat disaster, there was another exodus from Tristan, again reducing the population to some 60 people. Among those who left were all of Tom Glass's children except his daughter Jane, who eventually was married to a shipwrecked Italian sailor, and again for a couple decades the name Glass was absent among the people of Tristan da Cunha.

News of the lifeboat disaster brought the eyes of the world upon the little community in the ocean, and it became clear that the British authorities as well as the rest of the world looked upon Peter Green as the undisputed Chieftain of the island. Andrew Hagan was completely ignored, both by the islanders and by the world. In June 1898, at the age of 82, he committed suicide. Four years later, Peter Green died. He was 94.

RETURN OF THE GLASSES

It was a reduced community that struggled along on Tristan da Cunha at the beginning of this century. It now numbered little more than 70 persons in some 12 to 14 households. The trade with passing ships had been reduced to a trickle as the sailing vessels vanished from the open sea, and the community was entering a period of extreme isolation and poverty. After Peter Green's death in 1902, there was no one on the island quite able to fill his place. The British authorities were looking in vain for a substitute. An officer of a visiting navel ship reported: "There is no form of government, and the men were curiously averse to any individual being considered to have more influence than the rest" (Further Correspondence 1903:14). On the whole, the community was as anarchistic and atomistic as ever before.

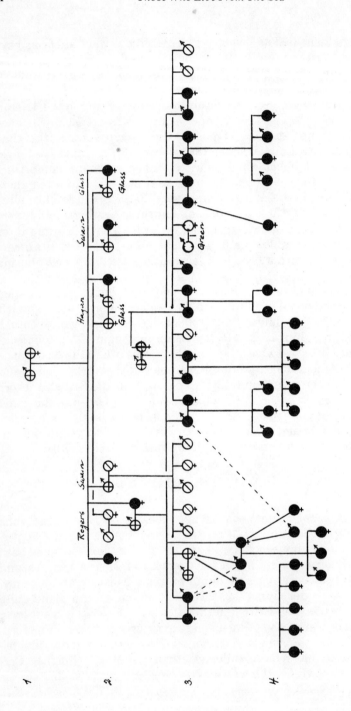

FIGURE 6   The Swains, 1905

⊘ - emigrated

⊕ - died on Tristan

The Swains, the Greens, and the Repettos

New alignments were being established as another generation grew to maturity. In particular, after the lifeboat disaster, one new social set appeared to be taking shape as the Swains separated themselves from the Greens, and the Rogerses from the Glasses, and joined together into a very close-knit group through extensive intermarriage in the third Tristan generation. In fact, all of Joshua Rogers' five children married Swains, their cousins, establishing strong and lasting ties between the two existing Swain families and the Rogers family (Fig. 6). The group eventually even included a returned son of Tom Glass and a kind and unpretentious son of Andrew Hagan, both of whom married Swains.

With the departure of all the Cottons after the lifeboat disaster, and with the complete loss of the Swain support, the Green set was sharply reduced. Just after the turn of the century, it consisted of only two families: Henry Green, a grandson of Peter Green and Alexander Cotton, and his younger sister Frances, who was married to a recent arrival, Andrea Repetto, another shipwrecked Italian sailor (Fig. 7). This little group, however, remained the prestigeous elite of the community and the main carriers and guardians of its traditional values of dignity, generosity, and egalitarian anarchy, in direct continuation of the tradition handed down from Alexander Cotton and Peter Green.

On the whole, this was probably the most peaceful period in the history of this generally peaceful community, with latent structural tensions at a minimum.

The "Newcomers"

With the Swains claiming the allegiance of the one remaining Hagan family and of the one returning Glass as well as that of the whole of the Rogers family, the Glass set was reduced to practically nothing (Fig. 8). Soon, however, the state of harmonious anarchy was once again challenged by returning members of the Glass set.

The party arrived in March 1908 in the schooner *Greyhound* of Cape Town and included two sons of Tom Glass, Joe and Bob, and their cousin Jim Hagan, a son of Captain Hagan. The three of them had left Tristan after the loss of the lifeboat in 1885, had married three strong-minded sisters of Irish origin, whom they had met at the Cape, and after a varied career in the "outside world," were now returning with their families (Fig. 9). With them was also a young nephew of Jim Hagan. The obvious leader of the party was Bob Glass, the youngest son of Tom Glass.

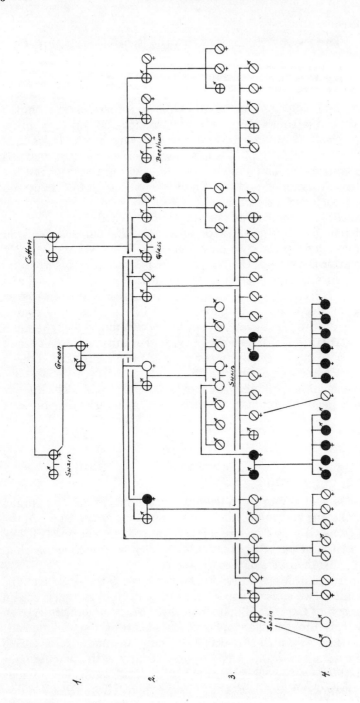

FIGURE 7   The Green-Repetto Set, 1905

⊘ - emigrated
⊕ - died on Tristan

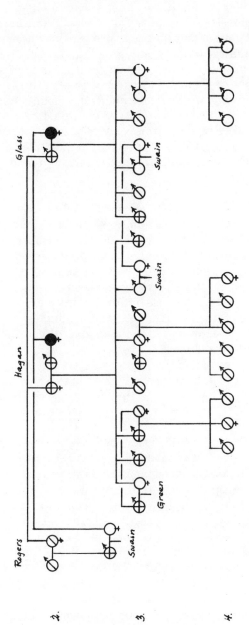

FIGURE 8   The Glasses, 1905

It soon became apparent that the "newcomers," as they were called, had designs on introducing changes in the Tristan community, and perhaps on establishing themselves in a position of power and authority. Bob Glass, no doubt, had ideas about how to improve the economic situation of the Tristan community, which would give him a prominent position as the manager of whatever business he might be able to start. His ideas were varied, and none of them seems to have gone beyond a rather vague planning stage. Having worked—by his own account quite successfully—as a "boat-steerer" (harpooner) in a whale ship, it was obvious that one of his ideas should be whaling from a shore base on Tristan, and it is reported that he once got a boat's crew with him and killed a whale. Another fairly obvious idea was commercial seal hunting on the neighboring island of Inaccessible.

At first, Bob Glass appears to have gained some support among the islanders, especially among the wavering Swains, who could be regarded as "renegade Glasses" since they all were affiliates of Joshua Rogers' family (see Fig. 6). Several of them had themselves been away from the island for varying periods and had learned the ways of the "outside world." Besides, Bob Glass's schemes, however vague, did offer some hope for prosperity in a community where the effects of increasing isolation were beginning to be severely felt. If Bob Glass had ambitions playing the role of an agent of change, therefore, he had a potential medium of change in the Swains, who must have experienced some degree of estrangement from the dominant Green-Repetto set.

Bob Glass, however, did not have the capital to start anything on his own, and he always managed to be on the wrong side of external influence and authority. There were disputes about the ownership of the Hagan property as well as about Peter Green's house, now occupied by the Repettos, but claimed by one of the newcomers. In the latter case, the minister, who happened to be in residence at the time had to invoke the authority of the British Government to avoid violence. On the whole, the arrival of the newcomers had introduced a new and different atmosphere on Tristan da Cunha, in sharp contrast to the usual harmony and tranquility of the island. Violence was in the air, and it is perhaps not surprising that, in the local traditions of these peaceful islanders, Bob Glass has come to be pictured as a ruthless, crafty villain, who would not shy away from criminal acts, including murder, "to make a name for himself." Soon his followers dropped away, and most of the newcomers returned to Cape Town.

From that time, Bob Glass became more and more an isolate in the community, not by communal decree, but simply as a consequence of the withdrawal of reciprocal relationships on the part of individual islanders.

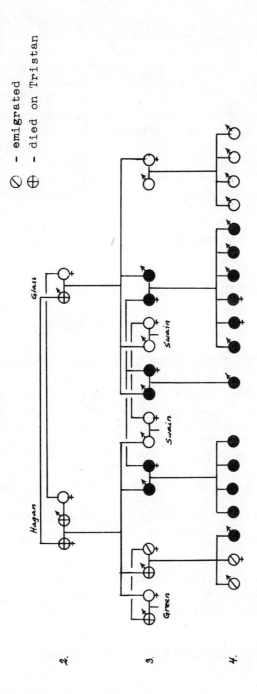

FIGURE 9 The Glasses, 1908
"The Newcomers"

Nevertheless, he continued to present himself to visiting ships as "head-man" of the island whenever he had a chance to do so. In the absence of a minister, he even functioned as an unofficial marriage officer and kept the birth, death, and marriage registers up to date. But as far as he attempted to go beyond this in directing the lives of others, he was simply ignored—like William Glass and Andrew Hagan before him.

So the traditional values of anarchy and individual integrity were once more confirmed, and the Repettos, continuing the Cotton-Green tradition, were solidly established as the dominant elite of the community, This time, the Glasses—now reduced to Bob Glass and most (but not all) of his immediate family—remained on the island (Fig. 10). But a certain estrangement from the rest of the community, especially from the Repettos, was in evidence. Bob Glass himself spent his later years almost as a semi-hermit in bitter resignation. He died in 1942, at the relatively young age of 70.

MODERN INDUSTRY MOVES IN

A Conflict of Values

Shortly after World War II, the extreme isolotion of the Tristan community came to an end. A South African fishing company moved in and established modern industry on the island. A factory was built and started operations processing crayfish tails for export, and two small fishing ships were operating in adjacent waters, employing islanders as fishermen. This not only brought a new affluence to Tristan; it also pulled the community back into the commerce of the world, with regular connections by ship and by radio to Cape Town and the world at large, and with a permanent colony of transient outsiders and their families living at the "Station" just below the "Village." It also brought an official administration to the island, with a resident Administrator sent out from England by the Colonial Office. A powerful agent of change had invaded the territory of a traditional folk community as the outside world established a beachhead on the island itself.

On the surface, there was an amazingly quick adaptation on the part of the islanders. They took to the use of money as a measure of material value and an exchange commodity with no difficulty. After some initial problems, they also soon learned the meaning of a labor contract, and because the new affluence brought by the fishing industry was recognized by all as something of value, the new enterprise was at first received with enthusiasm by the islanders.

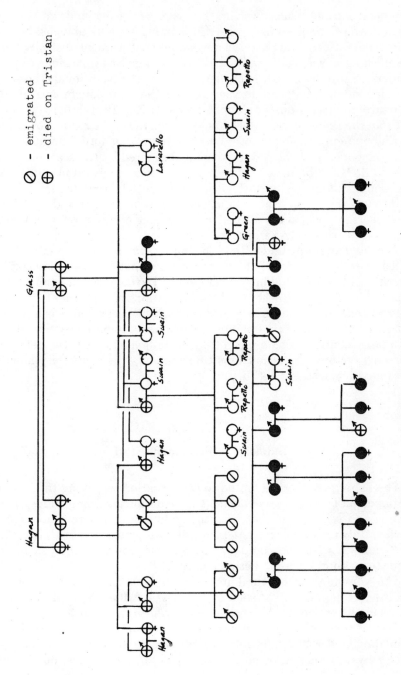

FIGURE 10 The Glasses, 1938

It soon became clear, however, that some of the demands and expectations of the fishing industry were interfering with established relationships, obligations, and patterns of conduct that were intrinsically tied to manifest expressions of traditional values of great importance to the islanders. A conflict of values ensued, in which the traditional ethos of the Tristian community was pitched against the materialism and commercialism of modern industry (Munch 1970a, 1970b; 1971:180–197).

From the point of view of the fishing company, the main problem was to find and engage a committed and reliable labor force. Because of the extreme poverty of the community (as measured by the scale of the outside world), and because of the obvious economic advantages offered by the fishing industry, no difficulties were anticipated; thus, the disappointment was great when it did not work out as expected. The blame was, as usual, put on the alleged laziness, lack of ambition, or even ignorance of the prospective workers.

The islanders fully understood the implication of contract labor but refused to accept the idea that a labor contract should always have priority over the obligations to kin and neighbors. To them, the one commitment was as binding as the other, and the obligations to a partner in a reciprocal relationship was infinitely more important because it was a personal rather than a contractual obligation. In fact, giving consistent priority to a labor contract would mean total estrangement from the network of personal reciprocal relationships that made up the comminity and gave the individual a status within it.

Industry's "Permanent Staff"

The fishing company adapted to the situation by giving the islanders an opportunity to work as independent fishermen, signing on for a day at a time and selling their catch to the company rather than working for wages. Only about a dozen islanders, who were prepared to accept a binding contract with the company, were continuously employed in what came to be known as the "Permanent Staff."

The company soon found its most reliable supporters among the Glasses. None of the six sons of Bob Glass who remained true to the Glass tradition, nor his two sons-in-law (whose wives, at least, continued to regard themselves as Glasses), had taken up the old man's dream of providing leadership in bringing Tristan da Cunha to affluence and prosperity by introducing a more commercial spirit. Besides, no one could shake the position of the Repettos had he wanted to, or penetrate the wall of inaction and passive resistance that he would probably meet had he tried. But in some of the new generation of Glasses there seemed to be much of the same resigned aloofness that I had found in old Bob Glass himself, as if they were outsiders observing the community with amazement, reluctantly adapting to it but not really a part of it, and often quite critical of its unchanging traditions. Obviously, their commitment to the traditional values of the community was fragile, to say the least. And with their somewhat estranged position in the community, their reciprocal relationships with other islanders were generally fewer and probably less binding. Most of them stayed pretty much within their own inner circle, and some of them were regular loners. They would easily find the rewards of the new industrial system greater than the losses they would suffer from abandoning the old ways.

So the Glasses did indeed play the role of a medium of change. They were the ones who first learned to give priority to a labor contract over whatever personal obligations they might have in the network of selective reciprocity that made up the community; since the fishing company would hire selectively on the basis of compliance with contract, soon more than half of the permanent staff of the company and the administration consisted of Glasses.

The rewards were not only material. The positions held by the permanent staff, such as beach foreman, store keeper, a man in charge of machines and engines, and even an assistant manager, gave a measure of responsibility, prestige, and even authority over other islanders. This appeared to give at least the Glasses among them a sense of identity as a group, a collective identification that they once gave symbolic expression by agreeing to grow beards as a mark of distinction. It also prompted them in some cases to make things difficult for non-Glasses on the permanent staff, sometimes resulting in replacements and an increasing monopoly for the Glasses. To be "Permanent Staff" was to them a privileged position that put them in a special trusted relationship with the company and its expatriate management. Ironically, it also gave them the opportunity (and privilege in their view—following the example of the company officers) to pilfer from the company stores, especially if the store keeper was a non-Glass, boasting among themselves about their exploits as "Permanent Staff."[8]

The Glasses were also the ones who most readily adopted not only the techniques but even the social attitudes of a money economy, who would engage in monetary transactions even with other islanders (which most of the islanders refused to do), and on the whole developed a more commercial attitude toward their fellow man, whether islander or outsider.

EXILE AND SELECTIVE MIGRATION

Evacuation and Resettlement

In October 1961, the industrial development of Tristan da Cunha was halted by a volcanic eruption that destroyed the factory and threatened to engulf the settlement. The island was evacuated, and the whole population of 263 islanders were brought to England and resettled in an abandoned Royal Air Force settlement at Calshot, near Southampton. There they became part of the unskilled labor force of a highly industrialized area, holding a variety of jobs. It was the hope of the British authorities that they would adapt to modern industrial society and settle permanently.

The Tristan islanders did not come entirely unprepared for such an adjustment. Ten years of contact with modern civilization through the fishing industry and the British administration on the island had given them at least some familiarity with modern technology, even with modern bureaucracy. But the presence of a permanent colony of outsiders and the extended contacts with the outside world had also given them a new awareness of their own collective identity as "Islanders" or "Trist'ns" as opposed to the "Stations" (the Station people). During their exile in England, under the spotlight of press, radio, and television, confronted with a strange society full of stress, worries, and crime, this new self-awareness of the Tristan islanders blossomed fully. Desperate to return to their island but abandoned by the authorities, this atomistic community of rugged individualists, who had never submitted to any internal authority, set aside their high ideals of anarchy and individual integrity and consolidated into a unified group under the firm leadership of "Chief" Willie Repetto. In this situation, all internal differentiations and structural tensions seemed to disappear, repressed and covered up by an overriding loyalty to "the People" and its cause. After two years of fighting disease, mental depression, and reluctant authorities, the islanders finally returned to Tristan da Cunha. Among the wavering Glasses, there was indeed some ambivalence about returning to the island. But all verbal dissent was soon silenced by the general demand for solidarity, and in the end most of the Glasses returned to Tristan with the others (Munch 1974).

Selective Migration

The consolidation of the community was only temporary. After resettlement on the island, the islanders immediately reverted to their traditional atomistic structure with its intricate network of overlapping and interlocking individual allegiances, and with complete freedom from any collective obligation to the community as a whole. The evacuation and two years of residence in England, however, had sown a seed of unrest among the islanders, which was only temporarily covered by the intense solidarity that developed in that strange milieu. Within a year, people started to talk about going back to England. By the end of the second year, it had developed into a regular migration fever. Rumors circulated on the island as well as in English newspapers that more than half the population, perhaps as much as 75 percent, wanted to return to England and modern civilization. The rumors were exaggerated. Nevertheless, on Easter Day, April 10, 1966, no less than 10 families comprised of 35 men, women, and children sailed from Tristan da Cunha a second time to settle in England, with an additional 10 persons expecting to follow in October.

These were not the first casualties of two years of close contact with modern civilization. When the islanders returned to Tristan in 1963, 13 of them remained in England. Another family of three returned to England immediately in the same ship that brought the main party of islanders back. A few others had followed. In the aftermath of the evacuation, the Tristan community had now lost almost one-fifth of its population by emigration, with an additional number ready to pull up stakes at the first opportunity, threatening to make it a fourth of the population.

This was not a movement staged by a rebellious youth against a conservative and domineering older generation. Of the 55 islanders who had either remained in England or returned there after resettlement, only 8 were young persons who had separated themselves from the community independent of their parents. The remaining 47 migrants left the community in family groups which included 17 dependent children. Of the 38 who left according to their own option, almost half were over 40, 10 were over 50, and no less than 6 of them were over 60 years of age. It could hardly be called a youth movement, even though almost half of the community members were under 25 and unmarried (as of October 1961).

What makes this emigration particularly interesting in the present context is that it consisted overwhelmingly of Glasses. Among them were 3 sons and a daughter of Bob Glass, and 9 grandchildren, all but 3 of them with spouses and some of them with children, numbering altogether 32 persons, well over half the group of migrants. Including 4 young people who had left the island before the volcanic eruption, and adding the 10 persons expecting to emigrate in October 1966, there were 69 actual and prospective emigrants from Tristan da Cunha since 1950, of whom 44, or almost two-thirds, were Glasses. This is more noteworthy since the Glass set was a comparatively small group in the community.

In fact, after the emigration of 1966, in a population now reduced to about 230, there were no more than a dozen or so Glasses left on the island, including children.

This was the third time in the history of the community that the Glasses had practically quit the island—another evidence of their estrangement and marginality in the community, accentuated by the role they were playing on the "Permanent Staff" of the fishing company. The obvious los er in this latest migration wave was the fishing industry. Just as a new in dustrialized Tristan appeared to be rising more vigorously than ever from the rubble left by the eruption and evacuation, those who were best equipped both in skills and in attitudes to play a leading role in this development were leaving the island. This, however, is what regularly happens when modern industrial society reaches its beckoning arm into a small rustic community, whether maritime or landlocked. Those who are ready to accept its values and value priorities, and who acquire the skills and, particularly, the attitudes that go with those values, often become strangers in their home and wander away to ever larger cities, where the promise of a social as well as material reward for their skills and attitudes always seems greater.

END OF UTOPIA

Second Return of the Glasses

To the remaining Tristan community, the departure of most of the Glasses might again mean a consolidation and a reinforcement of the traditional values and way of life as a marginal group, and a potential medium of change was once more removed from its midst. Throughout the history of this utopian community, an important factor in preserving its traditional conservatism as well as its homogeneity, concord, and relative harmony had been that the dissenters and the discontents could pick up and leave and be absorbed by the Outside World.

This time, however, things were different. Since the last great emigrations from Tristan da Cunha at the turn of the century, the industrialized, urbanized, and rapidly changing Outside World had grown so far apart from this maritime community that it could no longer readily absorb her renegade sons and daughters.

Among the many reasons the emigrated islanders gave themselves and others for wanting to leave England a second time, the most important ones were probably the most difficult to articulate because they lay buried in the unconscious attitudes and feelings of the Tristan Islanders.

From my conversations with these emigrants I gathered that most of them were lonely in the midst of the constant stream of humanity that surrounded them. And the more sensitive among them felt sorry for the English because they realized that they, too, were lonely, perhaps without even knowing it. The islanders had never before experienced anything like it. The last time they were in England, they had been together among themselves. Now they were strangers, extremely lonesome in a lonely crowd.

Within five months from the emigrants' arrival in England, telegrams were sent to relatives and friends on Tristan, telling them not to follow as planned, and by Christmas a large number of the emigrants had decided to return to Tristan. Over the next years, 26 of the latest emigrants were back, including 19 or 20 Glasses.

A Changing Community

What the returning emigrants came home to was a changing Tristan da Cunha. By 1970, the population of the island had grown to 275, not including expatriates in the fishing company and the administration. The company had greatly expanded its operations with motorized craft and heavy machinery and had built its own boat wharf producing glass fiber motor boats for its own use. Mechanical workshops for the repair and maintenance of tractors and heavy equipment had been established, and a number of specialized jobs had been created, some of them requiring special skills that were new and strange to the islanders; in some instances, young men had been sent to St. Helena for training at company expense. Also the administrative organization of the island had been growing in Parkinsonian fashion, greatly increasing the number of permanent jobs available to the islanders.

These developments meant a dramatic increase in the islanders' participation in the "modern" activities of the company and in the administration. Eventually, the majority of islanders were permanently employed, either by the fishing company or by the administration, and to be on the permanent staff was no longer a distinction and privilege for the few more "progressive" islanders. Only a minority of the islanders were still holding out, clinging to their traditional freedom by offering their services only as independent fishermen and refusing to accept a permanent job. But all were engaged in money-earning activities.

The traditional subsistence economy had not been abandoned, although there were a few islanders who were living entirely "off the canteen," that is in a complete dependence on cash. The total economy of the community still had its base in the growing of potatoes and the raising of cattle and sheep for home consumption, with important supplements from hunting and gathering of sea birds and their eggs on the neighboring island of Nightingale; and it was in these activities that the social structure of the community with its selective reciprocity still found its most important manifestation in the form of mutual aid and cooperation. The fishing company had recognized the necessity of not interfering with these activities and was willingly lending out tractors and motorboats for hauling and towing, obviously to reduce the time taken away from industrial endeavors. Consequently, the traditional oxcarts had practically disappeared, and although the longboats were still kept in good trim for the Nightingale trips, the homemade canvas dinghies were being neglected and falling into disrepair. An important outcome of this, however, was that a whole series of traditional cooperative efforts of the islanders were being eliminated, mutual services between islanders in selective reciprocity being replaced by services rendered indiscrimninately by the company.

The increased affluence and flow of money also had effects on social structure and forms of social organization. New status symbols had appeared that only money could buy, upsetting the traditional system and prestige and influence. For two or three young islanders—characteristically they happened to be Glasses—private cars had replaced the longboats as the most important instrument of self-expression, although on Tristan no wheeled vehicle can be driven more than five miles from home. Mechanical skills and administrative responsibilities were competing with boatmanship as the prime source of pride. On the whole, the patterns and symbols as well as the values of modern industrial society appeared to be asserting themselves within the community of Tristan da Cunha to a higher degree than ever before, at the expense of the traditional values of anarchy, equality, and selective reciprocity.

The Glasses had shown the way. In their estrangement from the community, they had been forced to become more self-reliant than most. Relatively free from reciprocal obligations, they had less difficulty accepting the alternative way of life offered by the fishing industry, thus taking on the role of a medium of change. Now, as this alternative had been widely accepted, the Glasses had lost an important mark of distinction. While the name is still present on the island, "the Glasses" as a discernable social unit seems to be disappearing, the descendants of Bob Glass now being absorbed by various other cliques and social sets as a new generation establishes new structural alignments.

NOTES

[1]Among the vast literature on industrialization and modernization, see, *e.g.*, Barnett's analysis, mainly in terms of personality types, of the acceptance and rejection of innovations (1953; 1964). An interesting point of view in terms of "vulnerability" and "existence rationality" is offered by Goulet (1973). See also Linton's distinction between "utility" and "compatibility" as a basis for the acceptance of innovations (1937:341f).

[2]On the concept of the "symbolic group" as a shared idea of collective identity, see Munch and Campbell (1963). On "socio-cultural symbolism," see Munch (1954, 1956:22 ff.).

[3]The author was a member of the Norwegian Scientific Expedition to Tristan da Cunha (1937–1938, under the leadership of Dr. Erling Christophersen, of Oslo, Norway (Christophersen 1946–68). The expedition spent four months on the island, December 1937–March 1938. In the summer of 1962, the author spent two months with the Tristan islanders at Calshot, England. After resettlement in 1963, the author returned to Tristan da Cunha for a stay of six months, November 1964–April 1965. In 1966, contracts were made with old emigrants from Tristan da Cunha in New London, Connecticut, and visits were made with recently-emigrated Tristan islanders in England during the summer of 1967. Archive studies were made in Cape Town (1937 and 1964), in London (1964, 1965, and 1967), and in New England (1966). For information of developments in Tristan da Cunha since 1965, the author is indebted to Mr. Roland Svenson, artist and writer of Nacka, Sweden, who visited the island in 1963, 1970, and 1973–74. Financial support was received from the Social Science Research Council (1962), the National Science Foundation (GS381, 1964–65), the American Philosophical Society (1966), and Southern Illinois University, Carbondale.

[4]On "primitive atomism," see Sumner and Keller (1927:I, 16 ff.; IV, 1 ff.). The above definition is that of Ruth Benedict as quoted by Honigmann (1968).

[5]For a more detailed discussion of the "atomistic integrity" of the Tristan community, see Munch (1971:180–186, 1970b).

[6]Documents pertaining to the early history of the Tristan community were discovered in 1932 in the possession of a granddaughter of William Glass residing in New London, Connecticut, and are now in the British Museum (Add. 43864). The full text of the above document is presented by Gane (1933:590). A brief history of the settlement of Tristan da Cunha may be found in Munch (1945:13–47, 1971:19–73).

[7]A crease in the paper has rendered a few words indecipherable. For the complete text of this document, see Gane (1933:593 ff.).

[8]Reference is made to a conversation that took place in the house of one of the Glasses in Calshot, November 18, 1962. The conversation was recorded on tape by Dr. J. B. Loudon, who was kind enough to furnish me with a transcript.

LITERATURE CITED

Barnett, H.G.
  1953   Innovation: The Basis of Cultural Change. New York: McGraw-Hill.
  1964   The Acceptance and Rejection of Change. *In* Explorations in Social
          Change. Zollschan and Hirsch, eds. 345–367. Boston: Houghton-
          Mifflin.

Boalt, Gunnar, ed.
  1970   Samhallen och Kulturer: Faltstudier och Makroperspektiv. Stock-
          holm: Natur och Kultur.

Brander, Jan
  1940   Tristan da Cunha, 1506–1902. London: Allen & Unwin.

Christophersen, Erling, ed.
  1946–1968 Results of the Norwegian Scientific Expedition to Tristan da Cunha
          1937–1938. Vols. 1–5. Oslo: Det Norske Videnskaps-Akademi.

Correspondence
  1887   Correspondence Relating to the Island of Tristan d'Acunha. Imperial
          Blue Book C.4959. London: Her Majesty's Stationery Office.

Further Correspondence
  1903   Further Correspondence Relating to the Island of Tristan da Cunha.
          Imperial Blue Book Cd.1600. London: His Majesty's Stationery Of-
          fice.

Gane, Douglas M.
  1933   Early Records of Tristan da Cunha: The Discovery in New London.
          United Empire 1933:589–598, 651–658, 709–713.

Gist, Noel P., and Anthony Gary Dworkin, eds.
  1972   The Blending of Races: Marginality in World Perspective. New
          York: Wiley-Interscience.

Goulet, Denis
  1973   The Cruel Choice: A New Concept in the Theory of Development.
          New York: Atheneum.

Honigmann, John J.
  1968   Interpersonal Relations in Atomistic Communities. Human Organi-
          zation 27:220–29.

Linton, Ralph
  1937   The Study of Man: An Introduction. New York: Appleton-Century.

Munch, Peter A.
  1945   Sociology of Tristan da Cunha. *In* Results of the Norwegian Scientif-
         ic Expedition to Tristan da Cunha 1937–1938. Christopherson, ed.
         Vol. 2, no. 13. Oslo: Det Norske Videnskaps-Akademi.
  1954   Group Identification and Socio-cultural Symbolism. Midwest So-
         ciologist 16:13–18.
  1956   A Study of Cultural Change: Rural-urban Conflicts in Norway. Oslo:
         Aschehoug.
  1970a Vardekonflikt och ekonomisk utveckling: ett socialt experiment på
         Tristan da Cunha. *In* Samhallen och Kulterer: Faltstudier och
         Makroperspektiv. Gunner Boalt, ed. Pp. 19–42. Stockholm: Natur
         och Kultur.
  1970b Economic Development and Conflicting Values: A Social Experi-
         ment in Tristan da Cunha. American Anthropologist 72:1300–18.
  1971   Crisis in Utopia: The Ordeal of Tristan da Cunha. New York: Thom-
         as Y. Crowell.
  1972   Race and Social Relations in Tristan da Cunha. *In* Gist and Dworkin
         1972:265–81.
  1974   Anarchy and *Anomie* in an Atomistic Community. Man N.S. 9:
         243–61.

Munch, Peter A., and Robert B. Campbell
  1963   Interaction and Collective Identification in a Rural Locality. Rural
         Sociology 28:18–34.

Sumner, William Graham, and Albert Galloway Keller
  1927   The Science of Society. Vols. 1–4. New Haven: Yale University
         Press.

Taylor, William F.
  1856   Some Accounts of the Settlement of Tristan d'Acunha in the South
         Atlantic Ocean. London: Society for the Propagation of the Gospel.

Zollschan, George K., and Walter Hirsch, eds.
  1964   Explorations in Social Change. Boston: Houghton-Mifflin.

*

10

Technological Change in a Grenada W.I. Fishery, 1950–1970 *

GEORGE M. EPPLE

Rhode Island College

The purpose of this paper is to examine a specific case of the impact of technological change in a traditional fishery on the east coast of Grenada, West Indies. The major change in technology involved the mechanization of the fishing fleet through the introduction of gasoline inboard engines, with concomitant changes in boat design and construction. The short- and long-term effects of these innovations completely transformed the east coast fishery from a small-scale traditional subsistence-oriented endeavor to a more modern coastal fishery producing principally for a cash income. A measure of the impact which such an innovation may have is that the introduction and acceptance of gasoline engines into the east coast fishery led to changes in virtually every aspect of the fishery and contributed to the development of a fishermen's marketing cooperative.

*Based on fieldwork conducted between June 1969 and June 1970 and sponsored by a National Science Foundation grant for "Doctoral Dissertation Research in Anthropology" (GS-2414) and a grant from the Research Institute for the Study of Man, New York, Dr. Vera Rubin, Director.

Inherent in the present analysis is the idea of a fishery as an ecological system which includes: (1) a natural resource—a variety of species of fish found above and along the insular shelf of Grenada; (2) a physical environment—including both the oceanographic and the physiographic characteristics of the coastal land areas of the island; and (3) a human factor—consisting of a population of fishermen, a technological repertoire utilized for the capture of the natural resources, a system for the distribution of the catch, and a cultural or ideological system which places certain constraints on the free interplay of other variables in the system. The term *fishery* is used to indicate an exploitative-productive unit consisting of a population of fishermen utilizing similar techniques to capture similar species of fish within the same general ecological niche. A fishery is a complex system and not simply a set of techniques associated with the capture of one particular species.

Assuming the systemic nature of a fishery, it follows that a change in one or more elements will initiate a process of adaptation tending toward establishing congruity between the parts of the system. Consideration of the Grenada case verifies this assumption. The magnitude of the impact of introducing gasoline engines is demonstrated by the changes that occurred: (1) the demographic pattern within the east coast fishery changed (2) new fishing areas were opened; (3) a more extensive internal distribution system developed; (4) there was a radical shift in the pattern of ownership of capital equipment; (5) the composition of work units was altered (6) the age-composition of the fishing population changed; (7) a new set of socioeconomic groups and relationships was generated; and (8) a fishermen's marketing cooperative was organized. The body of this paper will be concerned with describing and analyzing this chain reaction.

SETTING AND BACKGROUND

Before discussing the history of this particular case, some general information needs to be given on the contemporary setting and the relationship of the east coast fishery to other fisheries in Grenada. The research on which the present analysis is based was conducted during a 1 year field investigation in Grenville, Grenada, West Indies. The eastern Caribbean island of Grenada, located ninety miles north of Trinidad (see Map I) has a land area of only 120 square miles and a population of approximately 95,000. Economically, Grenada is almost totally dependent on foreign aid and the export of three main agricultural products: cocoa, bananas, and nutmeg. Other than tourism, which appears to have reached a peak, Grenada has little nonagricultural industry.

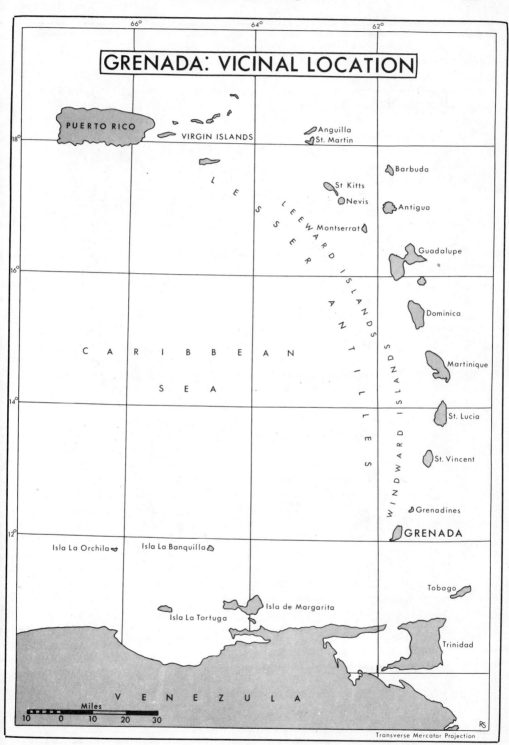

Map I

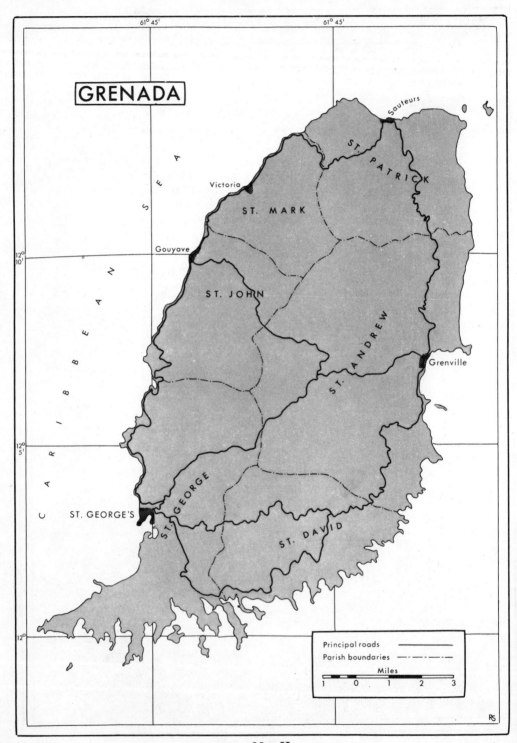

61° 45'   61° 45'

GRENADA

Sauteurs

ST. PATRICK

Victoria

S E A

ST. MARK

12°
10'   Gouyave

C A R I B B E A N   ST. JOHN

ST. ANDREW

Grenville

12°
5'

ST. GEORGE

C   ST. GEORGE'S

ST. DAVID

12°

| Principal roads | ——— |
| Parish boundaries | —·—·— |

Miles

1   0   1   2   3

RS

Map II

Grenville (pop. 1,747), the third largest town in Grenada, is located in St. Andrew's Parish on the east (or Atlantic) coast, approximately 14 miles from the capital of St. George's on the west coast (see Map II). The primary importance of Grenville is that it serves as the major marketing center for the eastern half of the island, its Saturday market rivaling that of St. George's. Although located directly across the island from the capital, communication is relatively easy; it is 14 miles—30 minutes by car—across the Grand Etang Road, or 45 minutes by way of the southern St. David's Road. Though most of the population of Grenville would be classified as urban lower-class by St. George's standards, there is a representative middle class population of business men, professionals, and civil servants, some of whom commute daily to St. George's.

Grenville's central location on the east coast contributes to its importance as a regional center. The St. Andrew's District Board, the police station, an agricultural extension office, the nutmeg processing station, a government fish market, a meat and produce market, and the Princess Alice Hospital—all located in or near Grenville—serve the entire eastern half of Grenada. The town contains four primary and two secondary schools, and Roman Catholic, Anglican, and Methodist churches. Branches of several of the largest retail stores in the island, a few whole-sale-retail firms, two supermarkets, a movie theater, and numerous smaller retail stores and shops provide customers with a wide range of goods and services.

Grenville's importance as a commercial center is enhanced by its protected harbor, the only sizable one on the east coast. Though access to the inner harbor is restricted by a narrow and twisting channel through a coral reef, several inter-island schooners make weekly stops carrying imported bulk goods, construction materials, livestock, and passengers between Trinidad and the islands to the north. A small pier and customhouse facilitate the servicing of these boats.

The town's status as a fishing center is evidenced by the location there of the largest fleet of mechanized fishing boats in the island producing the major landings of pelagic and demersal species of fish. In addition to functioning as the operating and marketing center for the St. Andrew's fishing fleet, Grenville is also the landing area for numerous fishing boats from the Grenadines and as far north as St. Vincent, 68 miles away. Most of these catches are sold in the local fish market, though occasionally a boat will land with a load of lobsters which are transported by car to the tourist hotels on the southeastern tip of the island. Fish from other parts of Grenada may also find their way to the Grenville market: truck loads of jacks from the west coast, pails of lambi (conch) from Sauteurs and Levera, or five gallon tins of titiree (small fry) from river mouths sold by the cupful by women and young girls. Some estimates rank Grenville as the Grenada fish marketing area handling the highest volumes of fresh fish and other locally produced marine resources. The contemporary importance of Grenville as a fishing center will be shown to stem partially from the effects of the introduction of mechanized boats.

A brief survey of the various fisheries of Grenada will help to place the east coast fishery in perspective and to indicate some of the contrasts between east and west coast fisheries which should elucidate some aspects of the changes which occurred on the east coast following mechanization. Traditionally, the fisheries of a country may be divided into four different types, based on the oceanographic, physiographic, and biogeographic features of particular zones. The four zones are designated as freshwater, onshore, coastal, and ocean (or deep-water). Both freshwater and ocean fisheries are of little or no importance in Grenada. The onshore fishery is carried out from the beach, in river mouths, or estuaries, and in bays and around coral reefs. Various types of beach seines, cast nets, pots, traps, and spear-fishing are used in this zone. Beach seining is the primary onshore method and accounts for nearly 40 percent of the total yearly landings in Grenada. Most of the beach seines are located on the west coast between St. George's and Victoria, and on Isle de la Ronde. The seines are moved from one beach to another on different days depending on where schools of fish have been sighted. Each of these seines has its own group of women vendors, who follow the net to whatever beach it is being used at that particular day. These women often have specific ties with members of the seine crew; they are usually the wives, mistresses or girlfriends of the eight man crew. Usually the women take the fish by car to the market in St. George's, although when there is a glut they will sell in the rural countryside. Large catches may be transported as far as Grenville in the back of a flatbed truck and sold directly from the truck. Beach seining is, therefore, a highly mobile type of fishing which does not necessitate the concentration of nets and net-crews in large population centers.

Coastal fisheries in the waters above the insular shelf are most highly developed on the eastern and northern coasts of Grenada where the grounds are relatively extensive (see Map III). The methods used may be divided into two general types depending on whether the species sought are demersal or pelagic. For demersal fishing, pots and bottom-fished handlines are the most common methods; for pelagic fishing trolling and drifting with handlines are the most common methods. This latter technique accounts for nearly 30 percent of the island's total annual catch and 75 percent of the catch on the east coast.

Trolling with handlines and either artificial or natural baits at the edge of the insular shelf is the predominant method of fishing for bonito, albacore, kingfish, dolphin, and occasional sailfish, marlin and yellow fin tuna on the east coast. This fishery is centered in a Grenville-based fleet

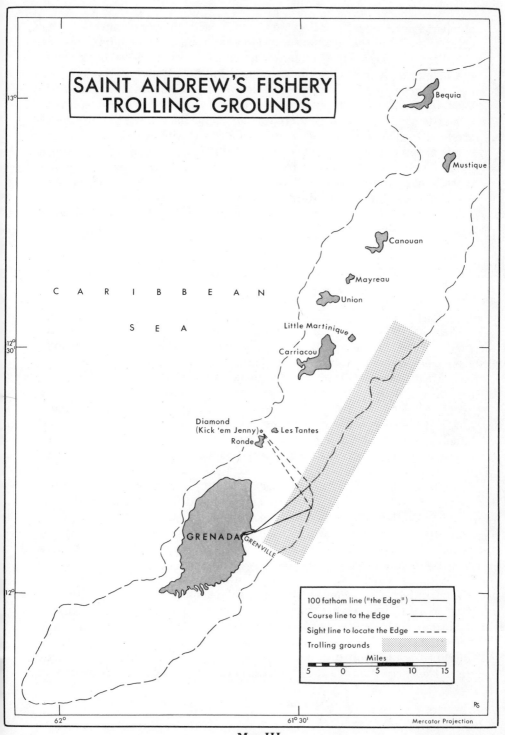

SAINT ANDREW'S FISHERY TROLLING GROUNDS

Bequia

Mustique

Canouan

Mayreau

Union

Little Martinique

Carriacou

CARIBBEAN

SEA

Diamond
(Kick 'em Jenny)   Les Tantes
Ronde

GRENADA GRENVILLE

13°

12° 30'

12°

62°   61° 30'

100 fathom line ("the Edge")	— — —
Course line to the Edge	———
Sight line to locate the Edge	- - - - -
Trolling grounds	

Miles

5   0   5   10   15

RS

Mercator Projection

Map III

of over 50 powered whaler-type boats, each carrying a two man crew. The great majority of the catches were sold to a group of 11 local fish vendors (until the development of a marketing cooperative in 1969–70). Most of the fishing is done during the early morning hours, and the majority of boats return by noon. To dispose of their catch, the boats land on a beach located only 20 yards from a government-owned fish marketing stall. As a boat lands, a group of vendors (or "dry-land fishermen") converge on the boat to examine the catch and bargain with the captain for the purchase of the fish. Once a vendor has bought fish, he then carries them a short distance up the beach to the market stall where they are immediately retailed directly to consumers. Thus the east coast handline fishery is far more centralized and less mobile than the west coast beach seine fishery, largely because of the consequences of technological innovation in the fishing fleet.

A CASE HISTORY
OF TECHNOLOGICAL CHANGE:

Prior to 1950, most of the fishing on the east coast was done from small, 8 to 12 foot rowboats ("transumes") and sailing canoes ("pirogues") operated by 1 or 2 fishermen in inshore or near-coastal waters. Most fishing utilized pots and banking in 5 to 20 fathoms for demersal species of fish, such as grouper, rock-hind, and snapper. The use of beach seines on the east coast was infrequent due largely to a lack of suitable clear bottom areas for hauling nets to shore. Fishing effort, at that time, was dispersed along much of the east coast, the fishermen living and working in small villages and scattered bays. Thus, what fishing was done tended to produce only small catches, used principally for the subsistence needs of the fisherman, or for limited distribution (on a casual barter or reciprocal basis with neighbors) within the small local community. While little is known of this period, discussion with some of the older fishermen indicated that their catches were rarely large enough to require more extensive distribution and that fish vendors or hawkers were not common on the east coast.

Following World War II, a significant change occurred as a result of the introduction of inexpensive inboard gasoline engines from Europe (the most common were one- or two-cylinder Stuart engines). Experimenting with those engines, the Government fisheries staff and local fishermen found they could be used efficiently and inexpensively in modified double-ended whaler or pirogue type boats. During the decade from the early 1950s to the early 1960s the mechanization of the fishing fleet was encouraged by government programs of loans and subsidies for the purchase and construction of powered fishing boats. A total of $50,000 EC (Eastern Caribbean Currency; $1.00 EC = $0.50 US) in loans was made, but the program was stopped in the early 1960s due to low pay-back rates on previous loans. By this time, however, the motorized whaler had become the standard fishing boat for the east coast, and individual fishermen and non-fisherman investors continued to purchase new boats and engines. By 1970, there were more than 125 powered whalers operating in Grenada, with at least 60 of these based in the Grenville-St. Andrew's Bay area. The following pages will examine some of the consequences of this rapid mechanization of the east coast fishing fleet.[1]

The extension of fishing grounds was one immediate consequence of the introduction of mechanized fishing boats. Motorized boats could travel faster and were not dependent on the wind, so that the fisherman could venture further out on the insular shelf without worrying about the direction and strength of the tides, currents, and winds. Faster boats meant that the fishermen could get to the more distant fishing grounds up to 20 miles from shore and still be able to return to their home ports the same day.

The opening of new grounds led, in turn, to changes in the species composition of the fishermen's catches. Before extensive mechanization the largest portion of the catch consisted of demersal species, such as hind, grouper, and various reef fish. After mechanization much greater emphasis was placed on handline trolling for the larger pelagic species, such as black-fin tuna, bonito, and billfish. In part, this change was a result of the faster and more constant trolling speeds of the motorized vessels. Tuna, bonito, and albacore generally strike baits trolled at relatively high speeds, a factor which seriously limited the productivity of sailing craft in this type of fishery.

Mechanization favored changes in other, associated aspects of fishing technology. For example, the increasing importance of handline trolling for larger species of fish increased the desirability of imported nylon and monofilament lines and leader material. Some fishermen still use cotton or linen handlines, because they feel these materials are less slippery than nylon when wet; other fishermen prefer the synthetics because they are less susceptible to rotting and have a much higher breaking strain which may mean fewer lost fish and gear. Other foreign-made tackles and gear began to be imported in larger quantities, including Japanese-made feather "baits" (lures) and tube lures for tuna, bonito, and albacore.

The basic change in technology created changes in the composition of work units. The older transumes and pirogues were most often manned by a single fisherman, though at times two or more men would go banking together. For powered whalers, two-man crews are standard: the captain stands in the stern to steer and fish one deep-running handline, while a bowman (crewman) sits or stands in front of the engine box amidships and fishes two handlines from bamboo outriggers. Occasionally three-man crews may go trolling and groups of three to five men may use a large whaler for banking. Unfortunately, I was unable to reconstruct with any certainty the possible effects which this change in the unit of production may have had on interrelationships among fishermen or within the community

Two interrelated changes resulting from the mechanization of fishing craft were: a change in the internal marketing system for fresh fish, and a shift in the location of the production units from rural, isolated villages and bays to the more heavily populated coastal towns. For reasons stated previously, fishermen using powered boats made substantially larger catches than had been common with the banking-pot fishing carried on from sailing boats. Larger catches meant that all of the fish could not generally be consumed by the fisherman's family or through the informal exchange networks within the village.

According to several informants, the distribution problem was solved temporarily by the fisherman himself transporting fish to other areas along the coast, including Grenville, and selling them there. Soon a few itinerant hawkers began to appear at the landing beaches to purchase fish, which they then transported and sold in inland villages and as far away as St. George's. Most likely, these vendors were women fish-hawkers from St. George's and the west coast where they normally worked in association with the beach seines. Alternatively, some of the fishermen began to land their catches directly at Grenville, to be sold there before returning to their home villages. With the average daily landings of fish increasing as more fishermen acquired motorized boats, the need for more permanent middleman-vendors arose. It was not long before some of the older fishermen, who could no longer fish on a regular basis, began to assume a middleman function for groups of fishermen within their neighborhoods. It is quite likely that these ex-fishermen/vendors (now referred to as "dry-land fishermen") gained acceptance among the fishermen more easily than the itinerant vendors from other areas; many of my fisherman-informants stated that, while they felt that all vendors "advantaged" (cheated, or took advantage of) the fishermen in their bargaining over the sale of fish, one had to be more cautious in dealings with vendors from other parts of the island. A local vendor had to maintain some degree of cordial relations with the fishermen with whom he would deal every day, or they might refuse to sell to him. It would seem logical that when a niche was created for permanent fish vendors on the east coast, some fishermen played on existing networks established while operating as fishermen in establishing themselves as full-time vendors. Such vendors provided a necessary service in disposing of catches too large for the individual fisherman to consume or distribute through traditional means. Thus, one effect of mechanization was to stimulate the development of new distribution and marketing channels, thereby transforming a primarily subsistence-oriented fishery into a mixed subsistence-cash income occupation.

Change in the marketing-distribution system was directly related to a movement of fishermen from rural villages to the town of Grenville. As indicated earlier, mechanization led to larger catches of fish, which in turn created the need for distribution outside the small villages traditionally occupied by fishermen prior to the 1950s; some fishermen solved this problem by landing catches directly at Grenville. Gradually, some fishermen began to move to Grenville, or nearby areas along St. Andrew's Bay; some merely anchored their boats near Grenville and maintained residences in their home villages, others moved both their boats and residences to the Grenville area. The results of this process are obvious in the concentration of mechanized fishing vessels found in Grenville today, and in the existence of enclaves of fishermen's residences in certain areas around Grenville. One such area just to the south of the main part of town is referred to as La Baye and is generally considered to be populated predominantly by fishermen; other enclaves include Soubise and Marquis (see Map IV). Additional evidence of this process is that during the period of research at least three crews and their boats moved to Grenville, while none left for other areas.

The attractiveness of Grenville (and the larger St. Andrew's area) as a base of operations for fishing is implicit in the description given earlier of Grenville as a major focal point for all types of social and economic activity for the eastern half of the island. Further, Grenville has the only well-protected harbor other than St. George's; the larger 25 foot powered whalers could not be hauled onto the shore as easily as small transumes and pirogues, something which was essential for protecting boats at the more open beaches and bays of the east coast. Thus, movement to Grenville both facilitated the marketing of fish and provided safer anchorage for the fishermen's boats.

Another consequence of mechanization was a shift in the pattern of ownership of capital equipment correlating with the considerably greater expenses involved in building and outfitting a boat and purchasing and installing an engine. Prior to mechanization, nearly every fisherman owned a boat; but, when the first inboard engines were introduced, few fishermen had sufficient funds to purchase them and build suitable boats.[2] Loans for the purchase of engines were scarce and few fishermen had the necessary collateral to get regular bank loans. The glamour of the

Map IV

new engines and the increased profits from fishing attracted a greater number of young men willing to work for others but unable to buy boats; less conservative, and enamoured with the prospect of having money to spend, few of these younger fishermen saved enough of their earnings to buy their own boats. When the government loan scheme was established, the primary beneficiaries were those same fishermen who already owned one or more engine boats and were thus better risks. Many others who did receive equipment before the scheme ended never repaid the loans. When the boats or engines needed replacement, they had no funds, and most were forced again to fish for other owners. The most successful fishermen today are those who managed to acquire a mechanized boat early and used the profits to purchase additional boats. A survey of the lists of engines purchased in the years between 1960 and 1970 clearly indicates that the same small group of fisherman/boat-owners periodically purchased new engines, while few new names of fishermen appear. Thus, in 1970, 6 of 17 fishermen who owned boats controlled 58 percent of the boats owned by fishermen. In addition, 5 of the 11 owners of only 1 boat had owned another boat prior to their present one. Thus, control of capital equipment by fishermen was highly centered on a few individuals.

These circumstances created an ideal opportunity for the entry of outside entrepreneurs into fishing. It was not known who had been the first nonfisherman to build a boat, nor what his motives had been, but the idea soon caught on. At the time of the study, 57 percent of the powered whalers in the St. Andrew's fishery were owned by nonfishermen. Financing a fishing boat provides a reasonably good investment for a person with access to a small amount of capital. Returns from this type of investment can be good and the risk is not unduly great. A boat will pay for itself in one or two years, depending on the success and industriousness of the crew. If kept in good condition, the boat and engine will last four to five years before needing major repairs or replacement. Though boat ownership is not time consuming, it is best if the owner lives nearby so that he can check on the boat and crew frequently. Minor engine repairs are needed often, and if the owner is not available to arrange for these, the boat may sit idle for some time. Also an owner is much more likely to be cheated out of a portion of his share of the profits, if he is not present occasionally to check on the landings and collect his money. For these reasons, most of the nonfisherman–owners are middle- or lower-middle-class business or professional people who reside in or near Grenville.

Mechanization, therefore, has substantially altered the pattern of ownership of fishing boats: whereas in 1950 at least 90 percent of fishermen owned boats, in 1970 not more than 25 percent of the full-time fishermen owned boats. Even during the year of research, this shift continued as three times as many new boats were financed by nonfishermen as by

fishermen. It seems reasonable to assume that the present trend will continue, unless changes occur making it possible for more fishermen to purchase their own boats. Were the Government to reinstate a loan scheme
designed to aid fishermen in purchasing boats, engines, and equipment,
the balance might be altered. Alternatively, one aim of a newly active cooperative is to improve the fisherman's ability to purchase his own equipment by increasing earnings and changing attitudes toward savings. The
success of the cooperative may depend partially on its ability to accomplish this aim, since a fisherman who owns his equipment has more to
work for than simply putting a few dollars in his pocket each day and is
more likely to be committed to the cooperative program.

Mechanization has had an effect on the age-composition of the fishing
population. As noted in connection with changes in ownership patterns,
more young men were attracted to fishing because of the glamour of the
new engine boats. Any motor-driven vehicle is a prestige-enhancer
among young Grenadians; it is not surprising then that many younger
men have turned to fishing and taxi-driving. The care which young fishermen lavish on their boats, frequently repairing, painting, and decorat-
ing them, reminds one of the effort expended by American teenagers of
the 1950s on their hot rods. Even the names chosen for boats reflect the
influence of the young and their heroic idols: Astronaut, Hondo, Atracan
Star (from a movie which played at the local cinema), and Bad John.
While specific age comparisons could not be made between 1950 and
1970, the average age of the full-time fishermen in 1970 was well under
30, and the older fishermen recalled that there were many more older fishermen before mechanization. In fact, the change in age composition may
be directly related to the change in fishing methods associated with
mechanization, in that a majority of the pot and banking fishermen of today are older men; pot fishing and banking are considered to be less
strenuous than handlining, since one does not go out as often, and does
not encounter as rough water. Whatever the reasons, it seems reasonable
to conclude that the average age of east coast fishermen today is lower
than for the same group in the early 1950s.

That mechanization created new economic roles and relationships is
demonstrated in the change from single to two-man crews (resulting in
the labels "captain" and "bowman"), in the origin of the "dry-land fisherman," and in the creation of a category of non-fisherman–boat-owners.
Entirely new sets of economic relationships came into existence: captain-
bowman, fisherman-vendor, fisherman–boat-owner, vendor-consumer,
fisherman-townsman. These developments changed the organization of
the east coast fishery drastically.

A less direct consequence of mechanization was the evolution of new
forms of social organization among fishermen. It has been established

that mechanization stimulated a migration of fishermen to the urban center of Grenville, where they became but one of a large number of occupational categories (and one most often ranked lowest on a socioeconomic scale by other townspeople), rather than the major occupational group of the small rural fishing village. For reasons too complex to be discussed more fully here, this migration with its consequent exposure to the urban environment, greater contact with mass media (particularly cinema), and more complex social stratification produced a "machismo"-oriented self-image among these fishermen-townsmen and a disruption of many of the social, kinship, and familial based associations of small village life. One apparent adaptation in response to this change has been the formation of informal male peer-groupings among the fishermen.[3] These informal social groups, whose memberships consist entirely of fishermen, provide the setting for the expression and testing of male values; support the values attached to fishing; and influence the behavior of its members through various informal sanctions. A major focus of research, these informal social groups proved to be an essential part of the fisherman's ability to cope with the urban-like milieu of Grenville.

"TAKE-OFF" FOR A COOPERATIVE

Though not a direct result of the mechnization of the east coast fishing fleet, the formation of a fishermen's marketing cooperative at Grenville in 1969–1970 appeared to be a response to a need for more comprehensive forms of organization stimulated by technological innovation (Epple 1971 and 1973). It can be argued that the sequence of changes discussed in the second part of this paper created a kind of "take-off" stage for economic development.

The various effects of mechanization outlined earlier resulted in the creation of a dependency relationship between the fishermen and other segments of the community which had not previously existed. First, many fishermen could not afford to purchase the new boats and motors and had to work for those who did own boats. Second, the change in the organization of the fishery led to the development of a firmly entrenched middleman fish-vendor group, on whom the fishermen became dependent for an outlet for their fish.

These two factors established a basis upon which the idea of the cooperative could grow. Most of the fishermen expressed a desire to own their own boats, and most felt the vendors were taking unfair advantage of them and making excessive profits.[4] The formation of the cooperative changed this situation drastically. Operating primarily as a marketing organization, it offered to purchase all of the fish that its members could catch, thereby providing a guaranteed market. The cooperative established a set wholesale price slightly above the average paid by the vendors prior to the cooperative, and agreed to redistribute the profits from the cooperative's activities in the form of a rebate. The actual price paid by the cooperative was therefore well above that which the vendors had been offering. The effects of this on the productivity of cooperative members were noticeable; they began fishing longer and going out more frequently; and soon the cooperative, though only controlling one-third of the boats, was accounting for more than one-half of the total daily catch at Grenville.

Many of the fishermen perceived the cooperative as a chance to overcome these problems and to establish greater individual autonomy. Thus, the effects of the change in technology were to establish a basis for the acceptance of the cooperative innovation. As a rule, a cooperative of this type would be more likely to gain acceptance if it allowed the fishermen to perceive themselves in a dependent relationship vis-à-vis other sectors of the fishing industry. The effect of mechanization was to transform the east coast fishery from an independent-producer subsistence fishery to a dependent, share-worker, cash-based fishery, thereby creating the dependent relationship and economic imbalance which favored the formation of the cooperative.

It was not the technological innovation around 1950 that created the cooperative; it was the changes in the fishery caused by the new technology that generated conditions conducive to the implementation of a cooperative form of organization. Within the context of technological change, it was the prospect of another technological innovation which actually stimulated the growth of the cooperative. In 1967, a small group of fishermen from St. Andrew's, under the leadership of a local representative of the Cooperative Department, began to formulate plans for a fishermen's cooperative. Nearly two years elapsed between the first meeting of fishermen and the actual registration as a cooperative body. This delay would have been considerably longer had it not been for the catalytic effect of a Government announcement of plans for a fish marketing project to be financed jointly by the Grenadian Government and Canadian External Aid funds. The project, originally conceived in 1966 and involving a survey of the island by a team of Canadian consultants, had provided the initial impetus for the formation of a cooperative. The plan called for the installation of a flake ice plant with storage facilities for fish, and trucks for transporting fish to the other markets. In 1969, revisions in the plan stipulated that a cooperative should be responsible for operating the facility. As a result, the membership of the St. Andrew's Fishermen Cooperative Marketing Society—hitherto little more than a social club—felt it was imperative that they move ahead as rapidly as possible with the aim of proving and improving their ability to fulfill the management requirements of the project. Without this incentive, the development of the cooperative might have remained at a standstill for a much longer time.

CONCLUSIONS

Examination of a specific case of technological innovation in a traditional West Indian fishery indicates that a change from oar- and sail-powered to mechanized fishing craft produced changes in other aspects of the fishery—demographic, economic, technological, social, and organizational—which in turn created a "take-off" stage leading to the formation of a fishermen's marketing cooperative. The extent of the resultant changes in the east coast fishery following mechanization supports an approach which views a fishery as an ecological system consisting of a natural resource(s), a physical environment, and a human-cultural component. A change in technology—part of the human-cultural component—generated changes not only in other aspects of the human-cultural component; but in the physical environment component—in the opening of new fishing areas; and in the resource component—in the exploitation of new species, and in the relationship between all three components. Assuming the ecological systemic nature of a fishery, one should expect that a change in one aspect is likely to have far-reaching effects on the entire fishery—particularly in small-scale traditional fishing industries.[5]

NOTES

[1]Discussion of the consequences of mechanization are, of necessity, sketchy, because this area was not of major concern to the original research project. The outlines of the change are, however, adequate to establish the far-reaching impact of this innovation.

[2]Anderson and Anderson (1964:43–44) note a similar phenomenon in the Danish fisheries.

[3]These groups are similar in structure and operation to the "crews" described by Peter Wilson for Providencia and other areas of the Caribbean (see Wilson 1969, 1971, and 1974; and Epple 1973).

[4]In fact, the fishermen's belief that the vendors were "advantaging" them is supported by the analysis of extensive data on the transactions involving vendors and fishermen. During the six months prior to the cooperative, the regular vendors paid an average of less

than 40ᶜ per pound for fish, whereas the cooperative during its first six months of operation paid an average of 44ᶜ; the average retail price throughout this period was over 50ᶜ per
pound. Expressed in another way, prior to the cooperative, the vendors were making a
mean net profit of $4.50 on each load of fish they purchased (18%). Before the cooperative,
fishermen had a mean daily income of $4.20, compared to $5.53 in the six months after the
cooperative began operating.

⁵The data in this paper were cross-checked against and substantiated by the following
bibliography.

LITERATURE CITED

Adams, John Edwards
    1970   Marine Industries of the St. Vincent Grenadines, West Indies. Ph.D.
            dissertation, University of Minnesota.

Anderson, A.M.
    1968   A Fish Marketing Project for Grenada, UNDP/FAO Caribbean
            Fisheries Project. Mimeo.

Anderson, Robert, and B.G. Anderson
    1964   The Vanishing Village: A Danish Maritime Community. Seattle:
            University of Washington Press.

Archambault, Jean
    1967   Un Village de Pêcheurs (Deshaies) en Guadeloupe. Univérsité de
            Montréal. Unpublished manuscript.

Aronoff, Joel
    1967   Psychological Needs and Cultural Systems. Princeton, New Jersey:
            D. Van Nostrand.

Aubin-Roy, Jacques
    1968   Vieux-Fort (Guadeloupe): Techniques et Coopération dans un Vil-
            lage de Pêcheurs. Univérsité de Montréal. Unpublished manuscript.

Benoist, Jean
    1959   Individualisme et Traditions Techniques Chez les Pêcheurs Martini-
            quais. Les Cahiers d'Outre Mer 12, no. 47:265–85.

Comitas, Lambros
    1962   Fishermen and Cooperation in Rural Jamaica. Ph.D. dissertation,
            Columbia University.

Corbeil, Andre
  1969   Saint Francois: Village de Pêcheurs (Guadeloupe). Univérsité de Montréal. Unpublished manuscript.

Davenport, William
  1956   A Comparative Study of Two Jamaican Fishing Communities. Ph.D. dissertation, Yale University.
  1960   Jamaican Fishing: A Game Theory Analysis. In Yale University Publications in Anthropology nos. 57–64. Mintz, ed. New Haven: HRAF Press.

Devas, Raymond P. O.P., M.C.
  1964   A History of the Island of Grenada. St. George's, Grenada: The Government Printer.

Edel, Mathew
  1967   Jamaican Fishermen: Two Approaches in Economic Anthropology. Social and Economic Studies 16:432–439.

Epple, George M.
  1967   Decision Making Processes in a Trinidadian Fishing Village. Brandeis University. Unpublished manuscript.
  1971   Group Dynamics and Economic Change in a Grenadian Fishing Community. Paper presented at the Northeastern Anthropological Association Meeting, Albany, New York, April 1971.
  1973   Group Dynamics and the Development of a Fish-Marketing Cooperative: The La Baye Fishermen-Townsmen of Grenada, West Indies. Ph.D. dissertation, Brandeis University.
  1973a   "The Heavy Thumb" in a West Indian fish market: Compensatory Mechanisms as Responses to Economic Change. Paper presented at the American Anthropological Association Meetings. New Orleans, Louisiana.
  1975   Technological and Organizational Factors in the Development of a West Indian Fish-Marketing Cooperative. Paper prepared for the Society for Applied Anthropology Meetings, Amsterdam, The Netherlands. March 1975.

Greaves, Nathaniel M.
  n.d.   A brief outline on the fisheries of Grenada. Mimeo.
  1968   Comments on A.M. Anderson's Report. Letter from Fisheries Officer to Chief Agricultural Officer (Extension), 26 November.
  1969a   Fish Marketing Project for Grenada: Report from Fisheries Officer to Chief Agricultural Officer (Extension). Mimeo.
  1969b   Fisheries Survey. Mimeo.
  1969c   Conversation at Ministry Office with N.M. Greaves, Fisheries Officer. 4 June. Tape transcript.

Guardian, The Trinidad
  1970   Fish Distribution in Grenada Uneven. The Trinidad Guardian. Port-of-Spain, Trinidad.

Idyll, Clarence P.
  1971   The Potential for Fishery Development in the Caribbean and Adjacent Seas. Marine Bulletin No. 1. Kingston, Rhode Island: University of Rhode Island.

MacDonald, Judy Smith
  1971   Inlaw Terms and Affinal Relations in a Grenadian Fishing Community. Mimeo.
  1972   Cursing and Context in a Grenadian Fishing Community. Mimeo.

Price, Richard.
  1964   Mágie et Pêche á la Martinique. L'Homme 4:84–113.
  1966a   Caribbean Fishing and Fishermen: A Historical Survey. American Anthropologist 68:363—83.

Price, Richard
  1966b   Fishing Rites and Recipes in a Martiniquan Village. Caribbean Studies 6(1):3–24.

Price, Richard, and Sally Price
  1966   A Note on Canoe Names in Martinique. Names.

St. Andrew's Fishermen Co-operative Society, Ltd.
  1970   Memorandum from the St. Andrew's Fishermen Co-operative Marketing Society, Ltd. To: The Honourable Premier, Minister of Agriculture. Grenville, Grenada, May 22, 1970.

Strachan, C. Basil
  1970   Report on Visit to St. Andrew's Fishermen Co-operative Society, Ltd. March 13, 1970. Mimeo.

Thompson, E.F.
  n.d.   Fisheries of British Honduras. Development and Welfare in the West Indies, Bulletin No. 21.
  1945   Fisheries of Jamaica. Development and Welfare in the West Indies, Bulletin No. 18.
  1946   Fisheries of the Caymen Islands. Development and Welfare in the West Indies, Bulletin No. 22.

Torchlight
  1970   Organizing our Fishermen. Editorial, October 30, 1970. St. George's, Grenada. Grenada Publishers.

1971a   Fishy business. Editorial, July 16, 1971. St. George's, Grenada. Grenada Publishers.
1971b   Preliminary Figures by Parishes for Grenada Census. St. George's, Grenada. Grenada Publishers.

UNDP/FAO: Caribbean Fisheries Development Project
1966   Project Report for 1966–67. Barbados.
1967   Report on Project 1967–68 and Work Plan 1968–69. Barbados.
1968   Draft Report of the Third Meeting of Liason Officers, Barbados. October 1–4, 1968.

Vidaeus, Lars
1969   An Inventory of the Grenada Fishing Industry. UNDP/FAO: Caribbean Fishery Development Project. Mimeo.

Wilson, Peter J.
1969   Reputation and Respectability: A Suggestion for Caribbean Ethnology. Man (N.S.) 4(1):70–84.
1971   Caribbean Crews: Peer Groups and Male Society. Caribbean Studies 10(4):18–34.
1974   Crab Antics. New Haven, Yale University Press.

*

11

Environment, Technology, and Time-use Patterns in the Gulf Coast Shrimp Fishery[*]

DAVID R. M. WHITE

Southern Methodist University

The temporal feeding patterns of various species of shrimp under various circumstances combine with purely technological factors to produce distinctive time-use patterns in different technologically-grounded segments of the Gulf Coast shrimping fleet. This discussion focuses on time-use and its context vis-à-vis techno-environmental and general sociocultural variables.

Graeme Salaman has recently referred to the "temporal organization" of work activities as one of the "restrictive factors" which impinge on activities and interests beyond the work situation; among these are the opportunities for establishing and maintaining friendships outside an occupational group (Salaman 1971b:404). My interests parallel Salaman's, although I begin by identifying certain technological and environmental

*An earlier version of this paper was presented to the Session on technological change and its effect on maritime communities, 34th annual meeting of the Society for applied anthropology, Amsterdam, March 19–23, 1975. The paper is based on 18 months of research done in 1971 and 1972–73, during which time I worked as a crewman on various shrimp trawlers.

sources of time-use patterns and follow these patterns beyond the individual and occupational levels to their effects on community and extra-community social organization. Unlike Salaman, I shall demonstrate that temporal organization may also be seen as socially creative rather than merely "restrictive."

One aspect of time-use patterning is the rather simplistically defined dichotomy of work versus leisure. Nearly 20 years ago, C. Wright Mills (1956:222–23) pointed out that for traditional craftsmen there is no sharp dichotomy between work and leisure as is the case with most middle-class white collar workers; more recently Salaman (1971a:54) has shown that the same vagueness applies to members of many occupational communities, such as the one described here. Parallel distinctions are employed in this paper, such as the relative amounts of time shrimp fishermen spend at sea and on shore or, while at sea, the relative amounts of time they spend on less immediately productive activities than fishing. It seems preferable, however, to leave these distinctions apart from the work-leisure dichotomy. A more productive approach is to focus on the social constraints or opportunities which are imposed or allowed by various time-use patterns, regardless of the work-leisure context.

Consideration of time-use patterns will be limited here to those included within the seasonal cycle; the bulk of attention is devoted to the repetitive cycle of fishing trips and shore activities, and to the daily cycle of activities and social interactions at sea.

TECHNOLOGY AND ENVIRONMENT

The Gulf Coast shrimp fishery is described here from the vantage point of a single community in Alabama which is heavily involved in the fishery.[1] Initially the focus is on the various interfaces of environment and technology, demonstrating the relatively restricted applicability of available technology within the spatiotemporal constraints set by the environment. This is followed by an outline of the time-use patterns observed within the contexts of different sets of technoenvironmental constraints.

The commercial shrimp fishery on the U.S. Gulf Coast developed essentially within the twentieth century, and is an industrialized fishery.[2] This does not mean, however, as is often implied, that machines are omnipotent and muscles outmoded. A rather wide range of technology is deployed by the fishery, giving differential access to (1) the various species of shrimp exploited by the fishery and (2) the ecological zones along the Gulf Coast in which the various species of shrimp are to be found. The spatiotemporal habits of shrimp (both seasonal and daily) in various habitats are thus pertinent to the time of day and year that a given type of technology may be successfully used.

Two major classes of boats are involved in the present-day Gulf Coast shrimp fishery; these are referred to as "bay boats" and "Gulf boats." In view of the range of technology and spatiotemporal behavior among the latter, I have found it analytically convenient to separate the Gulf boats into two groups; the arbitrary dividing point of 70 feet long is used to separate small Gulf boats from large.[3] Bay boats vary in size; and smallest in the local fleet is less than 30 feet and the largest is slightly more than 50 feet. Vessels culturally defined as bay boats and Gulf boats are overlapping in size, as the smallest Gulf boat is only 45 feet. The largest local Gulf boat in 1973 was a little over 80 feet.

All boats in the shrimping fleet are engine driven, but the responsibilities of the power systems vary considerably. Some bay boats today have no provision for picking up nets or lifting the anchor other than muscle power, and until quite recently many were driven by salvaged automobile engines and had only six-volt electrical systems. Early winches were improvised devices which men hoped would work but did not count on; some bay boats still utilize these jury-rigged "mule systems," but others have shifted to standard manufactured winches.

The smaller Gulf boats and most present-day boats are powered by small diesel engines, have 32-volt electrical systems sufficient for deck lighting and operating a wide variety of electronic equipment, and have commercial power take-off units which drive winches capable of handling heavy lifting. The largest Gulf boats are run by large diesel engines and have small diesel auxiliary engines which allow 110-volt electrical systems capable of providing for air conditioning and color television, as well as powering a full range of available electronic equipment. Some of these boats are equipped with heavy-duty hydraulic winches.

Larger boats, obviously, are capable of working deeper waters. Bay boats seldom carry enough net cable to work depths in excess of 10 or 15 fathoms; the smaller Gulf boats are only occasionally equipped to work depths approaching 50 fathoms and work predominantly inside the 30 fathom line; and early in 1973 the largest Gulf boats were seldom working beyond 70 fathoms.[4]

Two important functions of a boat's size are (1) the "carrying capacity," that is, the amount of fuel, fresh water, food, and ice for preserving the catch which a boat is able to carry, and (2) the "comfort facilities" which a boat has. The smallest bay boats had no bunks, no running water, and only a sterno stove for heating coffee or canned beans; most present-day bay boats and all Gulf boats have bunks, running water at least in the galley, butane stoves, and possibly a television set or stereo tape deck for entertainment. The largest Gulf boats are equipped with air conditioning, hot-water showers, toilets, and occasionally with exotica such as electric refrigerators and water coolers.

These factors combine to determine how long a boat is capable of staying away from port. As a general rule, however, the larger the boat the less closely its trips approach the maximum capability. Bay boats usually make trips of 1 to 3 days; small Gulf boats most often make trips of 5 days, but can (and sometimes do) stay out 10 days or longer; large Gulf boats make trips of 10 to 20 days, or more.[5]

Even the smallest of bay boats are technologically capable of working either day or night or both, according to the free choice of the fishermen; but shrimp, though small, are on the whole powerfully capricious creatures, and it is largely *their* "decision" as to when the men can work.

The Gulf Coast shrimp fishery currently depends on three species of shrimp, all bottom feeders, which have relatively distinct habitats and behavior: white shrimp *(Penaeus setiferus)*, brown shrimp *(P. aztecus)*, and pink shrimp or "hoppers" *(P. duorarum).*

White shrimp are found predominantly in inland waters (bays, sounds, and lagoons), often in very shallow water where only the smallest bay boats can safely work. Highly seasonal, they are found in Gulf waters during a small portion of their season only; even then, they are generally not found in quantity much beyond 5 fathoms and are rarely found beyond 10 fathoms. White shrimp feed during daylight hours, and are seldom found at night.

Brown shrimp and hoppers are also found in shallow water, but less reliably than in deeper water; the offshore limit of their range has not been determined by shrimpers. Hoppers tend to be found on hard bottom, whereas brown shrimp tend to be found on muddy bottom; deep-water bottom tends to be muddier. Both species are seasonal, but less so than white shrimp, particularly in deeper water. Brown shrimp and hoppers differ most significantly from white shrimp in that both feed only in the dark. Most inshore bottom is well lit during daylight hours, but in offshore and/or muddy waters, the bottom is dark both day and night. Thus the important difference here is not between brown shrimp and hoppers, but between different areas of their occurrence.

We may distinguish, broadly, between three ecozones which are exploited by the shrimp fishery: (1) a shallow-water zone, beginning at the inland shorelines and extending out to the 5 or 10 fathom line in the Gulf; (2) an inshore zone, beginning where the shallow-water zone ends and extending to a depth of 30 or 40 fathoms, and characterized by bottom shallow and sandy enough to be well lit during daylight; and (3) an offshore zone, beginning where the inshore zone ends and characterized by bottom deep and/or muddy enough to be dark even during daylight.[6] Shrimp follow different feeding patterns in these areas: zone one contains white shrimp feeding during daylight hours, and brown shrimp feeding at night or, if the bottom is sufficiently muddy, also during the day; zone two contains brown shrimp and hoppers, feeding at night only; and zone three contains brown shrimp, and possibly hoppers, feeding around the clock.

These feeding patterns are directly connected with work patterns; trawl nets recover shrimp only when they are on the bottom, feeding.[7] There are four resultant work patterns or patterns of time-use:"working days," "working nights," "working days and nights," and "clocking."

Working days is the pattern followed predominantly by bay boats. When working days, boats either drop anchor or return to port at night; potential dragging hours are from dawn to dusk. Small Gulf boats also on occasion spend several days working exclusively for white shrimp, usually in the fall of the year. They are hesitant to do so, however, because this forces a choice between two counterproductive strategies: either changing over to smaller nets, which lower the catch (Alabama state law forbids a boat in inshore waters to drag nets in excess of 50 feet total width), or running the risk of being caught pulling oversize nets.

Working nights is, in essence, the inshore work pattern for hoppers and brown shrimp. This pattern may be followed in zone one, but is most characteristic of zone two, and is therefore followed predominantly by the smaller Gulf boats. Boats following this work pattern anchor during the day, and the crew sleeps. Dragging begins at dusk and ends at dawn or shortly after. Large Gulf boats may also pursue this work pattern if the comparative catch situation at any given time warrants staying inshore; some habitually work inshore at least part of the year.

Working days and nights is a seasonal pattern, employed during a brief time of the year when white shrimp expand their range slightly, into the Gulf. It consists of working zone two at night for hoppers and brown shrimp, and running inshore to work zone one for white shrimp (preferably in legal areas[8]) during the day. This is again predominantly a small Gulf boat pattern, secondarily followed by large Gulf boats. Boats following this pattern do not anchor, and the captain and one or more crewmen alternate wheel watches while the others sleep in two or three hour stretches. This is a rather exhausting work pattern; not only is the boat constantly active, but relocation efforts are necessary twice during every 24 hours.

Clocking is also a work pattern characterized by working both day and night; it is mostly limited to large Gulf boats working in zone three where the same species of shrimp feed day and night in the same location, although small Gulf boats may venture into the peripheries of this offshore area if weather permits. This work pattern seems to be the ideal one from the standpoint of vessel efficiency, for with it boats are never idle.

As recently as 1968 this was not a usual work pattern, although it was being discussed as a possible benefit of electric rigs (Captiva 1968:141).

Bay boats may also work both day and night in zone one, if there are white shrimp present during the day and brown shrimp at night. This seems roughly equivalent to clocking but bay fishermen consistently refer to it as working days and nights.[9]

TIME USAGE

The four work patterns just discussed are only one aspect of time usage, and they must be put into larger context. We may begin with seasonality.

The bay fishery is most markedly affected by seasonality. White shrimp are the most seasonal species, and although there are legally closed seasons in inland waters the bay fishermen in effect "close" the bay themselves long before the conservation department does so. A majority of the bay fleet ties up for the winter while the fishermen turn to oystering or to some other economic activity; a minority of the boats either migrate to other parts of the coast to continue shrimping or re-rig for trout or mullet fishing.

Most of the smaller Gulf boats migrate to other parts of the Gulf Coast during the winter, as do many of the large Gulf boats. The latter may continue to work their usual areas, due to lesser resource fluctuations in the deeper water, but if they migrate they tend to range farther away from the home port than the smaller boats.

Although winter is, broadly, the off season, there are certain areas of the Gulf Coast which provide higher catch levels than others and some which produce more during the winter than at other times. There are also areas which peak during the spring or fall months. The smaller Gulf boats tend to work out a catch-maximizing migratory cycle within a radius of 150 to 200 miles from their home port; the largest boats may range throughout the Gulf Coast area and even beyond. The complexities of the cycles, which differ from port to port and even from boat to boat, cannot be discussed in detail here. The important facts to note are (1) that shrimpers from any given port are likely to be in year-round contact with shrimpers from other ports; (2) that the relative statuses of indigene and stranger are fluctuating and reversible according to the season; and (3) that the larger the boat the more frequent the contacts with strangers.[10]

The significant time units within the seasonal cycle are, for shrimpers, fishing trips rather than the usual calendrical units. Shrimp fishermen reckon time just as everyone else in the United States does, yet for their work, the standard calendar only provides a set of reference points for significant temporal events rather than a structured unit framework. This may also be noted for the seasonal cycle; it is not, for example, a fixed rule that the good season begins in May or in June, but that the season begins when the shrimp show in quantity.

Trips are repetitive time units, coming one after the other, ideally with only short intervals between each. Trip lengths vary, as noted earlier, according to the boat, but there is, for all shrimpers, a similar conceptual framework of time as being divided into these somewhat irregular and circumstantially defined cycles. Social plans and upcoming events are discussed primarily in terms of trips: "I promised my old lady I'd take her to Apalach to see her Mama after this next trip" or "Well, boys, 'bout three more trips—if we're lucky—an' it'll be Christmas!" For most boats, a trip is considered to be "made" only when a certain predecided catch is attained rather than when a set period of time has elapsed.

I commented that the calendar does not provide a unit framework according to which temporal events are necessarily structured; the context of such subjugation, when it does occur, is one of the more interesting aspects of time usage within the fishery.

If we compare trips with the idea of a work week, we see within the shrimp fishery a range of time usage which goes to extremes on either side of the circumscribed 5-day, 40-hour work week characteristic in America.

Let us consider the bay fishery; the pattern is complicated because many bay fishermen work part time at something other than fishing, sometimes even during the peak season. On the average, bay boats work three or four days per week. It may be only one or two days; for full-time shrimpers, it may be five. Weekly time expenditures of the boats range from 12 to 60 hours, or if a boat is working days and nights, up to 100 hours or more. Even so, the average bay fisherman spends less than 40 hours per week away from the dock. Furthermore, these hours are chosen at the discretion of the fishermen, and the three or five-day week may (or may not) consist of three or five one-day trips. There are days during any week when a man does not go out, and a strenuous week may be counterbalanced by a week at the dock. It is essentially the fisherman's choice whether he takes off the middle of the week or the weekend or scattered days here and there, and under many circumstances a bay fisherman may come home to his family every night if he so chooses.

In contrast with the bay fishery, the large Gulf boat fleet makes trips well over a week long. Ranging up to 20 or 25 days in duration, the trips swallow weeks; and there is little tendency whatsoever to distinguish between Sundays and Wednesdays except that the termination of a trip should occur on a weekday so the catch can be promptly unloaded (fish-houses are uniformly closed on Sunday and sometimes on Saturday after-noon). Statistically, there is a slight tendency for large boats to come in toward the latter part of a week and, after taking two to five days off, to go back out during the first half of the next week. Often enough, how-ever, these boats are in on Tuesday and back out by Friday.

In between the bayfishery and the large Gulf boats are the small Gulf boats. Although the most efficient usage of these would seem to dictate a trip between 8 and 12 days long, the majority of boats in this fleet seg-ment (62.5%) were never observed to make trips in excess of 5 nights. These boats leave the dock on Monday or Tuesday and return on Friday or Saturday. Other boats in this fleet segment, however, make trips up to 14 days in duration.

It is not only that larger boats make longer trips; they do not balance this out with proportionally longer stays on shore, and they spend more total time at sea. Over a three-month period during the summer of 1972, the bay fleet was at the dock 63.3 percent of the time, whereas small Gulf boats spent 58.9 percent of their time at sea and large Gulf boats were at sea 69 percent of the time.

Only one time unit within the trip cycle has genuine significance under all work patterns utilized by the shrimping fleet. This unit is the "drag," the length of time between setting the nets out and picking them up. A drag lasts, on the average, three to five hours, but this varies considera-bly depending on circumstances.[11] A boat must remain in constant mo-tion during a drag, and should be steadily searching for, or maintaining its location in relation to, shrimp. We have discussed the various work patterns, which are in essence different ecologically-based ways of or-ganizing drags within a larger spatiotemporal context.

If a boat is working days or working nights or even (considering the intervening relocation) working days and nights, drags are subsumed un-der the day-night dichotomy. When a boat is clocking, however, this dis-tinction becomes of minimal important to the organization of activities on board the vessel. It is literally true, as a crewman on a large boat com-mented, that "There ain't no day and night out here." Temporal orienta-tion is quickly lost, so that one wakes up expecting to see the sun and sees the moon instead; to place an event in temporal context one will say, for example, "I had this dream last drag. . . ."

The temporal organization of activities within the drag need not con-cern us here. There are variations to be observed but these are in large part idosyncratic and circumstantial rather than directly attributable to technological, environmental, or broad sociocultural factors.

We have seen that overall time investment, that is, time spent at sea, steadily increases with larger boats; the same is true of total time spent dragging. Different trends emerge, however, if we examine activities only in regard to time spent at sea. Large Gulf boats still invest more time dragging and more man-hours of task performance per trip than either Gulf boats or bay boats, but bay boats rank second, above small Gulf boats. Bay boats have the option of one-day trips, sometimes working both day and night, and their drags are more frequent and require proportionally more processing time than those of Gulf boats, whereas small Gulf boats are committed to longer trips during which they generally work only at night.

Time-use patterns vary, not only according to the size of the boat, but also according to the season. We have already noted that time investment generally decreases during the off season for the bay fleet. For boats which migrate, however, the qualitative aspects of time-use modification seem possibly more important than the quantitative aspects. The seasonal shift in time investment patterns depends directly on techno-environmental factors, but whether the shift represents an increase or a decrease in work time depends, quite simply, on how we define work time. If we define it as time spent away from the home port, work time investment increases significantly. Some boats may be away from the home port 100 percent of the time for two or three months in a stretch. A great deal of this time, however, is spent (due to bad weather and poor catches) at anchor or tied up to the dock in some "strange port," with the result that much less time is invested in dragging than during the good season (10–20%, rather than 30–50%). The crew can take a bus or hitchhike or drive back home occasionally, but they may spend less than 15 percent of their time there. During how much of this time is the crew working? Is it 10 percent, or 85 percent, or some compromise figure in between?

This is only one of the many aspects of time-use which might be noted to demonstrate that inadequacy of the work-leisure dichotomy. One man told me that you are "working" *only* when you are "catching shrimp." It is irrelevant whether you are home with your wife, or dragging where there are not shrimp; if you are not *catching* shrimp you are not working. But leisure cannot be the inverse of work thusly defined! It may be that, from a personal vantage point, leisure is a sense of temporary release from productive responsibility; it may be that leisure can come only when one has produced "enough" for the moment. In this view, it is the off season which provides the least respite, and it may be, then, that leisure is not nearly so much a matter of time per se as we generally assume.

Thus our primary concern here is with the general ramifications of time-use patterns, not merely their effect on nonwork activities.

SOCIOCULTURAL RAMIFICATIONS OF TIME USAGE

Time-use patterns have two different effects on community social organization. There is a progressive disinvolvement in the community as
new time-use patterns are generated by increased levels of technology,
and there is also a progressive development of occupational closure within and beyond the community. "Community disinvolvement" is intended
to imply two different processes: the lessening of participation in the institutions and activities of the spatially defined land-based community,
and the weakening of social ties with certain individuals in that community.

"Occupational closure" refers to a refocusing of social relationships
into a milieu centering around the occupational group itself, whether this
is seen as a local fleet segment, the Gulf Coast shrimping fleet, or the
fishing profession as a whole. Occupational closure has an effect of di-
verting individual social relationships away from the local community as
it is spatially defined and toward a wider activity-defined social network.
At the same time, occupational closure contributes to maintenance of the
identity of the spatially-defined community versus nearby nonmaritime
communities. In effect it is not so much that the community is being
weakened by development of the fishery, though the process of community disinvolvement might seem to have such implications, as that its base
of definition is shifting.

It should already be apparent how the trip cycle for the different
groups of boats might coincide with the social cycles of church services
and other community activities on shore. Bay shrimpers have relative
freedom to structure their working hours around whatever community
social activities or personal matters they are interested in: Wednesday
night prayer meetings, Thursday night seafood dinners at the church, or
dove hunting on opening day of the season. Gulf shrimpers, in contrast,
must limit their degree of community involvement. Men operating or
working on board a smaller Gulf boat may still, if the boat is operated at
slightly less than maximum efficiency, be able to attend Sunday church
services regularly, but in order to approach efficient use of a large Gulf
boat a man must be willing to sacrifice church attendance at least half of
the time and possibly more.[12] Likewise, the extended absence of Gulf
shrimpers from shore effectively curtails their participation in fraternal
organizations and certain other community social groups.

Another effect of the trip cycle is that of limiting potential friendships.
There are numbers of men in the local area with whom shrimpers could
establish friendships, were it not for the conflict between time schedules.
Men who work at jobs on shore with regular hours socialize on weekends,

not during the week; shrimpers, on the other hand socialize irregularly according to when they are on shore. Such conflicts are minimal for bay fishermen and men who run boats on a five-day trip basis; but men on larger boats cannot count on being on shore at all during many weekends and frequently find themselves on shore during the middle of the week, when they are limited to interaction with others who are in at the same time. Personal styles of interaction are obviously important, since brief visiting or a quick game of pool with a non-shrimper might be possible almost any night of the week, but longer visits or all-night drinking and guitar-playing sessions—in other words, all of the more intensive and/or time-consuming interactions which many shrimpers seem to prefer—are largely out of the question.

Thus close friendships beyond the occupational group are, theoretically, much more possible for bay shrimpers than for large-boat Gulf shrimpers. As the large Gulf boat fleet segment of the community is expanded, the time pattern impingement represents a progressive disinvolvement of shrimpers from the totality of potential social ties with non-shrimpers in the community; this is also a matter of occupational closure on the local level.

Another matter of no small importance is the amount of time men working on the various categories of boats have available for being with their wives and children. Obviously, men who spend 60 percent of their time on shore have more opportunity to involve themselves in the community than men who spend only 30 percent of their time on shore; they also have more time to participate in raising their children and in day-by-day household decisions. (The impact of fishery development on women's roles is thus significant, although this cannot be discussed here.)

The progressive disinvolvement with the community which a man experiences, varying according to the degree of technological development of the fleet segment with which he works, results from interactions at sea and time patterns within the trip as well as from trip cycles and overall time spent on shore. Particularly for men who spend 60 percent or more of their time at sea, these interactions are of considerable importance in establishing and maintaining primary relationships. Interactions at sea, external to those on board the vessel, are of two main types: indirect interaction via the two-way radios, and direct interaction by tying up together and visiting while not dragging.

Direct, face-to-face interactions among shrimpers at sea are highly affected by time-use patterns. Boats working nights frequently tie up with other boats during the day; meals may be shared, the crewmen of the two (sometimes three) boats visit and socialize, and the captains either relax and do the same or confer about rig problems, catch strategies, and the like. Some of the small Gulf boats tie up with one boat or another more often than they drop anchor alone; others do so infrequently, but the option is always open for boats working inshore. The same interaction pattern is open to bay boats working days; they may tie up together at night if they don't return to the dock.

The opposite situation prevails for clocking boats. If there is some pressing need, two such boats may agree to pick up their nets simultaneously and tie up, briefly, to confer about something which the captains are hesitant to broadcast, or to exchange needed supplies, but extended relaxed visits are out of the question when there are shrimp to be caught. The large Gulf boats, except those few that work inshore, are found tying up in the manner described above only when rough weather prevents dragging.

By considering both the possibility of face-to-face interactions at sea and the relative frequency and overlapping of time on shore for small boats versus large boats, we see that the small-boat work pattern allows face-to-face contact between numbers of friends and acquaintances with relative frequency, even at sea, whereas the large-boat work pattern is an obstacle to the maintenance of close friendships with anyone not on the boat, even on shore. One response to this, on the part of crewmen, is frequent changing of jobs—working on different boats in rapid succession—explicitly for the purpose of being with different "old buddies" at least once in a while. To the extent, however, that men do value their jobs and are hesitant to move from boat to boat simply in hopes of being with their friends, the large-boat work pattern eventually contributes to a lessening of intensity of friendships other than those between crew members on the same boat, and tends to increase the perception of friendship as a largely sporadic thing.

Another comparison between large and small Gulf boats is the degree of stratification within the crews. The heavier technology of large Gulf boats acts in itself to enforce a more strict division of labor among crew members; work patterns combine with this to produce considerable social distance between captains and crewmen of large Gulf boats, while minimizing the social distance or displacing it to a familial basis between captains and crewmen of small Gulf boats.[13] Differential age composition of crews, however, tends to partially counteract this trend; the larger boats generally have younger captains and less age spread within the crew.

When a boat is clocking the entire crew can get together only for peripheral social interactions or brief work conferences; even meals cannot be eaten together, since someone must stay at the wheel. Furthermore, the captain, regardless of how casual and friendly his behavior, is always preeminently the captain and must always be ready to give orders. But when a boat is dragging only at night, the anchor is dropped during the day and everyone can relax. The entire crew eats breakfast together; then sits and talks, or watches television, or plays guitars and sings together; and after a good day's sleep, sits together over coffee and talks before starting to work. Even when a boat is at rest, the captain remains captain, yet all of the men are capable of interacting—at least part of the time—simply as individuals rather than according to their work statuses.

Crewmen on either sort of boat interact freely with each other, even while working on the stern processing the catch, but small boats put the captain-crewman relationship on a more personal basis much more often than large boats. Thus the large boats can potentially reduce the relationship to that of employer (or 'foreman') and employee.

We may argue that an individual's perception of his degree of integration into the community structure depends, at least in part, on the extent and intensity of his relationships. Thus, the trend toward fewer face-to-face contacts (and concurrently decreasing numbers of friends and/or lessening intensity of friendships), and toward more impersonal relationships between captains and crewmen contributes to shifting foci of social identification. Certain channels of social interaction are being progressively closed; yet at the same time others are replacing them.

Indirect interactions at sea are a vital part of the social situation, compensating for the partial inability to participate in face-to-face interaction beyond the boat. The two-way radio allows men who work close inshore in the Gulf to talk with men working the bay or with men working offshore. Communications between the ecozones discussed earlier are minimal, since little direct benefit is derived from comparing information, yet the maintenance of contacts allows the relaying of messages from wives on shore with transceiver sets to boats far offshore via intermediately located boats.

Practically all communication among smaller boats is by means of open-channel citizen's band (CB) radios; crews of larger boats tend to increasingly depend on closed-channel VHF sets, but even they listen to and talk over the CB radios. Much information is shared, especially overheard information about the location or catch of other boats. This is particularly true if the information has been tentatively discarded as a basis for action. Other information is hoarded, being transmitted by pre-arranged codes over the CB among smaller boats or by closed-channel communication among larger boats. Small boats tend to be a bit more open with information transmitted in their radio conversations; but while they worry little about who hears what they say, many are highly sensitive about being talked to directly by a stranger. Large boats, in contrast, are closed-mouthed with information broadcast over the CB, yet are generally willing to talk to anyone around. Also, the CB tends to be regarded by small-boat men as an instrument of work and little else, whereas men on larger boats frequently use the CB during their wheel watches for carrying on extended social conversations with friends or acquaintances.

All of this may simply reflect the lost opportunity for face-to-face contact among individuals working on the large Gulf boats. It is important that with clocking indirect communication among vessels becomes feasible at all times, in replacement of the partial opportunity for direct communication among vessels following other work patterns. At any rate, regardless of the fleet segment, sharing of information is rarely so open as in the inshore Newfoundland fishery described by Stiles (1972), and secrecy and deception are seldom so pronounced as in the trawler fishery described by Andersen (1972). The important observation here seems to be that the indirect communication system allows the maintenance of social spheres at sea which are, to an extent, independent of and distinct from those of the land-based community.

I noted earlier that there is, logically, less opportunity for establishing friendships beyond the occupational group among men working on the larger boats, yet this progression is not as observable as might be expected. Generally, fishermen are friends with other fishermen, regardless of their opportunities for establishing friendships outside their occupational group. This relates to the matter of shared values and interests within the occupational group; even if one man runs a large Gulf boat and another runs a bay boat the two have certain interests in common which neither shares with a local farmer, even though the farmer's time schedule might match and be as open as theirs.

It is furthermore an observable fact that most close friendships are among men running boats of the same category. This involves both time-use patterns and common values and interests. It also involves age groups; as a general rule, young men become captains of the most advanced vessels of their time and, upon attaining ownership of a boat, men tend to grow old along with her. There are relatively few close friendships between Gulf shrimpers and bay fishermen, unless they have land-based links such as kin or common church membership. Friendships between captains of large and small Gulf boats are largely limited to men whose boats overlap areas of exploitation with relative frequency. Bay shrimpers are likely to include oystermen, crabbers, and mullet fishermen among their friends—who work in the same general area they do and who have similarly flexible time schedules.

This is a highly interesting trend in development of the extra-community social network. Remembering the regular seasonal migrations of shrimp fishermen, we find that friendships are established outside the community, based on the segmentation of the fleet along the technoenvironmental lines discussed earlier. Although any fisherman is likely to have friends in the local community who work boats in another segment of the fleet, he is likely to have as many or more friends and acquaintances (even though he may see them only during certain times of the year) in parallel fleet segments of other communities within his seasonal migratory range.

This has important implications regarding the effects of technology, environment, and time-use patterns on social contacts, and establishment of relationships between local communities; furthermore, it may help provide us with a different and more dynamic means of viewing communities themselves, and inter-community relationships within a regional context. An important note is that, given the relatively restricted migratory range of bay fishermen, their ties are less extensive in distance from the home port than is the case with Gulf fishermen. Men working the largest Gulf boats, however, are likely to establish friendships across a very wide range.[14]

It is in considering this latter development that I would argue for the creative dimension of time-use patterns. Rather than simply restricting potential social relationships, the temporal and spatial organization of the fishery has brought its participants into contact with individuals outside the local community and has allowed the progressive development of new and different fabrics of relationships. The same might be argued on an internal fleet level: the clocking work pattern, which has restricting effects on close personal interactions between captains and crewmen, seems thereby to be contributing to a lessening of the insularity of specific boat crews and to an increasing sense of stratified identity.

Thus far we have been discussing processes which are at least in part the result of environmentally regulated time-use patterns. A more complete understanding of these processes also requires brief mention of the rapid growth situation which characterized the fishery in 1971–73; nearly all of this was within the large Gulf boat fleet segment.[15] The growth of the fishery required an increasing recruitment of labor from outside the local community; likewise, with the increased capital investment required for large boats, outside ownership of boats has increased. In general, the effects of all this parallel those of the time-use patterns discussed here. Both the expansion of the fishery and the changing time-use patterns resulting from the technology and from characteristics of the new ecozones being exploited are contributing to a shifting focus of social interaction. The men who work on the boats are increasingly less able to identify themselves solely within the social fabric of the spatially defined community, which is based on church, family, and friendship; they must increasingly identify themselves with a wider group of people who have different sorts of interests, less personal and more economically oriented, in common with them. Men who work bay boats and small Gulf boats still tend to eulogize shrimping as a "way of life" rather than a mere job; even when they hate it, they love it. "It gets in your blood," they say. But men who were "raised" on the smaller boats and now work on larger boats tend to praise only their increased income. Many of them complain about the long trips—"It's like being in jail;" and also about the work pattern—"It's all work and no play. I feel like an old man at the end of every trip."

The changes resulting from rapid growth of the fishery are not being smoothly accepted. One major form of resistance to technological change, that of the underutilization of boats, has been discussed here. There are important aspects of underutilization, notably those relating to labor recruitment (e.g., the "kind of people" perceived to be willing to make 40-day trips) and to feedback effects on fishery resources, which cannot be discussed here.

SUMMARY AND CONCLUSION

The commercial shrimp fishery began its development with the introduction of the trawl net, which allowed movement into a new econiche (the open bay) where shrimp were more dependably available than was previously the case with shoreline seining. Subsequent technological developments allowed progressive expansion into new econiches in the Gulf, further and further offshore. The furthest areas were generally preferred insofar as it was perceived that there would be more shrimp where they had been worked over least.

Overall time investment increased in response to the increased monetary investment required for larger boats and the somewhat decreased short-term efficiency of the more advanced technology; one aspect of this is the increased travel time involved in reaching the production areas, and another is the expensive instrumentation which pays for itself only if the boat works under conditions and circumstances which prevent work without such technology.

Certain expansions of the fishery brought dependence upon either a different species of shrimp or the same species behaving in a different manner insofar as time was concerned. This modified the work patterns on board the boats which by reason of technological fitness worked predominantly in a given ecozone.

It is largely the technological level of a boat or fleet segment which regulates its total time investment, that is, time spent at sea; this is the aspect of time use which has the greatest direct influence on community social organization, leading to progressive disinvolvement of individuals with community social activities. A combination of technology and ecological strictures emanating from the behavior of the prey directly affects dragging time within the trip. This aspect of time use has marked effects on the social organization of boat crews, but it also has a feedback effect on community life insofar as the dragging time patterns of both bay boats and small Gulf boats allow relatively intense personal interactions among a wide range of individuals from the local community, whereas the dragging time patterns of large Gulf boats hinder such interactions. Furthermore, patterns of dragging time relate to segmental closures within the occupational group, both locally and in the inter-community social network.

A point of general theoretical concern is that "disinvolvement" and "closure" are not linear processes except with regard to specific and static contexts. A dynamic view shows that in most instances diminishment of one set of relationships merely leads to the elaboration of another set. Restricting land-based relationships leads to development of sea-based relationships; diminishing the closeness of ties within a crew leads to a refocusing of relationships between men belonging to different crews; and reduced opportunities for interactions between fleet segments from the same community leads to increased interactions between boats in parallel fleet segments from other communities. Thus disinvolvement in one context is a step toward reinvolvement in another, and closure from one point of view constitutes the opening of relationships from another. Qualitative aspects, of course, may differ.

There are also reactions from the diminished sectors; for instance, wives of fishermen intensify their relationships with each other when the men are at sea. Another example is that of a local church which responded to the seasonal absence of some of its members by establishing a close relationship with a church in the major off-season port. Also, the expanded network of relationships serves as an arena for labor recruitment, and it brings outside boats to local fishhouses when they are working in the area. Occupational relationships also lead to other sorts of social relationships; marriages are common between shrimp fishermen and women whom they have met in other ports, either through fellow fishermen, or by participation in the local community institutions of those ports.

Thus there is no simple indication that the community is being weakened by its rapid growth. Community institutions are changing, and many men are becoming increasingly less involved in land-based community activities, but there may be compensation in the resources which, at the same time, are being brought into the community from outside. Of course, whether fishery growth is bringing the sort of changes that community members want is an entirely different question. One also could ask whether the sort of growth to which the fishery is committing itself is to its own long-range advantage.

NOTES

[1]Historically a rather isolated riverine settlement, it is not in itself a "community" by Arensberg's (1955) definition. I use the term "community" a bit loosely here, following local usage but also Martindale's (1960) definition which sees the spatial dimension as a secondary consideration to that of systemic social integration (cf., Salaman 1971b:390). The latter implies to me that the concept of "community" may be applied at various levels of analysis.

[2]Shrimping was done to a limited extent during the nineteenth century using seine nets. The present-day fishery is based on use of the otter-trawl net, which must be pulled from a constantly moving boat. This net was introduced to the Florida east coast around 1913 (Idyll 1957:702, Owen 1973:18A) and reached the Alabama community discussed here in 1918. The shrimp fishery in Mississippi was prohibited by law from employing engines until the early 1930s (Ramos 1973), but I have been assured that it is impossible for a sailboat to make way against a headwind when pulling a trawl net, and apparently this law was not enforced. At any rate, the local shrimp fishery was developed exclusively with engine-powered boats.

[3]The distinction more commonly made by Alabama shrimp fishermen is between wood boats and steel-hull boats ("slabs"); this correlates in large part with the size distinction, but I find size itself to be the more sensitive indicator of spatiotemporal behavior.

[4]Only one year later, new and bigger boats were venturing out into depths approaching 200 fathoms, but the present discussion is confined to work patterns observed in 1971–73.

[5]The fact that even the largest boats in the fleet seldom make trips in excess of 25 days is a matter of sociocultural "obstinacy" rather than a technological limitation; some of them are in fact capable of 40-day trips.

[6]The depths listed here for the transition from zone two to zone three are general guidelines for the area between the Mississippi River and Mobile Bay. The boundary, in no sense fixed, is a function of both water depth and suspended sediment; on a cloudy day zone three begins closer inshore than on a sunny day and near the Mississippi River passes zone three may begin very close inshore and will vary according to seasonal fluctuations in the river's flow rate.

[7]The new "electric rigs" which use an electrical charge to coax shrimp up out of the mud, where they burrow when not feeding, may completely change the patterns of time use discussed here if they ever become widely accepted. Thus far, however, most shrimpers feel that these rigs are far too expensive.

[8]It was never clear to me whether the gear restrictions which applied to bays and lagoons also applied to Gulf waters within the three-mile state jurisdiction. The clearest answer to my questions was "Maybe—I don't know. But there ain't no enforcement in the Gulf, and that's what counts."

[9]Whether this usage reflects the different species being exploited, or relocations which may be necessary within the zone, or both, is unclear. It may simply be historical, with "clocking" being an innovative term which originated within the large Gulf boat fleet segment.

[10]Even in the home territory the deep water areas have a greater constant mix of boats from various ports.

[11]At the extremes, a drag will last as little as 1 hour (this is frequent with bay boats) or as much as 12. The primary determinant of this is the amount of fish and "trash" and the rate at which these are being taken into the nets. This is gauged by means of a small "try net" which is brought in at frequent intervals.

[12]A number of men have attempted running large Gulf boats according to the five-day trip cycle. As hired captains, they are almost inevitably fired for this. In November 1974, I learned that one of these men had acquired half-ownership in an 85 foot boat with which he makes five-day trips. As one of the most capable captains in the fleet, he *may* be able to meet his expenses in this manner, but there is much local opinion to the contrary. His own father is an outspoken critic of his insistence on attending church.

[13]The average Gulf boat crew consists of two or three men, captain included. Sometimes, depending on the size of the boat and the season, there is a third or fourth hand—the "fish-boy"—who is relatively unskilled. Bay boats have slightly smaller crews, sometimes being run single-handed and having at most three persons on board. Kinship ties predominate among bay boat crews, and are still prominent (though increasingly less so, the larger the boat) among the crews of Gulf boats.

[14]Given the infrequency of contacts, such friendships are likely to be instrumental rather than close; yet this merely parallels the progressive weakening of friendship ties discussed earlier.

[15]The local shrimping fleet increased from 65 boats employing less than 175 men in 1971 to 79 boats employing over 220 men in 1973. In 1971 the fleet was composed of 28 bay boats, 21 small Gulf boats, and 16 large Gulf boats; in 1973 there were 29 bay boats, 21 small Gulf boats, and 29 large Gulf boats. In a two-year span, the total fleet had increased by 21.5 percent, and large Gulf boats accounted for 93 percent of the total increase. When I left the field in 1973, 36 new boats (all large Gulf boats) were due to arrive by the summer of 1975. This would have been a four-year fleet increase of 76.9 percent; I was unable to obtain precise figures on my last visit to the community in May, 1975, but due to the general condition of the United States economy, the projected growth rate had clearly not been attained.

LITERATURE CITED

Andersen, Raoul
    1972   Hunt and Deceive: Information Management in Newfoundland Deep-Sea Trawler Fishing. *In* North Atlantic Fishermen: Anthropological Essays on Modern Fishing. R. Andersen and C. Wadel, eds. Pp. 120–40. Newfoundland Social and Economic Papers, No. 5. Institute of Social and Economic Research, Memorial University of Newfoundland. Toronto: University of Toronto Press.

Arensberg, Conrad M.
    1955   American Communities. American Anthropologist 57:1143–62.

Captiva, Francis J.
    1968   Modern U.S. Shrimp Vessels Design, Construction, Current Trends
            and Future Development. *In* The Future of the Fishing Industry of
            the United States DeWitt Gilbert, ed. Pp. 141–44. University of
            Washington Publications in Fisheries, New Series, Vol. 4.

Idyll, Clarence P.
    1957   Shrimpers Strike Gold in the Gulf. National Geographic 111
            (May):698–707.

Martindale, Don
    1960   American Social Structure. N.Y.: Appleton-Century-Crofts.

Mills, C. Wright
    1956   White Collar: The American Middle Classes. N.Y.: Galaxy.

Owen, Lyman
    1973   Veteran Fisherman, Gear Expert Honored by Giving Fish His Name.
            National Fisherman 54(7):18–19A.

Ramos, Ralph
    1973   The Last Great Schooner Fleet. National Fisherman: Yearbook Is-
            sue 1973. 54(13):78–79.

Salaman, Graeme
    1971a. Some Sociological Determinants of Occupational Communities. So-
            ciological Review 19(1):53–77.
    1971b. Two Occupational Communities: Examples of a Remarkable Conver-
            gence of Work and Non-Work. Sociological Review 19(3):389–407.

Stiles, R. Geoffrey
    1972   Fishermen, Wives and Radios: Aspects of Communication in a New-
            foundland Fishing Community. *In* North Atlantic Fishermen: An-
            thropological Essays on Modern Fishing. R. Andersen and C. Wadel,
            eds. Pp. 35–60. Newfoundland Social and Economic Papers No. 5. In-
            stitute of Social and Economic Research. Memorial University of
            Newfoundland. Toronto: University of Toronto Press.

12

Fisheries as Subsistence Resources: Growth and Decline of the Columbia River Salmon Fishery*

COURTLAND L. SMITH

Oregon State University

The last 10,000 years of human history has been a period of increasingly rapid growth, supported by the domestication of plants and animals. This period is also marked by increased energy capture, greater dependence on foodstuffs produced by industrialized agriculture, and formation of more complex social organizations.

This view, however, is deceptive of the process of human history. It masks the declines which too have characterized this period. Population declines have occurred, caused by: The great plagues in Europe during the fourteenth century; the impact of European-bred diseases, violence, and vice on native American populations; the playing out of resources in mining, fishing, and forestry; the failure of domesticated crops; and social action, or inaction, which has resulted in wide disparities in the distribution of resources.

*The research upon which this paper is based was funded, in part, by the Oregon State University Sea Grant College Program, supported by NOAA Office of Sea Grant, U.S. Department of Commerce under grant # 04-5-158-2. Dean Yates contributed some of the background data on the Columbia River salmon fishery.

Decline, too, has occurred in the United States fisheries position and the place of fish in U.S. subsistence patterns. In 1953 the United States ranked second to Japan and produced 10 percent of the fish caught. By 1971 the United States ranked sixth and produced only 4 percent of the world fish catch (United Nations 1973:150–151). The United States salmon pack between 1963 and 1972 was one-third the pack of a comparable 10-year period 30 years ago. The salmon harvest on the Columbia River in 1971 and 1972 was only 15 percent of the harvest in 1883 or 1884 (National Fisherman 1973, Pacific Fisherman 1950).

Tangible evidence for the decline of the Columbia River salmon fishery are the towns of Clifton, Brookfield, Bay View, Waterford, and Eagle Cliff. Once sustained by local salmon fisheries, they became ghost towns. Several writers have attempted to explain the decline in the Columbia River salmon fishery as an important subsistence resource (Bullard 1968, Lowell 1972, and Netboy 1958). There have also been numerous efforts to reverse the decline by developing fish hatcheries, by improving spawning habitats, by innovations in fishing gear and methods, and by increasing the social acceptance of the fishery.

However, is the decline in importance of the Columbia River salmon fishery as a subsistence resource due to the reasons commonly advanced: barrier dams, unscreened irrigation diversions, power generators, mining and pollution barriers, insufficient water flows, lethal temperatures, loss of natural foods, nitrogen poisoning, and overfishing? Review of the history of the Columbia River from the early 1800s to the 1970s[1] suggests that three processes failed to operate to continue the salmon fishery as an important subsistence resource. These processes are domestication, increased efficiency of production, and maintenance of a viable base of political power. While the case evaluated for these processes is the Columbia River salmon fishery, domestication, efficiency, and political power also provide insight into understanding the processes of growth and decline in other fisheries.

GROWTH TO DECLINE

How do societies grow so that energy capture, social complexity, and standard of living increase? Simply stated the economic growth of a society is one of increasing energy capture (Kemp 1971, Rappaport 1971, White 1959:40–56) which can occur in one of a combination of three ways:

1. Take resources from the environment.

2. Become more efficient in using resources.
3. Take resources from other people.

Fishing by its very nature is a process of taking from the environment. The concepts of overfishing and underfishing recognize this fact. Overfishing is a situation in which the harvesters take in excess of the requirements for maintaining the biomass, and the biomass of the resource declines. Underfishing is a situation in which the harvesters allow a portion of the mature population to die from "natural" causes. The balance between these two situations is *sustained yield,* which is the point of maximum harvest for human use without reduction to the biomass of fish available for harvest.

Sustained yield, a concept for balancing the capacity of the resource to maintain itself and at the same time provide for maximum human exploitation, does not have a very good record in protecting fish resources important to human populations. While this may be because fisheries management is inherently a political issue (Cooley 1963), a second problem with the sustained yield concept is that the amount of harvest which a fish population can sustain varies in accordance with other social needs for resource use. Estimates of the native American harvest of Columbia River salmon prior to Anglo contact indicate that the sustained yield was 18,000,000 pounds per year (Hewes 1947). Demands on the river and the watershed to serve other social needs such as hydroelectric power development, water diversions for irrigation, dilution of pollution, production of wood products, and overfishing have all contributed to alter the sustained yield (Fish Commission of Oregon and Washington Department of Fisheries 1972, and Richards 1968:251).[2]

The need for a fishery's management frequently goes unrecognized as the growth of a fishery continues with the opening of new areas and the harvest of new varieties. This process, called *resource substitution,* continues the taking from the environment while covering over the alterations which are occurring in the ability of the resource to sustain continued yields (Craig and Hacker 1940:196–197, Russell 1942:20–21, and Thompson 1950).

In the fisheries of the Pacific Coast, the process of resource substitution has made possible the continued harvest and packing of salmon. Resource substitution has occurred in both area and variety. The Columbia River spring chinook was thought by early salmon canners to be the best variety for packing; twenty years after the initial exploitation of the spring chinook in 1866 for canning, it was overexploited and the run size decreased. In order to maintain the salmon pack, other varieties of Columbia River salmon, including chum, coho, fall chinook, sockeye, and steelhead [3] were harvested and packed. The fall chinook season has been the dominant season since World War II. Yet in the opinion of early salmon packers the fall chinook was of little value, and this run was not fished commercially until the 1890's.

The salmon fishery on the Columbia River was started as a result of the process of resource substitution. Salmon canning was first tried in 1864 on the Sacramento River. Due to human alterations of the Sacramento River environment (principally hydraulic mining) which reduced the salmon runs, the first salmon canners, Hapgood, Hume and Company in 1866 opened a cannery on the Columbia River at Eagle Cliff, Washington Territory.

Production of canned salmon continued. The growth of the salmon pack was not due to domestication or improving efficiency, but from exploiting new areas and varieties. By taking from the environment the salmon pack was increased. Fisheries were begun in Puget Sound (1877), Oregon coastal streams (1877), British Columbia streams (1878), southeastern Alaska (1878), central Alaska (1882), western Alaska (1884), and northern Washington coast (1896).

In 1883 and 1884 over 80 percent of the United States Pacific Coast production of 790,000 and 750,000 cases of salmon came from the Columbia River. By 1936, 94 percent of the nearly 9,000,000 cases were packed in Alaska (Pacific Fisherman 1950). By that time most of the varieties of salmon and areas where they were available were fully fished or overexploited. Subsequently the pack decreased and more and more of the annual harvest was prepared fresh or in smaller cans for a luxury rather than a subsistence market.

Obviously, human existence depends on the exploitation of natural resources. We can always be expected to take from the environment. Sustained yield as a management concept, however, is too narrow and does not recognize relations between ecological processes and with other social needs. What are the characteristics, then, of the resources which become important in the subsistence patterns of an industrialized society? Three processes operate where natural resources become important for subsistence. These processes are domesticating, improving efficiency of production, and maintaining sufficient political power to assure decisions favorable to continued use as subsistence resource.

DOMESTICATION

Two major approaches are used to harvest fish resources. Commercial fishing is a hunting and gathering or capture technique employed in a marine environment. The commercial fishermen of the world in 1970 harvested most of the 69.6 million metric tons of fish (United Nations

1973:150) by searching out fish populations and harvesting them with nets, longlines, harpoons, traps, trolling, and so on. These techniques are essentially hunting and gathering techniques, and no attempt was made to control the reproduction of fish populations.

Roughly four percent of the 1970 fish and shellfish harvest was obtained by mariculture or aquaculture, a culture technique (Hickling 1968:7). Mariculture as a means of harvesting fish resources is a technique which employs the process of domestication. Domestication is a process whereby man exerts control on the reproduction process.

Zeuner (1963:57–59) suggests that the process of domestication consists of five stages. The initial stage is when the animal species has "loose ties with the social medium of man" and interbreeding with wild forms is still common. The second stage is one of "subjugating large numbers of the species and of making these individuals wholly dependent on the social medium of man." The outcome is a stock with distinct characters of domestication, such as different color, and change in body size or appearance. The third stage is the "intentional development of certain characters in the stock." During the fourth stage the domesticated stock becomes standardized and is different from the wild species and interbreeding with the wild species is highly undesirable. Finally, in the fifth stage, when the domesticated stocks "supply all the economic need the species in question could satisfy, except purely for sport, the wild relations were no longer wanted even for hunting."

With varying degrees of success humans have been practicing domestication since at least 8,000 to 10,000 B.C. Early experience was with land plants and animals, such as wheat, barley, corn, beans, squash, rice, sheep, goats, cattle, pigs, and chickens. Efforts to domesticate fish and shellfish resources have a much shorter history, only from about 1,000 to 2,000 B.C. (Hickling 1962, Iverson 1968, and Lin 1940).

By understanding the breeding process of salmon, improvement can be made on the reproductive efficiency of nature. Where salmon are allowed to spawn naturally and are in equilibrium with their habitat, only 2 or 3 of the 10,000 eggs released by the female and fertilized by the male live to breed again. Salmon hatcheries can improve on this rate of reproduction. However, most books on mariculture, aquaculture, and fish farming ignore or make only passing reference to the salmon propagation programs. This is because salmon hatcheries are, at best, at the initial stage in the domestication process.

Efforts to domesticate the Pacific salmon extend back to 1872 when the U.S. Fish Commission, created upon the recommendation of the American Fish Culturalist's Association, established the first salmon hatchery on the McCloud River in California. A hatchery was opened on the Columbia River system in 1874. The most successful early salmon hatchery was that of pygmy monopolist R. D. Hume (1961, Dodds 1959) who owned the fishery on the Rogue River in Oregon, and for over 20 years beginning in 1877 conducted his experiments in domestication of salmon. Hume, however, had difficulty convincing fisheries managers of the potential of artificial propagation of salmon. Finally, he convinced the U.S. Fish Commission and later the State of Oregon. In the 1890s the federal government and the states of Washington and Oregon began in earnest a program of salmon propagation on the Columbia River.

In spite of this early interest, beginning a century ago, the domestication of Pacific salmon remains at the initial level of Zeuner's stages of domestication. In fact, hatcheries have been conceived more in compensation for losses due to dam construction and other habitat losses, than as a mechanism of selecting for desirable attributes and significantly increasing the biomass of the resource to meet subsistence needs (Columbia Basin Interagency Committee 1957).

The last 10,000 years of the domestication of land plants and animals verifies the importance of domestication as a necessary process for establishing subsistence resources for complex societies. Domestication, however, is only one of the necessary processes.

EFFICIENCY

A second necessary condition for a resource to become important in a complex society's subsistence pattern is potential for better harvest efficiency. Improving efficiency is a process by which greater output is achieved per unit of effort.

Both domestication and improving efficiency lead to higher levels of energy capture for human societies. The additional energy capture can be used to sustain larger populations. The estimated world population in 10,000 B.C was about 5 million (Deevey 1960: 196); by 1975 world population was estimated to have increased 800 times to 4 billion. Additional energy capture can also be used to sustain a higher living standard as indicated by the 11.244 kilograms of coal equivalent consumed per capita in the United States which was over 5 times greater than the 1971 average for the world (United Nations 1972:354).

Increased energy capture converts into either population growth or a higher standard of living or both. If world population grows and nations of the world improve their standard of living, human populations have to seek new resources to exploit. The oceans appear as a large and untapped resource. Putting aside the problems that (a) vast areas of the oceans are not very productive and there are conflicting estimates for potential yields (Gulland 1971:246–255, Holt 1969, Idyll and Kasahara 1969:130–147), management and social policies operate against fisheries resources becoming important for human subsistence.

Very often what may be labeled efficiency is in actuality taking from the environment or taking from others. For example, in the Columbia River gillnet fishery, the gasoline engine in the early 1900s and more recent power-assisted equipment for hauling gillnets increased the quantity of fish which fishermen could harvest. How much of the increased quantity of fish harvested came from greater efficiency made possible by the gasoline engine and how much was taking from the environment or other fishermen?

The gasoline engine could also reduce the time spent by fishermen in obtaining their harvest. Fishermen, rather than catching the same quantity in less time, responded by fishing the same length of time and catching more. This led to management rules which caused greater inefficiency; fishing time was restricted to balance the estimated sustained yield with the efficiency of fishermen. This led to new innovations and new restrictions, and so on. In most managed fisheries, then, conservation rules force greater inefficiency rather than greater efficiency.

The gillnet fishery in the Columbia River had its fishing time reduced from 272 days in 1938 to 79 days in 1972. The average catch per gillnet remained constant at 9 to 12,000 pounds (Table 1). Thus fishing time balanced the number of fishermen and the efficiency of their gear with the quantity of resource available for harvest. The most efficient means for harvesting salmon were fishwheels and fish traps. These devices were outlawed in Oregon by public initiative in 1926. Washington followed suit in 1934. Innovations which make fishermen more successful, thus increasing the quantity of fish they can catch per unit of effort, meet with rules to outlaw or restrict use of the innovation.

Management criteria also allow for the social goal of open access. The impacts of management, where every harvester has equal access to the resource and in which the goal is sustained yield, is greater effort to produce the same quantity of resource. Economists Crutchfield and Pontecorvo (1969:111–117), analyzing the efficiency of harvest of Bristol Bay red salmon between 1934 and 1959, calculate that over 80 percent of the gear in 1955 was redundant. The yields for 1955–1959 were only "17 percent as efficient as in the base period" which was 1934–1939. For the Columbia River, Lewis (1973:18) found that 16 percent of the fishermen harvested 50 percent of the total value of landings. This, too, indicates that the annual harvest could be accomplished with fewer fishermen and less gear.

Managing for inefficiency is increased costs of production to society and marginal incomes for fishermen. Increased costs of production increase the cost to consumers, and where salmon prices competed with those of beef in the early 1900s (U. S. Bureau of Fisheries, 1914), in 1970 salmon was a food serving a luxury market. Per capita consumption decreased, for example, from 3.0 pounds of canned salmon in 1936 to 0.7 pounds in 1970 (U.S. National Marine Fisheries Service 1971:65). The process of reduced efficiency of harvest and serving only a luxury market typifies the evolution of the lobster, abalone, dungeness crab, shrimp, king crab, and prawn fisheries and is a process common to fisheries exploited by open access, hunting and gathering, and regulations based on sustained yield.

POLITICAL POWER

The progression of U.S. fisheries toward serving only luxury markets, too, relates to political power. Power is the ability to get actions favorable to one's position, or the probability of being able to carry out one's own will despite resistance from others (Weber 1947:152).

The power politics of the Columbia River salmon fishery are complex and conflictive. The first laws passed by Oregon and Washington were in 1878 and 1859, respectively (Wendler 1966). These laws were for the overt purpose of preventing overexploitation. In actuality, they were also a political ploy to get the federal government to increase funding for salmon hatcheries. Regulations since have been made in the context of several groups contesting one another for allocation of the fisheries resource. Fishermen were in opposition to one another, to processors, to sports anglers, to native American fishermen, and to foreign fishermen. Within each group there were internal conflicts. The general public very often sat in the role of final arbitrator as one side or the other brought issues before it for settlement.

Differences in the power of groups operate to allocate more of a resource to one group than another. Groups obtain their power in a variety of ways. No one way is commonly successful, but group number, importance of the group to society, the technology employed, the aggressiveness of leaders, etc. were all factors which governed a group's power to gain decisions favorable to its interests. The pursuit of power in decisions regarding the allocation of natural resources very often operates as taking from others.

Euro-Americans wrested allocation of the Columbia River salmon resource from native American harvesters in the early 1800s. Many

Astoria gillnetters and horse seining on the Columbia.

mechanisms were used. Native American fishermen were paid in currency, glass beads, tools, blankets, or liquor by the Hudson's Bay Company and others. Later, through conservation rules, property rights, and allocation of salmon habitat to other uses, more salmon were wrested from the native American. In 1959 and 1960 the Indian commercial harvest of Columbia River salmon was one-half percent of what it was prior to Anglo contact. A variety of mechanisms—disease, private property rights, violence, theft, money economy, and new technology—reduced the native American fisherman's competition for the salmon resource.

The process of taking from others did not stop with the competition with the native American. Fishermen competed with one another. The gillnetter competed with the trapman, the seiner, the fishwheel operator, the troller, and the sports angler for fish. Each group used conservation rules, violence, and appeal for public support to increase their power relative to other competitors.

Columbia River salmon were harvested from the mouth, up river 200 miles to Celilo Falls. Those closest to the mouth of the river had first chance at the resource. These were gillnetters from Astoria, Oregon, most of whom were immigrants from northern Europe. The gillnetter fished as close to the Columbia River bar as possible. As many as 50 gillnetters were estimated to have died each season during the 1880s. Drunkenness, bad weather, poor judgment were all causes, but the single most important cause was being swept across the bar and dying of exposure at sea (San Francisco Chronicle 1880). Just inside the bar was Baker's Bay where the trapmen from Ilwaco, Washington fished. The trapmen fished fixed gear called "pound nets."

From the appearance of the first trap in Baker's Bay in 1879, the gillnetters and the trapmen were adversaries. They used various forms of violence, terrorism, intimidation, and in 1896 the national guards from the states of Washington and Oregon had to mediate the conflict. The gillnetters were organized since 1879 as the Columbia River Fisherman's Protective Union. The union was the most powerful organization of fishermen on the river. Until 1896 the union had the power to bring fishing on the river to a halt. When fishing stopped near the mouth of the river, it improved up river where other fishermen operated. Up river at the Cascades and Celilo Falls were the fishwheels of the Warren and Seufert families and others (Donaldson and Cramer 1971:111-13). Native American fishermen also fished the upper river. Each of these groups strove to harvest as much of the salmon resource as they could. Through conservation rules, intimidation, legal action, and legislation each tried to limit the quantity of the salmon resource available to the other. One example of this was in 1908 when upriver and downriver interests presented initiatives to the citizens of Oregon which would ban each other's gear. Both

Gifford and Prentiss Photo, Oregon Historical Society

Fish trap and fish wheel.

Seattle Historical Society

initiatives passed and for a short time effectively closed the river to commercial fishing.

Fishing at Celilo Falls.

Added to conflicts between populations of fishermen was the fact that
salmon processors, up until 1896, were just as independent as the fishermen. After 1896, the year in which most of the processors joined the Columbia River Packers Association (the "Combine"), processors were better able to seek decisions favorable to their interests.

The Columbia River forms the boundary between the states of Washington and Oregon, and thus these two political entities had to be coor-
dinated when considering management regulations. The result of this diversity of interests, not unlike the world fisheries situation, was that decisions were arrived at slowly—usually after they could have significant
impact. The industry as a whole was not well integrated and had no well-
organized base of power which could obtain favorable decisions. Many
major management regulations were imposed or attempted by initiative
referendum. In 1926 by initiative petition, fishwheels and traps were
banned on the Oregon side of the river. Eight years later the same ban
was won on the Washington side. Seines were outlawed in 1949. In 1964

Oregon sports anglers tried to outlaw gillnets. This initiative failed after 1,000 Astorians mounted 29 buses and took their case to the citizens of Oregon.

Gifford and Prentiss Photo, Oregon Historical Society

Seufert response to 1926 Ballot Measure Election.

The participants in the fishery on the Columbia River were never able to amass enough political power to pass the legislative and public decisions favorable to the enhancement of their industry. One reason for this was internal conflicts which kept them a "house divided." A second reason was the other social needs in irrigation, power development, flood control, recreation, and so forth which the river was to meet. Finally with declines in the production of salmon, the price increased, and groups of consumers were lost. Fewer consumers meant fewer people concerned with salmon as a subsistence resource, and thus less legislative power.

The circular process of decline in supply, increase in cost, and loss of consumers is common to many fisheries which shifted from a subsistence to a luxury food resource. As a luxury food resource there is still a niche for fishermen to earn their livelihood; however, the political power to enhance their industry is lacking. There is little legislative power in providing food for a luxury market, and there are fewer people concerned with the plight of the fisherman and the fishing industry.

In the minds of fishermen who were interviewed in 1972 about the condition of their industry (Smith 1974), their weak political position was apparent. They saw this weakness as sports anglers obtained greater allocation of the salmon resource and as the distant water fleets of other nations took "our fish."

The political power has been absent to obtain decisions favorable to greater domestication of the resource, improved efficiency, and preventing the taking of segments of the resource by sports anglers and others. The salmon resource—like the lobster, abalone, dungeness crab, shrimp, king crab, and prawn—became a resource supplying a luxury rather than subsistence market, a market with only a few consumers who are willing to pay high prices. This severely limited the political power necessary for decisions of resource enhancement and improved efficiency of harvest.

CONCLUSIONS

These data about the growth and decline of the Columbia River salmon fishery show that the processes of domestication, improving efficiency, and a favorable balance of political power failed to operate to continue salmon as a subsistence resource. What predictions does this conclusion offer for the fisheries of the world?

Fisheries exploited by a hunting and gathering or capture technique, which is the technique by which the majority of fish and shellfish were harvested in the 1970s, would over the long run decline in importance because of overexploitation of the resource, because of the problem of declining fishing efficiency, and because of absence of sufficient political power. While the fisheries resources of the ocean may look vast, in 1968 they provided less than 5 percent of the protein consumed by humans (Holt 1969:188). Estimates of the sustained yield from the oceans vary but they range from 3 to 30 times the 1970 world fisheries harvest. If world population increases and if demands for improved standards of living mount, food from the sea by hunting and gathering does not pose a viable long term alternative.

The pattern in all fisheries managed in accordance with sustained yield, allowing open access, and hunting and gathering techniques for exploitation, has led to over-exploitation which increases costs of production and loses consumers. Attempts to prevent over-exploitation reduce the efficiency of fishermen. In this situation the fishery often evolved to provide for only a luxury market.

Will this mean that mankind will turn from the sea? On the contrary, there will probably be a rush to control and divide up the sea's fields and pastures so that domesticated mariculture can be practiced. Man is a territorial animal, and he has divided up the land areas as resource surpluses have become resource deficiencies. Quite likely some of the next world conflicts will occur over control of the sea's resources. Witness the conflicts of the early 1970s between Britain and Iceland, Peru and the United States, the United States and the Soviet Union, and developed and developing nations over access to the resources near their national shorelines.

Suggesting that the seas should be reserved for mankind sounds noble, but in the light of the last 10,000 years of human history, it is unlikely to occur. Did the English common pastures last? Was the New World left open to the peoples of the world? Humanity has perhaps come a long way, but have we proceeded to a condition of altruism where we no longer take from one another? The territoriality documented by the concept of community, private property, and the institution of nation state is still a strong force which will shape new power alliances geared to domesticating and improving the efficiency of harvest from the sea to meet the subsistence needs of human populations.

TABLE 1   Comparative Gear Efficiency[a]

Gear	Case I[b] 1889—92	Case II[c] 1930—35 (Pounds/year)	Case III[d] 1963—72
Fishwheel	90,100	[e]	[e]
Trap (pound net)	26,500	12,000[f]	[f]
Haul Seine	59,000	45,600[g]	[g]
Gill Net	12,400	10,100[h]	9,300
Troller	[i]	12,800[i]	2,900[i]

a These are representative examples. Additional data which provide similar results can be found in Cobb (1911), Fiedler (1929 and 1931), Radcliffe (1919), and Sette and Fiedler (1929).
b Wilcox (1895:244–247).
c Oregon State Planning Board 1938:45–47 and 66–67).
d Smith (1974).
e Fishwheels were banned in Oregon by a 1926 initiative. They were legal in Washington until 1934. An average of one man was required to operate each fishwheel (Fiedler 1929:568 and 1931:982 and 985).
f Traps (pound nets) were banned in Oregon in 1927. While fishwheels were important on the Oregon side of the river, fish traps were not. Traps remained in Washington until 1934. An average of 0.8 men were required to operate a fish trap. (Fiedler 1929:568 and 1931:982 and 985).
g Haul seines were banned in Washington in 1935 and in 1949 in Oregon. The average number of men operating a haul seine was 11 (Fiedler 1929:568 and 1931:982 and 985).
h An average of 1.5 men worked each gillnet (Fiedler 1929:568 and 1931:982 and 985). With power-assisted equipment one man could handle the equipment.
i Trolling became possible off the Columbia River bar with the introduction of the gasoline engine in the early 1900s. Data available for 1963–72 were for all licensed vessels and for the entire Oregon coast. The figure given is underenumerated.

NOTES

[1]Craig and Hacker (1940), Daily Astorian (1966), DeLoach (1939), Gile (1955), Hayden (1930), Miller (1958), and Rubenstein (1966) provide historical summaries of the Columbia River salmon fishery. In addition, original materials held by the Bancroft Library at the University of California, Berkeley, the Oregon Historical Society, the Columbia River Maritime Museum, and special collections at the University of Oregon have been consulted in preparing the historical aspects for this paper.

[2]The exact sustained yield of Columbia River salmon is difficult to calculate. In addition to the variety of different runs, fish produced by the Columbia River system are caught by salmon trollers from the Southern Oregon Coast to Alaska as well as by sports anglers, gillnetters, Indian fishermen, and some by the distant water fleets of other nations.

[3]Steelhead are a trout; however, they are canned as salmon.

LITERATURE CITED

Bullard, Oral
    1955   Crisis on the Columbia. Portland: Touchstone Press.

Cobb, John N.
    1911   The Salmon Fisheries of the Pacific Coast. Bureau of Fisheries Document No. 751. Washington: G. P. O.
    1921   Pacific Salmon Fisheries. Bureau of Fisheries Document No. 902. Washington: G. P. O.

Collins, J. W.
    1892   Report of the Fisheries of the Pacific Coast of the United States. *In* Report of the U. S. Commissioner of Fish and Fisheries for 1888. Washington: G. P. O.

Columbia Basin Inter-agency Committee
    1957   Columbia River Basin Fishery Program. Portland.

Cooley, Richard A.
    1963   Politics and Conservation, The Decline of the Alaska Salmon. New York: Harper and Row, Publishers.

Craig, Joseph A., and Robert L. Hacker
    1940   The History and Development of the Fisheries of the Columbia River. Bulletin of the Bureau of Fisheries 49(32):133–216.

Crutchfield, James A., and Giulio Pontecorvo
    1969   The Pacific Salmon Fisheries, A Study of Irrational Conservation. Baltimore: The John Hopkins Press.

Daily Astorian
    1966   Columbia River Salmon Packing Industry Observes 100th Year. 13, Dec. 8, 1966. Astoria, Oregon.

Deevey, Edward S., Jr.
    1960   The Human Population. Scientific American 203(3):194–201.

DeLoach, Daniel Barton
    1939   The Salmon Canning Industry. Corvallis: Oregon State College.

Dodds, Gordon B.
    1959   The Salmon King of Oregon: R. D. Hume and the Pacific Fisheries. University of North Carolina Press.

Donaldson, Ivan J., and Frederick K. Cramer
    1971   Fishwheels of the Columbia. Portland: Binfords and Mort.

Evans, J. G.
    1969   The Exploitation of Molluses. *In* The Domestication and Exploitation of Plants and Animals. Peter J. Ucko and G. W. Dimbleby, eds. Chicago: Aldine Publising Co.

Fiedler, R. H.
    1929   Fishing Industries of the United States, 1928. Bureau of Fisheries Document No. 1067. Washigton: G. P. O.
    1931   Fishing Industries of the United States, 1929. Bureau of Fisheries Document No. 1095. Washington: G. P. O.

Fish Commission of Oregon and Washington Department of Fisheries
  1972   Status Report, Columbia River Fish Runs and Commercial Fisheries,
          1938–70. Clackamas, Oregon and Olympia, Washington.

Gile, Albion
  1955   Notes on the Columbia River Salmon Industry. Oregon Historical
          Quarterly 56:140–65.

Gulland, J. A.
  1971   The Fish Resources of the Ocean. London, England: Fishing News
          (Books) Ltd.

Hayden, Mildred V.
  1930   History of the Salmon Industry in Oregon. M. A. thesis, University
          of Oregon.

Hewes, Gordon W.
  1947   Aboriginal Use of Fishery Resources in Northwestern North Ameri-
          can. Ph.D. Dissertation, Department of Anthropology, University of
          California, Berkeley.

Hickling, C. F.
  1962   Fish Culture. London: Faber and Faber.
  1968   The Farming of Fish. London: Pergamon Press.

Holt, J. S.
  1969   The Food Resources of the Ocean. Scientific American
          221(3):178–94.

Hume, Robert, D.
  1961   A Pygmy Monopolist: The Life and Doings of R. D. Hume, written
          by himself and dedicated to his neighbors. Madison: State Historical
          Society of Wisconsin, University of Wisconsin.

Idyll, C. P., and Hiroshi Kasahara
  1969   Food from the Sea. *In* Exploring the Ocean World. C. P. Idyll, ed.
          New York: Thomas Y. Crowell Company.

Iversen, E. S.
  1968   Farming the Edge of the Sea. London: Fishing News (Books) Ltd.

Kemp, William B.
  1971   The Flow of Energy in a Hunting Society. Scientific American
          224(3):104–15.

Lewis, Robert C.
  1973   Preliminary Economic Analysis of Management Alternatives for

Limiting Harvest Effort by Oregon Commercial Fisheries. Fish Commission of Oregon. Mimeo.

Lin, S. Y.
1940   Fish Culture in Ponds in the New Territories of Hong Kong. Journal Hong Kong Research Station 1(2).

Lowell, Steve
1972   The Tragedy of the Columbia River. National Fisherman, Yearbook Issue 52(13): 18–23.

Miller, Emma Gene
1958   Clatsop County, Oregon, Its History, Legends, and Industries. Portland: Binfords and Mort.

National Fisherman
1973   Pacific Packers Report. National Fisherman 52(12).

Netboy, Anthony
1958   Salmon of the Pacific Northwest: Fish vs. Dams. Portland: Binfords and Mort.

Oregon State Planning Board
1938   A Study of Commercial Operations on the Columbia River. Salem.

Pacific Fisherman
1950   Yearbook. Pacific Fisherman 48(2).

Radcliffe, Lewis
1919   Fishing Industries of the United States. Bureau of Fisheries Document No. 875. Washington: G. P. O.

Rappaport, Roy A.
1971   The Flow of Energy in an Agricultural Society. Scientific American 225(3): 116–33.

Richards, Jack A.
1968   An Economic Evaluation of Columbia River Anadromous Fish Programs. Ph.D dissertation, Department of Agricultural Economics, Oregon State University.

Rubinstein, Mark E.
1966   The History of Concentration in the Canned Salmon Industry of the United States. Bachelor Honors Thesis, Department of Economics, Harvard College.

Russell, E. S.
1942   The Overfishing Problem. Cambridge: University Press.

San Francisco Chronicle
    1880   Located in Bancroft Scraps, Volume 33:77, Sept. 21, 1880. Berkeley: Bancroft Library.

Sette, Oscar E. and R. H. Fiedler
    1929   Fishing Industries of the United States, 1927. Bureau of Fisheries Document No. 1050. Washington: G. P. O.

Smith, Courtland L.
    1974   Fishing Success in a Regulated Commons. Ocean Development and International Law Journal 1(4):369–81.

Thompson, William F.
    1950   The Effect of Fishing on Stocks of Halibut in the Pacific. Seattle: University of Washington Press.

United Nations. Statistical Office. Department of Economic and Social Affairs
    1973   Statistical Yearbook, 1972. New York: United Nations.

U.S. Bureau of Fisheries
    1914   Canned Salmon Is Cheaper Than Meats. Washington: G. P. O.

U.S. Bureau of the Census
    1972   Statistical Abstract of the United States. Washington: G. P. O.

U.S. National Marine Fisheries Service
    1971   Fisheries of the United States, 1971. Current Fishery Statistics No. 5600. Washington: G. P. O.

Weber, Max
    1947   The Theory of Social and Economic Organization. A. M. Henderson and Talcott Parsons, trans. Glencoe: The Free Press.

Wendler, Henry O.
    1966   Regulation of Commercial Fishing Gear and Seasons on the Columbia River from 1859 to 1963. Fisheries Research Papers, Washington Department of Fisheries 2(4):19–31.

White, Leslie A.
    1959   The Evolution of Culture. New York: McGraw-Hill Book Company.

Wilcox, William A.
    1895   Fisheries of the Pacific Coast. *In* Report of the Commissioner for the Year Ending June 30, 1893. U. S. Commission of Fish and Fisheries. Washington: G. P. O.

Zeuner, Friedrich E.
    1963   A History of Domesticated Animals. Hutchinson of London.

13

Primitive Accumulation in Small-Scale Fishing Communities*

JAMES C. FARIS

University of Connecticut

INTRODUCTION: THE TAXONOMIC PROBLEM

The classification of small-scale fishing communities poses a problem in anthropology. Existing evolutionary taxonomies which focus (cf., Service 1962) on types or forces of production rather than on the way production is organized and planned (relations of production) are no help. These yield classifications such as the common sequence of hunters and gatherers (which includes fishers), agriculturalists, and industrialists. This is the equivalent of (and makes about as much sense as) a biological classification which lumps together whales, fish, and submarines, and separates them from bats, birds, and airplanes. Such a biological classification is absurd because the theory of evolution forms classifications and taxonomies, showing why these things are not related (even though they all have water or air in common, respectively). No such general theory

*Though acknowledgement of their ideas and contribution in no way commits their responsibility, I want to thank F. Antler, W. Roseberry and W. Leap for their immense help.

guides social science, however, (or rather, no such theory has been widely accepted), so we have no methodology for eliminating potential members from our taxonomy. By virtue of the link to water, scuba divers, plumbers, longshoremen, and naval personnel become relevant to a classification with fishers.

We must not look at the resource base or type of production, but to the organization of production—the social relations people enter into and the types of productive forces employed. This allows us to avoid any focus— for example hunting and gathering (and fishing)—which requires lumping the trawlermen of Hull-Grimsby with indigenous Australian hunters. The Kwakuitl, then, would no longer be an embarrassment to classificatory efforts because they are hunters and gatherers with a class-based incipient state organization and slavery (Ruyle 1973). *It is not the type of activity, but the way the activity is organized—its potentialities and contradictions—that should be the focus of informed classificatory efforts.* The fishing communities about which we are talking are, in the conventional anthropological formulation, hunters (or gatherers); but this label reveals very little of scientific interest about these communities (cf., Faris 1975, for an expanded critique of such classifications).

Other taxonomies have lumped such small-scale fishing communities with peasant agricultural communities (Leap 1977), in that both control aspects of their production to produce subsistence plus a commodity for exchange (or sale) in markets external to the local society—markets over which they have no control. This latter classification makes sense from the Newfoundland perspective. Newfoundland outport fishing communities traditionally produced a finished product, whose processing they controlled, in ways very similar to peasant agriculturalists. Certainly the organization of production had more in common with peasant agricultural communities than with industrial fishing enterprise, such as offshore draggers (essentially factory ships) or land-based hunters and gatherers (such as indigenous Australian society).

The present paper will explore both the similarities and the differences between fishing peasants and agricultural peasants, to help make clear some of the structural constraints and processual determinants of such societies. It will focus not on differences in the forces of production between the two, but on the similarities of organization, planning, and social relations of production in the societies. Indeed, the forces of production are totally different in these two types of peasant communities. But much of their social relations of commodity production are similar. We must avoid nomenclatures which describe such differences as separate modes of production (cf., Terray 1972 for an example of this tendency, and Meillassoux 1972:98 for an unfortunate endorsement). The modes of production, then, in the two types of peasant communities are best regarded as the same.

The forces of production are in perpetual contradiction with the social relations of production in all human societies. That is, a contradiction exists between the way production is organized (including work planning as well as distribution of the product, e.g., control) and the skills, tools, and techniques (and their control) which realize the production. It will be argued that the essential scientific and informative differences between agricultural peasants and fishing peasants rests in the specific nature and potentialities of the contradictions between the forces and relations of production in each case. This will allow us to examine the possibilities in each system; to see what potentialities exist for differential accumulation of capital and differentiation in the community, and the implications of the development of the forces of production (or relations of production) and their relative determinance; and to understand at what points other modes of production, such as industrial or finance capitalism, may penetrate and dominate local systems.

AGRICULTURAL PEASANTRIES

In classical peasant communities of feudal Europe (cf., Berthoud 1972a), the limitations on the development of the forces of production were many. Very common was the lack of capital for investment (as well as lack of investment opportunities) in development and research. The surplus appropriated by nonproducers (commonly in the form of product) was usually consumed—as under manorial feudalism. Thus, the social relations of production frequently inhibited the development forces of production beyond what peasants themselves might be able to do, such as differential cropping systems and consequent development of different hand tools (see Boserup 1965 for details of such possible agricultural development).

The surplus appropriated by landlords or those otherwise in a position to command a portion of peasant production thus demanded consumption—there was little or no opportunity for investment. This constituted an important contradiction in such societies, and was a problem resolved with—indeed necessitating—the emergence of capitalism, a mode of production enabling such appropriation to be invested. Moreover, the possibilities were now present for private accumulation by peasants themselves in agricultural production, and hence, differentiation with the peasant community. Roseberry (1976) has shown the implications of inefficient rent extraction in peasant communities where total capitalist rationalization (i.e., proletarianization of peasants) is inhibited because of factors such as marginal productivity. Rent may be extracted in the form of labor, product, or money. Each form may evolutionarily precede the others, or they may all occur simultaneously. But as Roseberry notes (1976:51):

> rent does not necessarily extract all of the surplus product; it may also extract less than or more than the total surplus. For instance under labor rent, while the peasant is simply granted a subsistence plot, the peasant might produce a surplus product beyond subsistence needs. Under rent in kind, the direct producer may produce a surplus of cash crop commodities because of particularly good environmental conditions in a given year. Under money rent, the market price for a commodity may be particularly good in a given year. If rent were computed on the basis of previous or average market conditions, the peasant would be able to pay the rent with a smaller portion of the total product, thus retaining a surplus. Claimants of peasant rent will of course attempt to respond to these conditions, but the response is necessarily a slow one since they do not control the production process. It is thus possible for some peasants to retain a surplus product after the payment of rent. It is also possible, indeed likely, for rent to absorb more than the surplus produced by the peasant unit.

Under capitalism, peasant communities became part of a world system which witnessed extraordinary developments in productive forces, and thus the social relations of production no longer appear to be fetters on the development of the forces of production. Where it increasingly favors the organic composition of capital, capitalism will attempt to penetrate the agricultural sector, and to increasingly rationalize peasant production. In this process, landed property may cease to be the central means of production (cf., Berthoud 1972b:192) for certain peasant agricultural modes of production. In others, however, intensification and increased investment in the land itself is the penetration strategy. This contrasts with the situation in peasant fishing communities in significant ways; though capitalist rationalization increasingly must, where it is productive, force peasants in both agricultural and fishing communities to sell their labor rather than the products of it. It is, however, on the implications for accumulation by peasants themselves that we will focus; though it will be argued that in so doing, we are able to understand more clearly the dynamics of capitalist rationalization as well.

FISHING PEASANTRIES

In the traditional Newfoundland outport fishing community such as Cat Harbour (Faris 1972), access to the common property resource was unlimited or arranged by drawing lots to known fishing sites (cf., Alexander et al 1974). These were known locally as "spots of ground" or "berths" (see Faris 1966, for a discussion of sea floor topology in Cat Harbour and techniques of exploitation and processing). This distributed access equitably (or at least randomly) to those in possession of the necessary gear needed to fish such a site. For more than the first half of the twentieth century, this gear was commonly a cod trap: a net box of many hundreds of pounds of net set on the floor of the sea, into which ground-fish (bottom-feeding species such as cod) were directed by means of a long net "leader." This cod trap was hoisted to the surface by crews normally requiring about four men, who removed the fish and set the trap again. These fish were then taken ashore to be processed—usually by "shore crowds" composed principally of women (wives and daughters of the fishing crew)—into a finished or semi-finished product: salted fish, sold to buyers later in the year after the fishing season was over.

Plate 2   Hauling cod trap. Crew composed of three brothers and the son of one. Cat Harbour, Summer 1964.

This particular productive pattern has aspects which differentiates it from production of agricultural peasantries. First, in the absence of ownership of the resource, there is removed the possibility of selling or renting access to it (see below for the response of the State to this circumstance). This effectively removes the opportunity for accumulation of capital that would characterize an agriculturalist's opportunity in fixed resources such as productive land. Thus, expropriation by way of rent of the resource was not possible. The possibility of such a situation as, for example, the ownership of particular trap berths or sites is eliminated, as the product of the resource, fish, is mobile and may not always move through a particular berth each year. The only possibility for effective (i.e., long term, enabling inheritance and investment of capital and labor) control of the means of production would be the adoption of a farming technology on the spawning grounds of the fish (a situation most possible in shellfish farming, but not likely in the Newfoundland inshore ground fishery). Thus, control of the means of production (here defined as the ocean with fish in it) beyond the necessary access and forces available to produce from it, is not a possibility for primitive accumulation in the traditional Newfoundland outport.

To describe the means of production of the fishery as simply a common property resource, however, fails to penetrate the economic implications of the phenomenon. Of course the mobility of the product of the resource inhibits ownership as a means of alienating it from producers. But more important for our theoretical comparisons between the two types of peasant production is that labor cannot be embodied in the resource. The resource is, as Marx has suggested, the subject of labor and cannot become an instrument of labor (1967:178–181).[1] Thus we may question Meillassoux's discrimination of agricultural peasantries as those which—because the resource (land) is an instrument rather than a subject of production—are oriented about control over reproduction (subsistence and women) rather than control over the means of production (1972). In the Newfoundland outport fishing communities the resource is clearly the subject of labor, yet the community social relations of production are remarkably similar to those of agricultural peasantries.[2]

Though labor is expended in extracting fish from the sea, labor is not (normally) embodied in the resource per se, making it the receptacle of value. Thus, it is because it is not possible to capture and embody labor in the resource itself—only in its product—that makes its ownership economically problematic.

One means of overcoming this situation is to develop the forces of production to allow pursuit of fish rather than their harvest in fixed berths (as in the current inshore fishery). This alternative is being pursued in

Plate 1   Light-salted cod drying. Sold on world market as finished product. Cat Harbour, Fall 1964.

Newfoundland with the appearance in the past decade of increasing numbers of huge dragger fleets (primarily foreign) which pursue the fishery in
a distinctly predatory way (cf., Andersen and Wadel 1972). This "hunting" type of production effectively denies access to fish by inshore fishers
as it catches the fish that would normally come closer to shore to be "harvested" in the fixed gear of the traditional inshore fishery. Moreover, this
predatory type of production requires sophisticated forces of production
and immense capital outlay (not to mention the support of the State). It
is as beyond the reach of peasant fishers as the purchase of combine harvesters and tractors is beyond the reach of peasant agriculturalists. And
it requires abandonment of long-term concern for the future of the resource (cf., Antler and Faris (In press), just as certain intensive fertiliza-
tion techniques (Harris 1973) and destructive monocropping (Gross
1971) in peasant agriculture ultimately destroy the resource. Of course
such penetration by industrial capital also forces peasant producers to
give up their relations of production—to increasingly sell their labor as
they can no longer sell their product.

From the perspective of the local outport, there are other fetters on
primitive accumulation in addition to the inability to capture labor in the
resource. This is seen in the inability to successfully control the forces of
production. The various instruments of production are, of course, herit-
able; but the partibility of the estate has always inhibited capitalization
in the traditional Newfoundland outport.

The instruments of production include land for the installation of fishing premises: stages, stores, boats (and since World War II, engines);
and extensive gear: cod trap(s), nets, grapples, line, and so on. In the traditional outport it took a great deal of time to acquire all the items necessary to pursue the cod trap fishery. A cod trap itself might require years
to knit, or if purchased, an accumulation requiring years (cf., Breton
1973). Boats were constructed from local materials as their purchase required outlay beyond reach—even if there were a market in boats—and
could be expected to last, with care, almost 20 years. Beside the trap
skiff, there were the numerous smaller boats necessary. And in Cat Harbour, the bridges, stage heads, and other parts had to be newly constructed each year because the severe ice damage each winter forced
fishers to dismantle and store them. Engines, grapples, line, and twine
for nets all had to be purchased—an outlay requiring several years to
save (or several years to pay off if purchased on credit). This all meant
that it was very difficult if not impossible for a young man in his lifetime
to inaugurate an entire set of required materials himself. It required not
only the help of others to construct and assemble the necessary items,
but financial outlay normally in excess of available funds over a series of
years. Debt—caused by uncertain catches, market prices, and (at least

for the northeast coast) weather—was avoided if possible (though because of these same conditions, was often a fact of life).

Thus the usual means of acquiring at least a portion of the necessary gear was through inheritance. And the usual means of acquiring the labor necessary for the construction of most of the remainder necessary (as well as labor necessary for the realization of production itself) was through offspring—offspring whose payment was subsistence until they established their own domestic unit. But the demands for labor and the reproduction of labor power (requiring numerous offspring) also acted to divide the instruments of production in the transmission of property by the centrifugal force of inheritance. A portion of the estate (the total of which is necessary for the process of production) went to each son: a boat without gear to one, a cod trap without a boat to another, and so on. This helped each son (who ideally by this time would have young sons of his own) begin to establish his own independent economic unit, but as it was only a portion, production was inhibited given no innovation in the forces of production. Until the other necessary items were constructed or purchased (those items inherited by other siblings), production was hampered:

> sons inherit land equally. The same applies to fishing gear, but unfortunately a cod trap, a boat, an engine, or fishing premises are not divisible as is land, and a father can only hope that by giving a piece of gear to each son, he divides the inheritance equally among them. This means, of course, that unlike the division of resources in an agricultural community, none of the inheritors have all the necessary items required for a complete and independent economically-productive unit of his own . . . (Faris 1972:89).

This phenomenon of the partible inheritance of an impartible estate required considerable renewed investment for each generation and effectively inhibited the accumulation of capital (by consuming it) which might have otherwise lead to significant differentiation. The local work organization constituted both the enabling conditions for the operation of the fishery with the production forces available, and the fetter upon the development of different productive forces.[3]

Innovation in the instruments of production themselves was difficult; experimentation was inhibited, as a possible seasonal failure meant disaster. Any capital changes in the forces of production were discouraged because of the lack of capital; without a change in the social relations of production, overcapitalization resulted given the existing work organization (a frequent outcome of attempts to invest in small home-built schooners to be used in the Labrador fishery by northeast coast fishers).

Instead of concentration and capitalization, or other development of the forces of production, outport fishing labor was put into reproduction and expansion of the base, not in intensification of embodied labor. There was a constant siphon of labor (and/or capital) into the reproduction of the production forces in each generation.

Theoretically then, it is the inability to embody labor in the resource that causes such high reproductive costs each generation in peasant fishing communities. The resource remains a subject and cannot become an instrument of production. Labor is embodied in other instruments required for production; but the instruments are fragmented each generation by partible inheritance, consuming labor and capital in their continual reproduction.

MECHANISMS AND IMPLICATIONS OF
CAPITALIST PENETRATION

Capitalism must constantly seek to rationalize itself, to create an increasingly favorable organic composition of capital. That is, it must constantly attempt to capture surplus value; by control over the means and forces of production, the capitalist can command the sale of labor rather than product. The capitalist thereby seeks to pay as little as possible for labor power, so to maximize the capture of surplus value—the difference between the value of labor in the product (which includes all labor embodied in its production) and the value of labor power which the capitalist must pay in the form of wages.

This rationalization must, of course be profitable for the capitalist. In peasant settings it may require more investment to control resources and instruments of production than it is possible to glean in returns in the short term. The inherent tendency to invest, then, may be in contradiction to unfavorable returns from such investment in some sectors. Such is frequently the case in peasant commodity production, and is one of the reasons such production is maintained in the face of increasingly rationalized capitalism.

There are other tendencies, however, which inhibit capitalist penetration of peasant production. One is the commonly noted tendency to force the costs of reproduction of labor power in the urban sector onto the rural infrastructure. Thus, in areas of peasant production, urban proletarians may require the support of rural relatives to supplement their subsistence in the towns. The Newfoundland outport increasingly acts as a bedroom community for people who work seasonally in the urban centers of the mainland. And thus infrastructure costs in the form of homes, schools, medical care, and so on are saved, and those costs of the reproduction of labor power in the urban settings are transferred to the rural area. The end result of all these contradictory tendencies in capitalist penetration and rationalization is commonly increasing misery in both the rural and urban areas. Of more particular interest here is the actual capitalist investment strategy in the rural fishing community.

As noted, the inability to embody labor in the resource and the situational requirement to continually consume labor in the generational reproduction of the forces of production pose, for the capitalist, a particular investment problem somewhat unique to the peasant fishing type of production. We have detailed elsewhere (Antler and Faris In press) some of the ways in which this is realized; here several features may be abstracted relevant to capitalist penetration which relate to the enigma posed by the problems documented in embodying labor.

As mentioned, in peasant fishing communities the instruments of production may be the agency of penetration (capital-intensive gear, large boats, etc.), requiring increasing proletarianization of the work force. Command over the means of production in the absence of landed property is much more difficult. This usually proceeds by State intervention so that rights of access are exclusive and controlled. This can lead to the selective creation of a class of rich fishing peasants, or to the proletarianization of all fishing peasants—forcing them to sell their labor as hands on corporate trawling fleets who now have exclusive access. This is brought about by denying rights of access to small peasant-controlled vessels in various ways: use of licensing regulations which force them into capital-intensive gear, refusal of the State to enforce territorial claims (thus allowing foreign trawling fleets to exploit the fishery), selective pricing for offshore fish versus inshore fish, resettlement schemes (which remove fishers from access to the shore), and a complex system of transfer payments (unemployment benefits, welfare, etc.) which favor selling labor rather than product (cf., Antler and Faris In press; Alexander et all 1974 for details). The maturation of the State-capital nexus thus has come to facilitate a penetration which would have otherwise been difficult, given the unique problems of the embodiment of labor in peasant fishing production.

Though on the basis of indigenous capital accumulation, fishing peasants are faced with obstacles not present in agricultural peasant situations, fishing communities are not ipso facto poorer than agricultural peasantries. But it does not mean that the possibility for differentiation within the community based on resource management is lessened; agricultural peasants can, on the basis of labor embodied in landed property and the way in which rent is extracted from such resources (cf., Roseberry 1976), accumulate differentially. There are few structural mechanisms for such differentiation in peasant fishing communities.

Of course situational circumstances (demography, etc) may always bring about differentiation in fishing communities; we are not concerned with such individual and essentially random features in this essay, but with the *structural* constraints on differentiation and accumulation. Indeed, differentiation which exists in fishing communities is—based on the experience of Cat Harbour—traditionally a function of such random demographic features as lack of sons or daughters for recruitment to production units and premature deaths or injuries, and accumulation in other types of petty commodity production, such as sale of outport agricultural produce, small timber mills, fish oil processing plants, retail mercantile outlets, and successful speculative investment in schooner-based Labrador fishery. Of course traditionally other types of production have been, like the seasonal work in exterior labor markets and domestic agricultural production, normally a constant fact of existence. But these are usually necessary as reproductive expenses for the dominant type of production, the inshore fishery; and are forced onto fishers by the low market price of fish. This usually means that only by establishing an outport situation in which labor can be embodied and hired—such as in the timber mills, oil-processing facilities, or other types of commodity production—can the accumulation leading to differentiation actually occur. And, of course, it commonly has occurred (cf., Faris 1972:114).

The most common form of capitalist rationalization, in fact, is to penetrate such ventures—to increasingly extract surplus value by controlling processing. This removes the fisher's control of a finished commodity, and today most inshore fishers sell their product fresh rather than salted (though the buyers may continue to process it into a salted product, cf., Antler and Faris In press). This also inhibits holding the fish off the market for higher prices, as fresh fish must be sold immediately.

CONCLUSIONS

For indigenous development through primitive accumulation, it has been suggested that peasant fishing communities such as Cat Harbour, by the nature of the dominant mode of production, lack the same possibilities that peasant agriculturalists have. One consequence may be the ethos of egalitarianism among peasant fishers (cf., Faris 1972:100 ff.). Other secondary types of production, of course, offer investment opportunities—opportunities which are, to a significant extent, realized.

For the dominant type of production, however, the noticeable lack of diversification rests fundamentally in the inability to embody labor in the resource—to be able to capture labor for potential accumulation. The transmission of partible estates in productive forces (each portion of which was required for a single productive unit) constantly fractionalizes the necessary materials for a productive fishing enterprise, and acts as another brake on differential accumulation.

Different types of production (hunting, domestic agricultural production, etc.), in fact, act as support for the dominant form of commodity production. That is, they may be considered as expenses of reproduction of labor power for the fishing enterprise. And to the extent that their products are consumed and not sold, they constitute a reproductive portion of the peasant fishing mode of production, not a separate mode of production. This circumstance has made possible low prices for the products of labor, particularly during a period of immature mercantile capitalism in Newfoundland. And insofar as low prices are maintained, it is usually not possible for these other types of production (in which labor *could* be embodied) to form the basis for capital accumulation.

With the increasing rationalization of capitalism, the productive process of outport fishers had to be penetrated to force producers to surrender a greater amount of their surplus value (previously captured and held by them inasmuch as a finished product was offered and not their labor), and, increasingly, to require them to sell their labor rather than the product of it. Thus, whereas a possible capitalist rationalization in agricultural peasantries involves the alienation of the means of production (as well, of course, as control of the forces of production) for increasing proletarianization; in fishing peasantries, capitalist penetration strategy has to await and rely on State intervention.

NOTES

[1]Marx considers both the instruments and the subject of labor the means of production (1967:181), but in the case of the sea fishery, is forced to add: "It appears paradoxical to assert, that uncaught fish, for instance, are a means of production in the fishing industry. But hitherto no one has discovered that art of catching fish in waters that contain none" (1967:181n). In the present paper I regard the instruments of labor as forces of production—that is, those material objects and situations in which labor is embodied (tools, techniques, skills).

[2]We must take exception to other aspects of Meillassoux's thesis—particularly surrounding the object of production in such modes of production as we are discussing. This is discussed in Faris (n.d.).

[3]The economic and structural implications of the partibility of estates is considered in peasant agricultural communities as well (cf., Wolf 1972). But whereas such partibility may appreciably diminish the production of agricultural peasants (without development of the forces of production, newly acquired land, or emigration of those remaining), it does not stop it.

LITERATURE CITED

Alexander, D., et al.
  1974   Report of the Committee on Federal Licensing Policy and Its Impli-
          cations for the Newfoundland Fisheries. St. John's, Newfoundland:
          Memorial University of Newfoundland.

Andersen, R., and C. Wadel
  1972   Comparative Problems in Fishing Adaptations. *In* North Atlantic
          Fishermen: Anthropological Essays on Modern Fishing. R. Ander-
          sen and C. Wadel, eds. Newfoundland Social and Economic Papers
          No. 5. Institute of Social and Economic Research. Memorial Univer-
          sity of Newfoundland. Toronto: University of Toronto Press.

Antler, E., and J. Faris
  In press Adaptation to Changes in Technology and Government Policy: A
          Newfoundland Example. *In* North Atlantic Maritime Europeans. R.
          Andersen, ed. The Hague: Mouton.

Berthoud, G.
  1972a   Dynamics of Ownership in the Circum-Alpine Area. Anthropological
          Quarterly 45(3):117–24.
  1972b   From Peasantry to Capitalism: The Meaning of Ownership in the
          Swiss Alps. Anthropological Quarterly 45(3):177–95.

Boserup, E.
  1965   The Conditions of Agricultural Growth. Chicago: Aldine.

Breton, Y.
  1973   A Comparative Study of Work Groups in an Eastern Canadian Peas-
          ant Fishing Community: Bilateral Kinship and Adaptive Processes.
          Ethnology 12(4):393–418.

Faris, J.
  1966   Cat Harbour: A Newfoundland Fishing Settlement. Newfoundland
          Social and Economic Studies, No. 3 (with appendix). Institute of So-
          cial and Economic Research. Memorial University of Newfoundland.
          Toronto: University of Toronto Press.
  1972   Cat Harbour: A Newfoundland Fishing Settlement. Newfoundland
          Social and Economic Studies, No. 3 (reissue minus appendix). Insti-
          tute of Social and Economic Research. Memorial University of New-
          foundland. Toronto: University of Toronto Press.
  1975   Social Evolution, Population, and Production. *In* Population, Econ-
          ology, and Social Evolution. S. Polgar, ed. The Hague: Mouton.
  n. d.   On the Concept of the Mode of Production. ms.

Gross, D.
1971 The Great Sisal Scheme. Natural History 80(3):48ff.

Harris, M.
1973 The Withering Green Revolution. Natural History 82(3):20ff.

Leap, W.
1977 Maritime Subsistence in Anthropological Perspective: A Statement of Priorities. *In* Those Who Live From The Sea, M. E. Smith, ed. St. Paul: West Publishers.

Marx, K.
1967 Capital, Vol. I. New York: International.

Meillassoux, C.
1972 From Reproduction to Production. Economy and Society 1:93–105.

Roseberry, W.
1976 Rent, Differentiation, and the Development of Capitalism Among Peasants. American Anthropologist 78(1):45–58.

Ruyle, E.
1973 Slavery, Surplus and Stratification on the Northwest Coast. Current Anthropology 14(4):603–631.

Service, E.
1962 Primitive Social Organization: An Evolutionary Perspective. New York: Random.

Terray, E.
1972 Marxism and Primitive Society. New York: Monthly Review.

Wolf, E.
1972 Ownership and Political Ecology. Anthropological Quarterly 45(3):201–205.

*

14

Maritime Subsistence In Anthropological Perspective: A Statement of Priorities*

WILLIAM L. LEAP

The American University

An interest in general anthropology, not maritime anthropology, led me to the discussion offered by this paper. Originally, I wanted to see what a general anthropological perspective, of the sort outlined in Boas (1938:1–6) might have to say about fishing as a cultural activity. To build this perspective, I had hoped to contrast anthropologists' comments on fishing with the comment participants themselves might make about the same activity, looking toward an etic/emic-ly derived unity of theoretical perspective. The limitations of the source materials soon became apparent. The linguistic aspects of fishing activities have been given only incidental attention in the monographs. Discussion within introductory textbooks (which are always good sources of anthropological position on any topic) seem merely to elaborate on Sumner's treatment of fishing as an expression of technological ingenuity (1909:115–18). Comments on the consequences of the implementation of this ingenuity, as in Murdock (1968) or Goggin and Sturtevant (1964) seem of interest only

*The assistance of the students in the departmental linguistics seminar, fall, 1973; and the contributions of Gary W. Hume, James Faris, Gibson Gardner, Steven Stout, and Amy Zaharlick are gratefully acknowledged.

where the total lifestyle would suggest the surplus and stability associated with plant cultivation, but where intensive fishing, not agriculture, forms the basis of the observable surplus and stability. It may not
be so serious a thing to understand the causal potential of one subsistence activity by evaluating its effects on those produced by a second
such activity, yet this implicitly assumes an equation between intensive
fishing and intensive plant cultivation when a clarification of the nature
of that equation may be more to the analytical point. Discussions of comparative or evolutionary economics have failed to provide that clarification. Edward Hahn, when considering the progress from savagery to
civilization, augments the traditional scheme by including horticulture
and pastoralism within the transition from hunting and gathering to
farming; the modification leaves fishing as another "pre-agricultural alternative" without comment. Tylor (1871, 1878) contains no substantive
discussion of fishing. However, Tylor (1881), and later Lowie (1934), do
allude to a pan-historical uniformity of fishing efforts; the significance of
those remarks will be considered in subsequent paragraphs. Childe
(1951:78) mentions early evidence of fishing within the archeological
record and discusses the subsequent technological florescence in association with this activity, but makes no attempt to consider the contribution such efforts may have made toward a "food producing revolution."
A similar absence of discussion on this point marks the work of Forde
(1949), Herskovits (1953), White (1959), and Sahlins (1972). Even the
monographs which focus attention on fishing communities (e.g., Malinowski 1922, Faris 1972) tend to view the community in singular terms,
omitting the alternative perspective which views them as specific cases
of a more general possibility of cultural expression.

   This paper is concerned with stating what should be said about the
fishing component of a people's cultural economy. First, the paper ex-
amines the conditions under which commitment will be made to fishing
efforts, and the consequences these commitments have on the total design of the subsistence strategy. The discussion (based on data originally
presented in Lee 1968) leads to the argument that, from an anthropological perspective, fishing is best considered as a kind of hunting activity. A
summary of a comparative linguistic analysis is presented to argue that a
similar assessment is made by speakers of 33 languages of the world
when referring to the fishing component of their community's subsistence effort.[1] The corpus is certainly not exhaustive, but the degree of
emerging regularity is suggestive of the existing cross-cultural observations out of which a cultural perspective on fishing activity can be constructed. Some implications of such a perspective are then explored.

I recognize that, following Ford (1949:372), fishing constitutes only one of the possibilities toward which the total focus of a people's subsistence economy may be directed. I know, further, that while such a possibility may occupy a major percentage of the total work effort, or may provide the major source of nutritional benefit, no single subsistence effort exists in complete isolation from the other components of the subsistence economy. Both of these points are well illustrated whenever discussions of the economic concerns of fishing communities are presented in the literature Diamond comments (1969:11) that the people of K'un Shen identify their primary economic pursuit as fishing, while

> in reality, most families depend on the income from several jobs. A household that relies on fishing, which brings in an average income of 600 NT a month in season, may also own a small plot of land for raising sweet potatoes, and the wife may earn extra cash by weaving hair nets or shucking oysters.

Fraser (1966:8) makes a similar point:

> While fishing . . . is considered to be the only important occupation by the people of Rusembilan, it is largely a seasonal occupation and directly involves only able-bodied men. The second most important occupation in these coastal villages is rice cultivation but it is engaged in by many only because it grows during the monsoon season when it is impossible to take the fishing boats out to sea.

It is not surprising, given " . . . this preoccupation with fishing," to find that ". . . the economies of Rusembilan and other coastal villages are unusually sensitive to fluctuations in the supply and demand for fish." Yet even so, Fraser concludes "[o]bjectively this sensitivity is not necessary, for the east coast offers opportunities for a wide variety of cash crop production."

Both examples suggest that fishing peoples need not concentrate their work efforts only within the fishing sphere. This puts a different perspective on Forde's observation ". . . we do not find single and exclusive economies but rather combinations of them" (1949:461). The combinations to which Forde refers represent the results of a decision-making process, a determination and subsequent ordering of subsistence effort possibilities and priorities by the participants within the given ecosystem.

What saves this from being treated completely as a particularistic de-cision—that is, one yielding only to context-sensitive variables—is that separate strategy designs resulting from specific ecological assessments can be shown to follow similar, pan-situational constraints. Richard Lee has noted, for example (1968:42), that ". . . all societies at all (geo-graphic) latitudes derive at least 20 percent of their diet from the hunting of animals," supporting the observation in his display (1968:46–49) of the relative percentages of effort devoted to hunting, gathering, and fish-ing in 24 Old World and 34 New World nonindustrial societies, where none of the hunting efforts were less than the percentage cited. This would imply that the hunting effort of any group which exceeds this pre-dictable percentage should be viewed as situationally conditioned, or "specialized" subsistence activity; since a similar sort of prediction can-not be made for gathering or fishing efforts, we are likewise led to view any occurrence of gathering or fishing in similar, situationally condi-tioned terms. The total amount of the work effort devoted to specialized hunting, gathering, and fishing cannot exceed 80 percent of the total sub-sistence effort, which gives an upper limit to the amount of effort which can be divided within the context-sensitive sphere. The resulting relative division of effort, when considered for the 54 societies within Lee's dis-play, yields only eight different subsistence strategies, each with its own relative frequency of occurrence within the sample, each with its own pri-mary subsistence emphasis.

Listed according to frequency of occurrence, the strategies are:

1.	Gathering, fishing, and little hunting	$g = f$	13 cases
2.	Gathering, some hunting, no fishing	$g > h$	12 cases
3.	Gathering, little fishing, little hunting	$g > (h = f)$	9 cases
4.	Fishing, little gathering, little hunting	$f > (h = g)$	7 cases
5.	Fishing, some gathering, no hunting	$f > g$	5 cases
6.	Hunting, fishing, some gathering	$(h = f) > g$	5 cases
7.	Gathering, some fishing, no hunting	$g > f$	4 cases
8.	Hunting, some gathering, some fishing	$h > (g = f)$	3 cases

Listed according to primary subsistence emphasis, the strategies are:

1.	Gathering, some hunting, no fishing	12 cases
2.	Gathering, little fishing, little hunting	9 cases
3.	Gathering, some fishing, no hunting	4 cases
4.	Gathering, fishing, little hunting	13 cases
5.	Fishing, little gathering, no hunting	7 cases
6.	Fishing, some gathering, no hunting	5 cases
7.	Hunting, fishing, some gathering	5 cases
8.	Hunting, some gathering, some fishing	3 cases

The data give support to Lee's argument (1968:41) that hunting is not an overwhelmingly dominant focus for subsistence strategies in nonindustrial societies. It would appear that hunting occupies such a primary place within the strategy only where the remaining effort is divided congruently between gathering and fishing, a strategy found in only 3 instances in the 54-entry sample; no instances are reported where hunting is the primary subsistence emphasis and where gathering and/or fishing efforts are lacking or occur only minimally (i.e., "little").

The concentration of primary effort on gathering or on fishing allows for greater variety in overall pattern. If there is primary concentration on gathering, fishing effort may equal the accompanying hunting effort (nine instances within the sample), or fishing may represent the sole concentration of the remaining effort percentage (four cases in the sample). If there is primary concentration on fishing, gathering effort may equal the accompanying hunting effort (seven cases) or may represent the sole concentration of the remaining subsistence effort (five cases in the sample).

A high frequency of recurrence comes from a subsistence strategy which places its primary concentration on gathering; an even higher frequency of recurrence arises if the subsistence strategy selects gathering and one other alternative for the primary concentration of effort. Here the consequences are much more specific: When fishing and gatherng are selected, the extent of specialized hunting effort is minimal. This is the most frequently occurring subsistence strategy within the sample. Similarly, if gathering and hunting are emphasized, the extent of fishing activity is minimal: This is the second most frequently occurring strategy in the sample. Conversely, the sample shows no instances where primary effort is divided between fishing and hunting; for primary effort to be concentrated in those two areas, primary effort must also be extended into the gathering sphere. There are five cases in the sample where this strategy is utilized.

The extent of gathering emphasis would appear to have a pivotal role within the tool design of a specific subsistence strategy. Recognizing that, we could proceed to clarify the conditions under which fishing may be included within a given strategy, yet the statement of these conditions is identical to the one we would need to make to clarify the occurrence of hunting within other such strategies. Neither fishing nor hunting can occur at all, without the presence of a gathering commitment; fishing and hunting do not co-occur as primary subsistence foci unless a substantial, if not identical, commitment is also being made within the gathering sphere; yet, either fishing or hunting can occur with gathering to produce an effective and widely occurring subsistence strategy. This parallel between the occurrence conditions of fishing and hunting suggests, from the point of view of strategy design, that fishing and hunting may represent the same kind of subsistence effort, differing only with respect to the commodity which serves as the focus of the subsistence effort. More than ecological logic can be used to support this claim. Inspection of fishing related terminologies in 33 of the world's languages (see listing in footnote 1) shows that specification of commodity reference, not terminological considerations, provides the distinction between fishing and other forms of subsistence, but particularly between fishing and hunting. Consistently this distinction is made in one of two ways.

(1) The terms for fishing qualify a more general "hunting" reference by combining the term for "hunting" with specific indication of the object being hunted: thus, Arabic *samak* "fish," *sayyad as-samak* "to hunt, chase, or pursue fish." Likewise, Celtic *piscis* "fish," *pisics fiadh* "to hunt (literally dig for) fish."

(2) Fishing is distinguished from hunting by deriving the term for the activity from the commodity itself. This is done either by deriving the verb from the noun reference through inflectional process: thus Classical Greek *ixΘus* "fish," *ixΘuaos* "to fish;" likewise, Hawaiian *i'a* "a fish," *lawai'a* "to fish (= fisherman);" or, treating the verbal and nominal expressions as identical lexical entries, differing only in the positions they occupy within sentence structure. Thus English *fish* "a fish, to fish;" Chinese *yu* "a fish, to fish."

In neither of these instances is a verb for "hunting" or an expression for "deep hunting," "rabbit hunting" or the like formed through analogous derivational process. In all of these instances, hunting reference is given in the abstract, without additional reference to the commodity being pursued, or connection to some other activity. Fishing reference, on the other hand, consistently seems to *require* some additional association within lexical reference, either (case 1) with hunting itself; or (case 2), with animals to which hunting reference does not apply, requiring the use of a more specific, commodity-based activity reference. Such a referential dependence would support the argument that fishing is not perceived as an autonomous subsistence activity; the implicit connection given to the hunting reference further strengthens the ecologically derived claim that fishing and hunting be viewed in complementary (dependent-independent) relationship.

The terms which identify the participant in fishing activity reflect the same sort of orientation and similar categorization principles. Again, the reference may be made in one of two ways:

(1) An independent term for "person" or "human being" is compounded with the term denoting the commodity involved in the participation: thus Old Icelandic *fisk* "fish," *fisk karl* "fishing man."

(2) A derivational suffix denoting "participant in" is added to the object (or more specifically, the object action) reference.[2] Thus Latin *piscis*

"fish," *piscator* "one who fishes;" Slavic *ryba* "fish," *rybolov* "fish catcher;" and similarly, Hawaiian *i'a* "fish," *lawai'a* "fisherman (= to fish)."

As the preceding investigation showed, it would again appear that participant reference is expresed in terms of commodity, not technological considerations. Taken as a whole, both sets of linguistic data strengthen the idea that fishing is not seen as an autonomous component of a people's subsistence activity; the terms themselves seem to define its specific place within the larger subsistence whole. The ecological data have shown that the parameters in which a fishing component will occur within the subsistence effort can be specified, and that the conditions which govern the extent of the commitment given to that component can likewise be predicted. For these reasons, the extent to which the terminological uniqueness of fishing activity should be given priority within anthropological analysis can be seriously challenged. Yet doing so will leave us with a question: To what maritime-related focus should anthropological perspective then be directed? The preceding discussion provides some basis for constructing an answer to that question.

First, recall that fishing best illustrates the kind of usufruct mentality which some might otherwise wish to attribute solely to hunting or gathering "primitives." Recent conflicts over "fishing rights" between Iceland and Great Britain, and likewise between Maine and New Hampshire, illustrate how relevant the question of "rights of open access" can be to the contemporary scene. The issue is relevant for a most critical reason. Ownership within the purview of fishing effort has little to do with the commodity in question; ownership, whether corporate or private in nature, arises solely within the portion of the total fishing effort which Andersen and Wadel (1972:158) have termed "management activity," the area which includes "the initiation and control over the fishing expedition, personnel, equipment and marketing." (It is the very presence of this "restriction over the control over resources" which lead these scholars to refer to fishing as "industrialized hunting" (1972:154).) Consequently, if the purview of control extends from the area of management to include the remaining details of the total production process (which could happen only when subsistence focuses on a non-mobile commodity or on a commodity rendered non-mobile) we expect that the work effort within the activity will become transformed, and the activity itself will be labeled differently. This is why shellfish collecting is consistently referred to as collection or gathering within the literature, and within native speaker expression.

Because the absence of commodity control is so implicit in any fishing effort, fishing by definition remains exempt from the set of historical processes whose effects within other subsistence spheres is identified as "the food producing revolution," processes which so drastically changed the character of the remaining segments of the total subsistence strategy. The kind of mainstream continuity which unites subsistence and industrialized fishing was noted by E. B. Tylor almost 100 years ago:

> Our fishermen carry on their business on a large scale, with their steam-trawlers and seines which sweep a whole bay, but their net-fishing is much of the same kinds as may be found among the peoples from whom we have taken our early examples of spearing and angling (1881:104).

Tylor's comment implies that change within the fishing-based focus of subsistence strategy, whether the synchronic (adaptive) or diachronic (linear historical) sense of that term, has followed an involutionary, rather than evolutionary pathway (Service 1972); to use the term that M. E. Smith has recently coined, the change exemplifies a process of accretive evolution (1972). This may be why Tylor was careful, even with his own observations of continuity and transhistorical similarity, not to refer to fishing as a cultural "survival." Fishing is certainly not a static and unyielding historical phenomenon, yet there are only certain aspects of the total fishing effort which may be susceptible to the development process. Andersen and Wadel have referred to "the acquisition of capital enabling the fishermen to adopt new technological organizational complexes" as "the major problem in intensive modern fishing operations wherever commercial fishing exists" (1972:157); however, they can make this comment only after previously noting:

> some features of one technological stage may still be present in others. Somewhat paradoxically, technological advance in fishing might under some circumstances increase uncertainty rather than reduce it. Even large capital injections have not reduced the *hunting nature* of fishing significantly; that [being] the lack of control over ecological variables. (1972:154)

If the area of participant control is limited to the management sphere, and if historical development is likewise limited to the management sphere, it is apparent why the specifics of management rather than the details of technological process have priority when participant, and analytical, interests are concerned. Fundamental here is a struggle waged for years in Northwest Coast studies: whether the florescence within that area is to be explained by commodity abundance or commodity scarcity. The misleading quality of that dichotomy becomes apparent in the light of Suttles' comment: "The limits to the exploitation in times of abundance may have been set less by the people's capacity to get food, than by people's capacity to store it" (1968:64, see also 1968:58 for elaboration). Indeed fish—qua fish—are useful only to the extent that something can be "done" with the catch. For this reason, as Fraser noted in both studies of Rusembilan, while only a small percentage of the community may be directly involved in the "fisherman activity," a much larger portion of the community becomes involved—as a participant within the management sphere, once the fisherman and his catch return home. It may well be that within the nature of this "additional involvement," the variability, vitality, and adaptability of fishing effort as cultural expression may be found. Consider the differences in strategy used by the people of Rusembilan, K'un Shen, and Cat Harbour when faced with the same management requisite to divide up the catch:

K'un Shen

Division on the basis of 25 shares:

1 share each for 15 participants in the crew
½ share for each of 5 who own the raft
1 ½ share each for 4 owning the net
1 ½ share for the owner of the raft which worked within the encirclement
(1969: 15) Diamond

Rusembilan

Division on the basis of 18 shares:

½ share for each of 12 crewman
½ share for each of 12 net owners
½ share for the steerer
¼ share for each of 4 netmen
¼ share for the person who washes the boat
1 share for the boat maintenance
1 share for engine maintenance
(1966:11) Fraser

Cat Harbour

Division between shares (full partnership with equal division of expenses and remaining profits) and shareman's parts (fixed percentage of the total catch prior to expenses).

$$\text{shares calculated according to:} \quad S = \frac{C - E}{n}$$

shareman's part calculated according to: $P = CX$

Where: C — total catch value (gross)
          E — expenses (of which P is one)
          X — determining factors (deduction of board and room, share crowd contribution, gear contribution, etc.)
          n — number of men entitled to full shares

(1972:107–08) Faris

Analysis of the cultural interpretation of priorities which lead to the use of such strategies tell us much more about the community's fishing commitment than will equally detailed analyses of technological specifics which produced the catch in the first place. It is this presence of participation beyond the fishing crew itself which led Fraser to Rusembilan as a fishing community, even though many people there pursue rice-growing during the rainy season, and even though the economic possibility of the nearby rubber plantations offers an equally viable alternative to maritime pursuits. As Fraser put it: "Fishing, boats, prices, nets and other topics related to fishing are uppermost in the minds of members of the community, men, women, and children, at all times" (1968:8). This concern is, of course, a response to a set of commodities over which the people themselves have no direct control; in this instance, the absence of direct commodity control is made even more complex by the external influence of the market economy in which Rusembilan, and other coastal villages are ". . . inescapably involved." Such external influence may not directly set the priorities within the technological sphere, but will directly influence the efficacy of efforts within management activity once the technological effort has been implemented, and as noted, the details of that influence may extend far beyond the fishing activity itself. Here, we may have the reason why the lifestyle of fishing communities is so frequently found to parallel the kind of lifestyle detail typologically characteristic of "peasant communities." Peasants, like fishing people (and perhaps for many of the same reasons) are not and cannot have full control over the details of the production forces from which their social organization and the ideological reference are constructed. The lifestyle of a fishing community is in effect built on consequences which nonfishing-based communities can experience only after food production; and the subsequent disjunction between production and distribution becomes stabilized historical fact. This makes the place of fishing communities within an evolutionary typology all the more intriguing for anthropological research.

NOTES

[1]Since the monographs which discuss fishing communities are characteristically devoid of linguistic information, reference had to be made to available lexical listings in dictionaries, grammars, and other such sources. The conversational validity of each item was cross-checked with native speakers in all possible instances. The languages considered were Modern English, Old English, Old Icelandic, Norwegian, Gothic, Modern German, Classical Latin, Classical Greek, Modern Greek, Old Irish, Modern Irish, Old Church Slavonic, Modern Russian, Baltic, Sanskrit, Hindi, Modern Persian, Tamil, Avestan, Arabic, Hebrew, Turkish, Vietnamese, Thai, Mandarin Chinese, Formosan Chinese, Hawaiian, Eskimo, Isletan Tiwa, Keresan, Salish, and Nootka.

[2]The English term *fisherman* is interesting in this regard: it includes both a designation of "participant" (the *-er* postfix) but also includes indication of sex of participant; such a lexical specification of sex of participant appears to exist only within the Germanic and the Sino-Tibetan language families.

LITERATURE CITED

Andersen, Raoul, and Cato Wadel
   1972   Comparative Problems in Fishing Adaptations. *In* North Atlantic Fishermen: Anthropological Essays on Modern Fishing. R. Anderson and C. Wadel, eds. Newfoundland Social and Economic Papers, No. 5. Institute of Social and Economic Research. Memorial University of Newfoundland. Toronto: University of Toronto Press.

Boas, Franz
   1938   Introduction. *In* General Anthropology. Franz Boas, ed. New York: D. C. Heath.

Childe, V. Gordon
   1951   Cultural Sequences in Savagery. *In* Social Evolution. Cleveland: World Publishing Company.

Diamond, Norma
   1969   K'un Shen: A Taiwan Village. New York: Holt, Rinehart, and Winston.

Faris, James C.
    1972   Cat Harbour: A Newfoundland Fishing Settlement. Newfoundland Social and Economic Studies no. 3. Institute of Social and Economic Research, Memorial University of Newfoundland. Toronto: University of Toronto Press.

Forde, C. Daryll
    1949   Habitat, Economy, and Society: A Geographical Introduction to Ethnology. New York: E. P. Dutton and Company.

Fraser, Thomas M., Jr.
    1966   Fishermen of South Thailand. New York: Holt, Rinehart, and Winston.

Goggin, John M., and William C. Sturtevant
    1964   The Calusa: A Stratified Nonagricultural Society (With Notes on Sibling Marriage). *In* Explorations in Cultural Anthropology: Essays in Honor of George Peter Murdock. Ward Goodenough, ed. New York: McGraw-Hill.

Herskovits, Melville J.
    1953   Economic Anthropology: The Economic Life of Primitive Peoples. New York: W. W. Norton and Company.

Lee, Richard B.
    1968   What Hunters Do for a Living, or, How to Make out on Scarce Resources. *In* Man The Hunter. Richard B. Lee and Irven DeVore, eds. Chicago: Aldine Press.

Lowie, Robert H.
    1934   Hunting, Fishing, Gathering. *In* An Introduction to Cultural Anthropology. New York: Farrar and Rinehart.

Malinowski, Bronislaw
    1922   Argonauts of the Western Pacific: An Account of Native Enterprise and Adventure in the Archipelagos of Melanesian New Guinea. New York: E. P. Dutton and Company.

Murdock, George Peter
    1968   The Current Status of the World's Hunting and Gathering Peoples. *In* Man The Hunter. Richard B. Lee and Irven DeVore, eds. Chicago: Aldine Press.

Sahlins, Marshall
    1972   Stone Age Economics. Chicago: Aldine Press.

Service, Elman R.
   1971   Cultural Evolutionism: Theory in Practice. New York: Holt, Rinehart, and Winston.

Smith, M. Estellie
   1972   Accretive evolution. Unpublished ms. presented at the Conference on Theory on the Fringe. SUNY College, Oswego.

Sumner, William Graham
   1906   The Struggle for Existence. *In* Folkways. New York: New American Library.

Suttles, Wayne
   1968   Coping with Abundance: Subsistence on the Northwest Coast. *In* Man The Hunter. Richard B. Lee and Irven DeVore, eds. Chicago: Aldine Press.

Tylor, E. B.
   1871   Primitive Culture: The Origins of Culture. New York: Harper and Row.
   1878   Researches into the Early History of Mankind. Chicago: University of Chicago Press.
   1881   Arts of Life. *In* Anthropology. Ann Arbor: University of Michigan Press.

White, Leslie A.
   1959   The Evolution of Culture. New York: McGraw-Hill.

*

Index

†